A Taste of Pennsylvania History

John F. Blair, Publisher
Winston-Salem
North Carolina

A TASTE OF PENNSLYVANIA HISTORY

A Guide to

Historic Eateries

and Their Recipes

DEBBIE NUNLEY & KAREN JANE ELLIOTT

The paper in this book meets the guidelines for
permanence and durability of the
Committee on Production Guidelines for
Book Longevity of the Council on Library Resources.

ON THE FRONT COVER, CLOCKWISE FROM THE TOP—
The Settlers Inn at Bingham Park in Hawley, Hyeholde Restaurant in Moon Township
Gabriel's Restaurant at The Inn at Olde New Berlin in New Berlin

Library of Congress Cataloging-in-Publication Data
Nunley, Debbie.
A taste of Pennsylvania history : a guide to historic eateries and their recipes / Debbie Nunley
& Karen Jane Elliott.
p.   cm.
ISBN 0-89587-193-9 (alk. paper)
1. Cookery. 2. Restaurants—Pennsylvania—Guidebooks. 3. Historic buildings—Pennsylvania.
I. Elliott, Karen Jane, 1958–   II. Title.

TX714.N86 2000
641.5'09748—dc21   00-039763

Design by Debra Long Hampton
Composition by The Roberts Group

To our families,
without whose support and patient understanding
this book would not have been possible

Contents

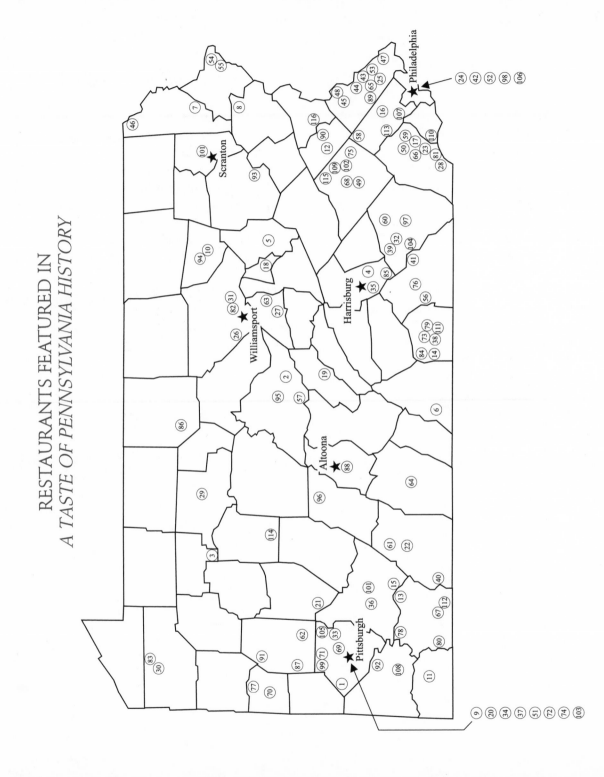

RESTAURANTS FEATURED IN
A TASTE OF PENNSYLVANIA HISTORY

RESTAURANTS FEATURED IN A TASTE OF PENNSYLVANIA HISTORY

1. Hyeholde Restaurant
2. The Hummingbird Room
3. Gateway Lodge
4. The Circular Dining Room, The Hotel Hershey
5. The Inn at Turkey Hill
6. The Mercersburg Inn
7. The Settlers Inn at Bingham Park
8. Skytop Lodge
9. Palm Court, Westin William Penn Hotel
10. Eagles Mere Inn
11. Willow Inn
12. Glasbern
13. The Barn Restaurant
14. Hickory Bridge Farm
15. Lesley's
16. Joseph Ambler Inn
17. Pace One Restaurant
18. Pine Barn Inn
19. At the Gables
20. Sunnyledge
21. 1844 Restaurant
22. The Inn at Georgian Place
23. Dilworthtown Inn
24. The Garden Restaurant
25. La Bonne Auberge
26. Gamble Farm Inn
27. Gabriel's Restaurant, The Inn at Olde New Berlin
28. Kennett Square Inn
29. The Towne House Inn
30. Venango Valley Inn
31. The Peter Herdic House
32. Groff's Farm Restaurant
33. Kleiner Deutschmann
34. The Church Brew Works
35. Appalachian Brewing Co.
36. Red Star Brewery & Grille
37. Penn Brewery
38. GETTYSBREW Pub & Brewery
39. Bube's Brewery
40. River's Edge Cafe
41. Accomac Inn
42. *Moshulu*
43. Centre Bridge Inn
44. Cuttalossa Inn
45. Golden Pheasant Inn
46. The Inn at Starlight Lake
47. Washington Crossing Inn
48. EverMay On The Delaware
49. Widow Finney's
50. Duling-Kurtz House
51. Victoria Hall
52. McGillin's Olde Ale House
53. Odette's
54. Dimmick Inn
55. Cliff Park Inn
56. The Altland House
57. Duffy's Tavern
58. Cab Frye's Tavern
59. General Warren Inne
60. General Sutter Inn
61. Green Gables Restaurant
62. Hotel Saxonburg
63. Lewisburg Hotel
64. Jean Bonnet Tavern
65. The Logan Inn
66. The Oak Grill, The Marshalton Inn
67. The Stone House
68. Perry's Temple Hotel Restaurant
69. Cross Keys Inn
70. The Village Inn Restaurant
71. The Pines Tavern
72. Mario's South Side Saloon
73. Blue Parrot Bistro
74. Klavon's Ice Cream Parlor
75. Landis Store Hotel
76. Roosevelt Tavern
77. The Tavern on the Square
78. The Back Porch
79. Dobbin House Tavern
80. The Lardin House Inn
81. Mendenhall Inn
82. The Thomas Lightfoote Inn
83. Riverside Inn
84. Cashtown Inn
85. Alfred's Victorian
86. First Fork Lodge
87. Harmony Inn
88. U.S. Hotel Restaurant and Tavern
89. Sign of the Sorrel Horse
90. King George Inn
91. Wolf Creek School Cafe
92. The Classroom Restaurant
93. Powerhouse Eatery
94. The Crestmont Inn
95. The Gamble Mill Tavern
96. The Miners' Rest
97. The Lancaster Dispensing Co.
98. Engine 46 Steakhouse
99. Wexford Post Office Deli
100. DiSalvo's Station Restaurant
101. Carmen's, Lackawanna Station
102. Bowers Hotel
103. Grand Concourse
104. Railroad House
105. Tarentum Station
106. City Tavern
107. The Jefferson House Restaurant
108. Century Inn
109. Whispering Springs Restaurant & Pub
110. Chadds Ford Inn
111. Farnsworth House Restaurant
112. Summit Inn
113. Gypsy Rose Restaurant
114. The Pantall Hotel
115. Deitsch Eck Restaurant
116. The Sun Inn Restaurant

Preface

We have been collaborating on activities since 1994. Originally, it was at elementary school, but now that our children are older, we have broadened our horizons. We have always shared the common interest of dining at unusual places and now are part of a ladies' group that meets once a month for the express purpose of seeking out unique dining experiences.

In our quest for new and different restaurants, we found a plethora of interesting places to suit our palate, our sense of adventure, and our historic curiosity. We so relished our discoveries that we wanted to share the joy. It occurred to us at the time that there was a book amongst all this research.

The dining establishments of primary interest to us fall into two categories. The first of these encompasses inns, taverns, and roadside hostelries that have been in business in the same locale for a considerable length of time. To be considered for this book, they needed to be of significant historic interest with respect to the location of the buildings, the memorabilia contained as part of the internal or external decor, or the cuisine served on a regular basis. The second type encompasses eateries housed in historic locations where elements of the buildings' original use are now part of the decor. Schoolhouses, train stations, and stores are examples of this type.

In trying to determine which restaurants to visit, we read everything we could obtain. We contacted county tourism offices for recommendations, cross-checked our information with county historical societies, and scoured local magazines and newspapers. We asked restaurant owners whom we had already met for their further recommendations. Finally, we surfed the Net in search of answers. As we made slow but steady progress, we discovered that everyone who was old enough to talk had an opinion about where we should visit.

In the process, we researched close to 900 establishments. Many of these, although old, had not maintained their historic integrity. In other cases, we approached a restaurant, slowed, and, after getting a full view, quickly pulled away. If we weren't prepared to go in, we certainly couldn't recommend it to our readers, regardless of how historic the building. Concerned about adequately representing the range of dining establishments across the 66 counties and 11 million people that make up the commonwealth of Pennsylvania, we narrowed the field to about 250 and made arrangements to dine.

Our favorite parts of the research were visiting the establishments, talking with the owners, the chefs, and the staff, tasting the food, enjoying the ambiance, selecting the recipes, and finally deciding which restaurants to include. We had a wonderful time from start to finish in choosing the 116 presented here.

The restaurants are organized into chapters based on common characteristics. Within each chapter, the restaurants are arranged in the order we visited them. We racked our brains for weeks to come up with catchy chapter titles. One of the most surprising chapters is the one called "Let Freedom Ring." When we started our research, neither of us anticipated finding so many links to the Underground Railroad.

Pen-and-ink drawings are traditional in books of this type for other states. Not wanting to break completely with tradition, we've introduced each chapter with a drawing of one of the establishments within. We thought it would create variety within the text if we used each restaurant's logo as the heading for its historic write-up. The variety and creativity of these was a pleasant surprise.

In just a shade over a year, we've gained an incredible amount of knowledge about a state in which neither of us was born. We've come across many delightful individuals who have generously shared their time and information. The stories they told us about their establishments are not only interesting but heartwarming as well. We hope that you enjoy this book as much as we have in putting it together!

CHAPTER 1

Dream a Little Dream

The Settlers Inn

"Out of a misty dream, our path emerges for a while," Ernest Dowson
wrote. In the case of the establishments in this chapter, that dreamy path
leads directly to a wonderful dining experience. The dream may be related to
the way the restaurant was started, out of someone's lifelong yearning, or it
might refer to the effect on each of us as we visit. Go and see if you
experience a dream come true.

HYEHOLDE RESTAURANT

CORAOPOLIS HEIGHTS ROAD
MOON TOWNSHIP, PA 15108
412-264-3116

As they were standing at the crest of a cornfield, William Kryskill told his bride, Clara, that he would someday build her a castle. That cornfield became the grounds of the castle called Hyeholde.

Work on Hyeholde began in 1931. The intent was to construct the building for use as a restaurant and living quarters. Over the next seven years, Bill and Clara spent the summer months operating Clark Studio Tea Room in Noank, Connecticut. Every September, they returned to the cornfield outside Pittsburgh to continue construction on their labor of love. Many of the beautiful materials used throughout the restaurant came from the old Stonesifer barn, which was located in what is now Robinson Township. The Kryskills carefully dismantled the barn and its stone foundation, reviving the materials as they created Hyeholde.

The first meals were served at Hyeholde in 1938, and the charming country restaurant became an instant success. It remained in the possession of the Kryskills until 1974, when it passed into the hands of Pat Foy, an experienced restaurateur. He is credited with maintaining the country charm of Hyeholde while creating its elaborate menu and list of fine wines.

As we entered the Great Hall, the slate floors, great beams, tapestries, stained-glass windows, and European furniture transported us to another time. The place settings were equally charming, a likeness of Hyeholde gracing the center of each plate. Hyeholde's ownership has also been transported—back into the hands of the Kryskill family. In 1991, the Kryskills' daughter, Barbara McKenna, and her husband, Quentin, purchased the restaurant. They have since maintained the exceptional menu and extraordinary service.

This was our first experience with Ostrich, so we ordered it as an appetizer portion and enjoyed every bite. The seasonal Mushroom Soup was warm and tasty on a chilly fall day. The entrées of Venison and Veal Medallions were every bit as good. We chatted with Barbara over our desserts of Chocolate Angel Cake in a Raspberry Compote and a Chocolate Martini (a martini glass filled with chocolate mousse in a chocolate shell). Her love for her parents and her passion for this place they created were mesmerizing.

Your fabulous dining experience in the medieval-like dining rooms may leave you wanting to enjoy even more of Hyeholde. On your next visit, you can order a gourmet picnic and enjoy it on the castle's beautiful grounds. Or you can request to be seated at the "chef's table" in the kitchen, where you can revel in the efforts of executive chef Chris O'Brien and his dedicated staff. Whichever option you choose, the service, the quality of the food, and the ambiance will make the entire experience an exceptional value.

❧ SHERRY BISQUE ❧

1 tablespoon vegetable oil
1 tablespoon butter
1 cup onion, chopped
¼ cup celery, chopped
1 teaspoon fresh garlic
2 cups tomatoes, peeled, seeded, and chopped
⅓ cup plus 2 tablespoons flour
12 cups chicken stock or water
12 ounces split green peas
1 bay leaf
1½ cups heavy cream
1 cup sherry
dash of apple cider vinegar
salt and pepper to taste

Place oil and butter in a pan and heat until butter is melted. Add onion, celery, and garlic. Sauté over low heat until transparent; do not brown. Add tomatoes and cook for 5 minutes. Add flour and make a roux. Cook for another 5 minutes. Add stock and bring to a simmer. Add split peas and simmer for 1½ hours. Add bay leaf and simmer for another ½ hour. Remove from heat and purée. Strain while still hot, then return to heat. Add cream and bring to a boil. Add sherry and vinegar and adjust salt and pepper. Serves 16.

❧ ❧ ❧ ❧ ❧ ❧

❧ PEPPER- AND CORIANDER-CURED ❧ SALMON GRAVLAX WITH CAPER MAYONNAISE

Salmon

3 pounds salmon fillets, cleaned
1 cup cracked black pepper
½ cup cracked coriander
1 cup kosher salt
¾ cup sugar
Caper Mayonnaise (see below)

Coat salmon with pepper, then with coriander. Mix kosher salt and sugar and coat salmon. Wrap in cheesecloth and let sit for 3 days. Remove cheesecloth, wash cure off, and dry salmon with a towel. Slice salmon thinly and serve on toasted rye bread with Caper Mayonnaise. Serves 18 as an appetizer.

Caper Mayonnaise

3 tablespoons prepared mayonnaise
1 tablespoon capers, chopped

Combine ingredients in a small bowl. Store covered in the refrigerator. Yields ¼ cup.

❧ ❧ ❧ ❧ ❧ ❧

the Hummingbird Room

PA 45
SPRING MILLS, PA 16875
814-422-9025

I could have made a meal on the bread alone. It was brought warm out of the oven to the table, and the herb aroma and flavor were delectable. Since Karen and I were dining separately on this occasion, I had no assistance in being conscientious.

At The Hummingbird Room, the menu can be described as French/continental, with choices for every palate. The prix fixe menu is a fabulous value. Guests may choose from four selections on the appetizer menu, which on the evening I visited were Lobster Bisque, Spinach and Leek Tart, Salad des Tomatoes (served with Black Truffle Vinaigrette), and Wild Mushroom Ravioli. A difficult choice! There were also four entrée choices—a fillet of beef, a game selection, a seafood option, and a vegetarian selection.

Although I did not opt for the prix fixe menu, I did try the Vegetarian Couscous, served timbale-style. The couscous were topped with chopped mushrooms, sautéed spinach, roasted eggplant, and roasted red peppers, finished with melted provolone cheese. The presentation was stunning, the flavor fabulous, and the service exceptional. I was very tempted to try the Peach Cobbler with homemade Cinnamon Ice Cream, but I refrained, since I'd had more than my share of bread before the meal!

The ambiance was subdued, allowing the food to speak for itself. The walls of the various dining rooms were painted in rich, deep tones, such as the navy blue in the room where I was seated. The tables were set with burgundy linen and floral china, creating a lovely combination. Hummingbird accessories were subtly displayed throughout the room.

The Hummingbird Room is a dream come true for owners Eric and Claudia Sarnow. After culinary school and a three-year apprenticeship in France, Eric returned to the United States and joined the staff of a highly acclaimed restaurant in Philadelphia. After the birth of the Sarnows' son in 1992, they set out for central Pennsylvania and started their first Hummingbird Room, a twenty-two-seat venture. Their following has grown, and the restaurant has flourished, allowing them to purchase one of Spring Mills' oldest residences for their current restaurant.

The structure in which The Hummingbird Room is located was once the residence of the Fisher family, one of the founding families of Spring Mills. It was built in 1847 and has been on the National Register of Historic Landmarks since 1977. Today, the brick building is attractively accented with sea-foam green shutters and white trim. As guests enter the intimate lobby, antiques such as an old organ and an antique clock catch the eye. I had been in the lobby several minutes, taking everything in, before I realized that the public-sale bill behind the reception desk advertised property of the Fishers. On that particular occasion, they were getting rid of a chestnut bay horse, two herds of young cattle, and a sow. Somehow, that poster strongly connected the past to modern-day life.

ZUCCHINI BLOSSOM TEMPURA WITH RED BELL PEPPER SAUCE

Tempura

16 large zucchini blossoms
½ pound ground beef (may substitute ground lamb, pork, or turkey)
¼ cup carrot, diced fine
¼ cup onion, diced fine
¼ cup celery, diced fine
1 teaspoon fresh ginger root, minced fine
2 pinches of salt
2 pinches of pepper
2 cups cooking oil
½ cup all-purpose flour
½ cup beer
Red Bell Pepper Sauce (see next column)

Rinse zucchini blossoms under water gently; let dry on paper towels. Combine beef, vegetables, ginger, a pinch of salt, and a pinch of pepper in a medium bowl to make stuffing. Gently pry open zucchini blossoms and fill with approximately 1 tablespoon of stuffing each. Gently twist blossoms to enclose filling. Heat cooking oil in a 2-quart saucepan on medium-high; oil is hot enough when water dropped on surface "dances." Mix flour, beer, remaining pinch of salt, and remaining pinch of pepper with a whisk until dry ingredients are incorporated. Dip stuffed zucchini blossoms into tempura batter, then immediately drop into oil; do not crowd. Cook approximately 2 minutes until batter is golden. Gently remove from oil with a strainer or a slotted spoon; set on paper towels to dry. Keep blossoms warm in a 200-degree oven on a baking sheet lined with paper towels until Red Bell Pepper Sauce is ready. Serves 4 as an appetizer.

Red Bell Pepper Sauce

2 red bell peppers, seeded and deveined, chopped coarse
1 cup dry white wine
2 cups heavy cream
2 sticks butter

Place first 3 ingredients in a 4-quart saucepan. Cook over medium-high heat until peppers are very tender and liquid is reduced by ½. Place mixture in a food processor; process until smooth. Add small pieces of butter 1 at a time with processor running; allow each to be incorporated fully before adding the next. Sauce may be served barely warm or may be reheated at a very low temperature on the stove. Serve with zucchini blossoms. Yields approximately 3 cups.

❦ TRUFFLES AU CHOCOLAT ❦

12 ounces fine-quality (Callebaut, Vahlrona, or Lindt)
  bittersweet or semisweet chocolate, chopped fine
½ cup heavy cream
¼ cup liqueur (Grand Marnier, Kahlua, Amaretto,
  Frangelico, Chambord, etc.)
8 tablespoons unsweetened butter, softened
1 cup powdered unsweetened cocoa

Put chocolate in a medium-sized, deep bowl. Bring cream to a simmer in a medium saucepan over medium-high heat. Reduce liquid by ½, stirring occasionally. Immediately strain cream through a fine sieve over chocolate; stir until chocolate is completely melted. Stir in liqueur until well blended. Swirl butter into chocolate mixture until incorporated. Cover and refrigerate ganache for at least 4 hours until very cold and stiff.

Using a melon baller or a teaspoon, scoop out 1-inch balls of ganache. Shape by rolling lightly between palms. If ganache becomes too soft to shape, return to the refrigerator until chilled again. Lay ganache balls on a baking sheet covered with parchment or wax paper and refrigerate until cool and firm.

Place cocoa in a wide, shallow bowl. Remove chilled ganache balls from refrigerator. Roll them gently between your palms to slightly warm them so cocoa will stick. Drop ganache balls into cocoa and roll to cover. Remove and store in a cool place or refrigerate. Yields 4 dozen 1-inch truffles.

❦   ❦   ❦   ❦   ❦   ❦

Gateway Lodge and Cabins

PA 36, BOX 125
COOKSBURG, PA 16217
814-744-8017

Nestled amid the trees in Cook Forest, Gateway Lodge looks as if a fairy tale is about to unfold. The lodge was fashioned out of pine and hemlock logs cut from the property. Its walls and trim are made of wormy chestnut. Oak plank flooring and heavy-beam ceilings create a warm, cozy, rustic atmosphere. Antiques and old family photos are displayed around the first floor. A weathered stone fireplace in the common room, just outside the dining room, invites guests to "sit a spell." The guest rooms echo this ambiance in their Early American furnishings, quilts, and braided rugs.

Except for an added staircase, the front porch, and guest amenities, the lodge stands as it was originally built. A favorite spot is the porch, where guests—perhaps in search of rest following an afternoon of hiking, fishing, hunting, canoeing, horseback riding, bird watching, or cross-country skiing—can take in the lush flora and abundant fauna surrounding the lodge. It was cold when we visited, but we tried the rope swing nonetheless. Other guests chose to relax in front of the Ben Franklin fireplace, located in the Tap Room. Old-fashioned kettles sat atop the stove, and a cast-iron coal bucket stood alongside. An old chessboard on a table in front of the fire completed the room's general-store atmosphere. Across the hall is the Game Room, where guests can enjoy a board game at one of the tables and where a sumptuous afternoon tea is served to lodge guests. During our visit, Cranberry Bread, cheeses, fresh fruits, and finger sandwiches were offered.

Dinner is served to the general public as well as to lodge guests. Visitors who wish to order from the à la carte menu do not need reservations. They are a must, however, for the four-course and seven-course dinners.

The rough-hewn walls of the dining room are lined with treasures of days long past. Tools, clothing, and other artifacts hang as they were stored by our ancestors. Twisted grapevines adorned with eucalyptus and white lights highlight the windows. The tables were set with pewter, and kerosene lanterns provide an additional glow. A striking wagon-wheel chandelier decorated with grapevine and memorabilia is the focal point of the room.

The food is as delicious as the atmosphere. We both chose one of the freshwater fish selections, served with a baked potato and tossed salad. The salad dressings were homemade, as was the warm bread, served with Honey Butter. Mmmmm! The dessert tray overwhelmed us with choices, from Fruit of the Forest Pie to Apple Dumplings to Amaretto Cheesecake. The Grand Slam Pie, reminiscent of cheesecake, had fudge chunks and caramel topping. The Chocolate Hazelnut Cheesecake was rich and delicious.

If you're dreaming of a good meal or just a place to get away, the staff at Gateway Lodge will do its utmost to make it all come true.

❦ FRENCH TOAST ❧

4 eggs
10 ¾-ounce can evaporated milk
1 tablespoon maple syrup
1 tablespoon vanilla extract
1 teaspoon cinnamon
½ teaspoon nutmeg
½ teaspoon Sugar in the Raw
2 loaves (approximately 12 1½-inch slices) home-
   baked bread
additional cinnamon and raw sugar

Combine first 7 ingredients. Dip each slice of bread into the egg mixture; make sure to keep stirring mixture so spices do not settle to bottom of bowl. Place dipped bread on a griddle and sprinkle with extra cinnamon. When bottom side is golden brown, turn over. Sprinkle with more cinnamon and raw sugar. Serve warm with maple syrup. Serves 6.

❦ SWEET AND SOUR FRENCH DRESSING ❧

1 cup sugar
1 cup oil
½ cup vinegar
1 teaspoon paprika
1 tablespoon dry mustard
10 ¾-ounce can condensed tomato soup
1 teaspoon salt
1 teaspoon celery seed
1 tablespoon Worcestershire sauce

Combine all ingredients with an electric mixer until sugar is dissolved. Cover and refrigerate. Yields 4 cups.

The
Hotel Hershey ®

HOTEL ROAD
HERSHEY, PA 17033
717-534-8800

Milton Hershey, the visionary who founded the Hershey® chocolate empire, once received a postcard from an acquaintance visiting Europe. On the front was a picture of the hotel that became the inspiration for the grand Mediterranean-style hotel that Mr. Hershey built. He was meticulous in his attention to detail, a fact that is obvious in the construction of the hotel's spacious main dining room, called The Circular Dining Room.

Having observed while dining in Europe's finest restaurants that guests of modest means or who weren't big tippers were often seated in the far corners of the dining room, Mr. Hershey grew to abhor walls and columns that divided space unnecessarily. Thus, he built his dining room with only two walls, one of which is the curved exterior wall. Large windows, beautifully decorated with patterns of flower vines and birds, overlook a reflecting pool and the beautifully landscaped formal gardens. The tranquility of this room is reinforced by the quiet but superb service.

The menu changes daily. The one staple here is chocolate, and lots of it. And you won't find it just for dessert, either. Some evenings, guests have the option of beginning their meal with a cup of Chocolate Soup. We were there at midday and enjoyed The Hotel Hershey's traditional buffet. A wide selection of fresh fruit, cold cuts, and cheeses was available, alongside five or six salad offerings. The Red Cabbage Salad was mild in flavor and crunchy in texture, while the Penne Salad, which featured shoepeg corn, was surprisingly sweet but very delicious. It was difficult to choose a favorite among those, the Couscous Salad, and the White Bean Salad.

The entrées were just as appealing, so we gladly sampled the Chicken Marsala, the Sliced Beef with Anchiote Garlic Mashed Potatoes, the Catfish with Parmesan Risotto, and the Fettuccine with Tomato Shrimp Ragout. Karen's preference was the catfish, by a slim margin, while Debbie was unwilling to declare a favorite.

When it came to the dessert table, we did our duty as purveyors of information to our future readers. We sampled them all! The Peanut Butter Pie, light in flavor, had a surprise layer of mini chocolate chips tucked between the filling and the whipped cream topping. For those interested in a fruity finish to their meal, there were several options, including Strawberries and Whipped Cream, served on slices of puff pastry, Apple and Blueberry Cobbler, and Pear Tart Frangipani. Of course, there was chocolate. Hershey's® Chocolate Cream Pie is a staple on the dessert menu. A brownielike Chocolate-Almond Torte and a fabulous Chocolate Croissant Bread Pudding, served with either Raspberry Sauce or Apricot Sauce, are also offered.

Feeling sated, we exited the restaurant and relaxed in the Moroccan courtyard just outside the dining room. To create this luxurious atmosphere, Milton Hershey imported Old World artisans to create the hand-painted tiles, the sculptured fountain, and the chestnut-railed balconies, complete with urns. The scene is so reminiscent of the movie *Casablanca* that we felt as if Humphrey Bogart might stroll through any minute. In this case, rather than "Play it again, Sam," he might say, "Let's eat again, Milton."

PUMPKIN SEED–CRUSTED LOIN OF VENISON WITH PEPPERCORN–PEAR GLAZE

2 6-ounce venison loin medallions, trimmed
salt and pepper to taste
4 tablespoons olive oil, divided
4 pears, peeled, cored, and diced fine
2 shallots, minced

2 small cloves garlic, crushed
2 cups bourbon
4 cups chicken stock
12 juniper berries in sachet
1 teaspoon cracked black pepper
2 cups brown sauce or good demi-glace
4 tablespoons Dijon mustard
3 cups pumpkin seeds, toasted and processed into crumbs
2 slices fresh bread, processed into crumbs

Season venison with salt and pepper and sear on all sides in 2 tablespoons of the olive oil. Set aside to cool. Add pears, shallots, and garlic to pan and cook for 1 minute. Add bourbon and flambé. When flame has died, add chicken stock, juniper, and pepper. Reduce by ½ and add brown sauce. Meanwhile, brush venison with Dijon. Combine pumpkin seeds with breadcrumbs and roll venison in mixture. Drizzle with remaining olive oil and roast at 350 degrees for about 45 minutes. Remove from oven. Slice venison into 6 to 10 equal pieces and place in a circle on 2 plates. Spoon the glaze between the pieces and serve. Serves 2.

CHOCOLATE BRIOCHE BREAD PUDDING

Ganache

2 ounces Hershey's® Baking Chocolate
6 ounces Hershey's® Special Dark® Chocolate
½ cup heavy cream

Chop both chocolates. Bring cream to a boil. Take off heat and stir in chocolates until smooth. Chill until set.

Bread pudding

9 ounces Hershey's® Special Dark® Chocolate
2½ cups milk
1 cup heavy cream
2 tablespoons sweet butter
3 eggs
¼ cup raw golden sugar
1 tablespoon vanilla
12 individual brioches or 1 loaf challah bread cut into
    1-inch cubes
Hershey's® Chocolate Syrup for garnish

Chop chocolate. Scald milk and cream. Take off heat and stir in chocolate and butter. In a separate bowl, stir eggs and sugar together.

Quickly stir some of the cream mixture into the eggs, then add the rest together. Stir in the vanilla. Pour mix over brioches and let sit until chocolate has soaked all the way through.

Place brioches halfway up individual 2-inch steel rings, followed by a small scoop of ganache. Fill top with remaining brioches and bake in oven at 350 degrees until set and firm. Serve warm on plates garnished with chocolate syrup in a free-form line design. Serves 8.

Note: Recipes reprinted with permission. Hershey, Hershey's, and Special Dark are registered trademarks or service marks used by permission of Hershey Foods Corporation and Hershey Entertainment and Resort Company.

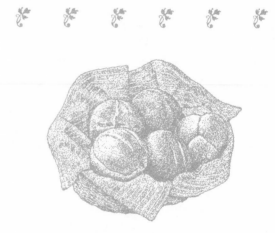

THE INN AT TURKEY HILL

991 CENTRAL ROAD
BLOOMSBURG, PA 17815
570-387-1500

Atop a knoll just outside the town of Bloomsburg is a white farmhouse dating back to 1839. The property on which it sits was part of a 1773 land grant from Thomas and John Penn. The location was originally called Last Trouble. Later, the farm became known as Turkey Hill, due to the large turkey farm on this site.

In 1844, representatives from the Duncannon Iron Company purchased the land and began mining it. Most of the ore was taken to iron mills in Bloomsburg, though some of it found its way to an iron furnace in nearby Lightstreet. Eventually, the ore beds were depleted, and some of the property was sold to build a school. By 1864, Turkey Hill School was providing education to children from a widespread area, a tradition it continued for quite some time.

In the mid-1940s, the farm was purchased by the local newspaper editor, who was also a gentleman farmer. He continued living there until the 1970s, when he began to feel that the modern-day world was getting a bit too close. Although he moved to another farm, he still maintained the home while also fostering a dream—a dream of turning the Turkey Hill farmhouse into a lodging property. In the early 1980s, he and his daughter began to explore the possibility of transforming it into an inn. Unfortunately, he passed away in 1984, before realizing his dream. His daughter and the rest of the family carried out the vision. Today, his grandson, Andrew Pruden, is the innkeeper at Turkey Hill.

Colonial furnishings in traditional colors decorate the rooms. The door of each guest room is adorned with a farm animal, on which the room number is shown. Guests staying in the stable will find their room identified by the name of one of the farm's horses in days gone by.

Located across the informal courtyard, past the gazebo and the pond, is the farmhouse, which hosts guests on its second floor and houses a fabulous restaurant on the main level. In the lobby, a Federal-style fireplace and built-in bookshelves painted a mossy green create a relaxing atmosphere. This was once the kitchen, and if you look closely at the wooden flooring, you can tell just where the original walls were. Down the hall and past the staircase is the home's living room, which now serves as one of the dining rooms. It is attractively decorated with murals depicting scenes from Columbia County. Back down the hall and across from the stairs is the original dining room, which still functions as such. Its beautiful stenciling and homey environment are much enjoyed by dinner guests.

The food here is superb. Many of the dishes contain exotic assortments of mushrooms. Our Asian Wild Mushroom Soup was scrumptious, as was the Duck and Mushroom Risotto. And those were just the starters! Jasmine Rice and Asparagus accompanied our Grilled Herb

Chicken with Crabmeat. The veal entrée was stuffed with garlic, pine nuts, fresh herbs, and golden raisins and served in a tomato-based sauce over a bed of tricolored pasta. It was truly exquisite. The Lemon Mousse that followed, served in a ladyfinger and pound-cake crust, was a wonderfully light end to a truly enjoyable meal.

If he could experience the lovely guest rooms, the excellent cuisine, and the stellar service at Turkey Hill, Andrew Pruden's grandfather would be very happy with the reality of his dream.

APPLE CIDER VINAIGRETTE

1 tablespoon parsley, chopped fine
2 tablespoons onion, chopped fine
¾ teaspoon salt
¾ teaspoon white pepper
scant ⅓ cup Dijon mustard
2 tablespoons lemon juice
¾ cup apple cider vinegar

¾ tablespoon garlic, chopped
2 cups olive oil

Place all ingredients except olive oil into a food processor and blend for a few seconds. Slowly add oil until dressing is emulsified. Yields 4 cups.

ASIAN MUSHROOM AND LEEK SOUP

1 tablespoon sesame oil
1 large leek, cut in half and sliced crosswise
¼ cup carrot, julienned
¾ teaspoon garlic, chopped
¼ cup shiitake mushrooms, sliced
¼ cup enoki mushrooms
¼ cup chanterelle mushrooms
¼ cup wood ear mushrooms
¾ teaspoon ginger, chopped fine
8 cups chicken stock
⅓ cup soy sauce
¼ teaspoon Thai red chili paste
cornstarch slurry (approximately 1 tablespoon
    cornstarch and ½ cup water)
salt to taste

Heat sesame oil in a large pot. Add leeks, carrots, and garlic. Sauté for 2 minutes. Add mushrooms and ginger. Add chicken stock, soy sauce, and chili paste. Bring to a boil and thicken with cornstarch slurry. Adjust seasoning as needed. Serves 6.

The Mercersburg Inn

405 SOUTH MAIN STREET
MERCERSBURG, PA 17236
717-328-5231

The birthplace of President James Buchanan, the town of Mercersburg was named for Hugh Mercer, a general under George Washington. Mercersburg, a charming, 225-year-old historic village nestled at the base of the Tuscarora Mountains, was an ideal location for the realization of Ione and Harry Byron's dream, the creation of a magnificent private estate. Their 21,000-square-foot Georgian Colonial mansion was originally named Prospect, after the stunning panoramic views of the Tuscarora Mountains. The home was designed in 1909 and completed just two short years later. It was the very first house in southern Pennsylvania to have electricity. Harry Byron was the owner of the leather tanning plant in Mercersburg. He was given permission by the borough to run electricity from his plant to his mansion, as long as he did not sell any of it.

The stately brick mansion with the distinctive slate roof is now known as The Mercersburg Inn, a country inn with fifteen guest rooms. Most of the rooms are used much as they were when the Byrons raised their three sons here. We were as impressed by the inside of the building as we were overwhelmed by the beauty of the outside.

Our attention was drawn to the white oak floors, the scagliola columns, and the impressive wrought-iron double staircase that curves to the second-floor landing from the immense entrance hall.

We found the fine-dining restaurant located in the original dining room to be magnificent. The high mahogany-paneled walls and the large marble fireplace created an elegant backdrop for the beautiful antique light fixtures. Built-in china cabinets with glass doors gleamed with crystal and silverware. Intimate tables for two or four were located around the edges of the room. On each, a single baby pumpkin embellished the plain white linens and small table lamps.

The service, as expected, was smooth and unhurried. We nibbled on warm, freshly baked bread while we decided between the à la carte menu and the five-course prix fixe. Having decided that we just weren't hungry enough for the prix fixe, we opted for the unusual, chunky Corn and Tomato Chowder, which was piping hot and extremely tasty. This was swiftly followed by Grilled Filet Mignon with Wild Mushroom Demi-Glace and Roasted Onion Buttermilk Mashed Potatoes. The potatoes were fluffy and the steak tender, but what we enjoyed most were the delicious Fried Green Tomatoes, which were breaded and wrapped in strips of basil. We expressed our pleasure to chef Kevin Carscadden, who popped into the dining room to ask if the meal was to our liking. He told us that many of the vegetables he uses are grown in the gardens belonging to the inn.

We tried to decide among the desserts—Hazelnut Cappuccino Crème Brûlée, Chocolate Macadamia Torte with Grand Marnier Sauce, and

Oven-Roasted Pears served in a Chocolate Cup with Caramel Sabayon—to no avail. Every item on the extensive menu was appetizing in the extreme, and so we retired defeated, to return and eat another day.

FRENCH BREAD CUSTARD

1 loaf French bread, crust removed, sliced 1½ inches thick
1½ sticks unsalted butter, melted
6 eggs
3 egg yolks
½ cup sugar
1 teaspoon vanilla
3 cups whole milk
1 cup heavy cream
¼ teaspoon nutmeg
2 tablespoons powdered sugar

Brush both sides of bread slices with melted butter and arrange bread in a 9-by-12-inch baking dish. Beat eggs and yolks together; add sugar and whisk well to combine. Add all remaining ingredients except nutmeg and powdered sugar. Whisk well. Pour custard over top of bread. Allow to sit for 5 minutes, then turn bread over. Refrigerate overnight.

Preheat oven to 350 degrees. Put baking dish into a larger pan. Pour hot water into larger pan until it comes halfway up sides of baking dish. Sprinkle custard with nutmeg. Bake 35 to 45 minutes until lightly browned and puffy. Dust with powdered sugar. Serves 8.

Note: A favorite breakfast item with guests of The Mercersburg Inn, this is usually served with fresh berries and maple syrup.

❧ ROASTED ASPARAGUS ❧
AND GOAT CHEESE SALAD

2 bunches pencil asparagus
6 cups fancy mixed baby lettuce
3 plum tomatoes, cut into 6 wedges each
18 cherry tomatoes, halved
salt and freshly ground pepper to taste
1 tablespoon extra-virgin olive oil
1 cup Goat Cheese Ranch Dressing (see next column)
6 tablespoons Highland Dairy Ester Run Chèvre (goat cheese)
6 crostini

Preheat oven to 350 degrees. Wash all vegetables. Cut asparagus into 2½-inch lengths. Set aside all but tips and the next lengths. Place these on half of a 12-by-24-inch piece of aluminum foil. Season with salt and pepper, then drizzle with olive oil. Fold foil over and seal edges tightly by folding several times. Roast in oven for 12 to 15 minutes, depending on thickness of asparagus. Remove from oven. Open foil and set aside to cool.

In a large bowl, toss cooled asparagus, lettuce, and dressing together. Spread 1 tablespoon Highland Dairy Ester Run Chèvre on each crostini. To assemble, arrange a plum tomato wedge at 12, 9, and 6 o'clock on each of 6 plates. Put a crostini at 3 o'clock. Place ⅙ of asparagus salad in center of each plate. Scatter remaining asparagus and cherry tomatoes on greens and edge of plates. Serves 6.

Goat Cheese Ranch Dressing

¾ cup goat cheese
½ cup mayonnaise
1½ teaspoons Dijon mustard
1 cup roasted onion purée
1½ teaspoons celery salt
¼ cup green onion, chopped
1 tablespoon cracked black pepper

Combine all ingredients in a mixer. Yields 2 cups.

THE SETTLERS INN

AT BINGHAM PARK

4 MAIN AVENUE
HAWLEY, PA 18428
570-226-2993

Just after the turn of the twentieth century, Hawley businessmen had a dream. As the construction of a hydroelectric dam progressed, allowing Lake Wallenpaupack to come into being, these men envisioned a hotel that would draw tourists to the downtown area. The Hawley Community Hotel was to include an assembly hall, a dining room, a coffee shop, and guest rooms. It truly was to be a community hotel. Building committee members went door to door throughout the town, selling shares of the hotel to residents who wanted to help make the dream come true.

And then came the stock market crash. Throughout the Great Depression and World War II, the building sat empty. It wasn't until the summer of 1948 that this Tudor-style hotel finally opened for business, its inaugural event being a wedding party for a local family.

Guests today know they're in for a treat the minute they enter the parking lot. Wildflowers border the stone paths, and their scents greet newcomers as they cross the porch and enter the lobby. Once inside, guests immediately get the feeling of having entered the warm hospitality of an English country house, thanks to the chestnut beams, the huge fireplace of native bluestone, and the Mission-style furniture.

The warmth continues in the dining room, which is decorated with heavy wooden tables and chairs with built-in pockets on the back. Upon asking about the unique design, we learned that the pockets were for hymnals and that the seats were garnered from a church not too far away. Other decor in the dining room, including the lighting, shows the obvious influence of Frank Lloyd Wright.

The inn's pleasant atmosphere was enhanced by the fabulous food. We enjoyed breakfast with Anastasia Paccione, the manager of The Settlers Inn at Bingham Park, on a sunny August morning. We started with warm Scones and Blueberry Coffee Cake as we mulled over the menu. They were scrumptious, and neither of us would have objected if we'd been allowed to fill up on just those. Debbie opted for the French Toast, created from the inn's homemade brioche and topped with a fresh fruit sauce. Yum! Karen took the day's special, a Baguette topped with roasted summer vegetables, a poached egg, and cheese. Yum, yum!

Had we been able to stay for lunch, we might have chosen Ham and Swiss with Maple Tarragon Mustard on Birdseed Multigrain Bread or Chicken Salad with cherries, toasted walnuts, and Lemon Balm Mayonnaise, served with Tea Bread. The dinner menu reads like poetry. The entrées include Beef Tenderloin Fillet with Red Wine and Onion Glaze, topped with Horseradish Breadcrumbs, and our favorite, Mignon of Venison on Squash Ribbons with Portabello Mushrooms and Raspberry Balsamic Glaze.

After touring the lovely guests rooms, each of which had a chenille teddy bear lovingly placed on the bed, we wandered through the gardens and down to the riverbank. As we were leaving, Anastasia handed us a care package of The Settlers Inn's homemade cookies and fresh-baked bread, which allowed us to enjoy the inn's warmth, bite by bite, all day long.

BIRDSEED MULTIGRAIN BREAD

1 cup milk
1 cup water
⅔ cup steel-cut oats
⅔ cup rolled oats
¼ cup bulgur (cracked wheat)
1 tablespoon salt
⅓ cup brown sugar, packed
¼ cup vegetable oil
1 tablespoon quick-acting yeast or 2 tablespoons regular yeast, dissolved in ¼ cup water
3½ to 4 cups bread flour
2 tablespoons sesame seeds
2 tablespoons flax seeds
2 tablespoons poppy seeds
2 tablespoons sunflower seeds

Combine milk, water, steel-cut oats, rolled oats, bulgur, salt, sugar, and oil. Let soak overnight. (To speed this up, heat milk and water and soak grains for about 3 hours.)

Preheat oven to 350 degrees. In a bread mixer or by hand, add yeast and 3 cups of the bread flour to the soaked mixture. Combine seeds in a small bowl. Add ¼ cup of this seed mixture to dough. Add additional flour to make a firm but slightly sticky dough. Knead 5 to 8 minutes to produce a pliable dough with some elasticity. Place dough in a greased bowl and let rise 1½ to 2 hours in a warm place until double in size. (On a cold day, this may take longer.)

Punch down dough and separate it into 2 pieces. Place in greased loaf pans and sprinkle with remainder of seed mixture. Bake for approximately 1 hour until browned. Cool slightly, then remove from pans to wire rack to cool completely. Yields 2 loaves.

Note: Steel-cut oats, bulgur, and flax seeds can be found in health food stores.

4 cups rich beef stock
salt and pepper to taste
½ cup heavy cream

Bring water to a boil in a saucepan. Add salt and rice. Simmer for 45 minutes until rice opens up. Drain and set aside. In a 3-quart stock pot, melt butter and sauté onions, carrots, and celery until soft. Add mushrooms and cook about 3 minutes. Add flour and cook on low heat, stirring occasionally, for 10 to 15 minutes. Add stock and simmer for 10 minutes. Add rice, salt, and pepper. Add cream just before serving and gently warm through. Serves 4 to 6.

WILD RICE AND MUSHROOM SOUP

3 cups water
¼ teaspoon salt
¹/₃ cup wild rice
2 tablespoons butter
½ cup onion, diced
½ cup carrot, diced
¼ cup celery, diced
4 cups specialty mushrooms (portabello, shiitake, or crimini), chopped rough
¼ cup flour

Skytop Lodge

PA 390
SKYTOP, PA 18357
570-595-7401

As you enter the lush grounds and first gaze at the lovely structure known as Skytop Lodge, you feel as if you've arrived at the impressive estate of a medieval baron. The expansive stone edifice, in perfect harmony with its mountain surroundings, is even more inviting than many of the mansions from the previously mentioned era.

Skytop was the creation of John Stubbs, Frederic Smith, Earl Mayne, and Sam Packer, who dreamed of building a grand resort in the Pocono Mountains. Located on a plateau three miles north of Canadensis, the resort was built on what were once eight contiguous tracts of farmland totaling twenty-five hundred acres. The visionaries then bought options on other area farms and purchased them when they went up for sale, increasing the acreage to as much as seven thousand acres. The property now encompasses fifty-five hundred acres. There are ample opportunities for guests to enjoy a wide range of outdoor activities. The plentiful hiking trails lead to breathtaking panoramas. To encourage hiking, the hotel provides two walking sticks tucked away in the closet of each guest room.

Inside the lodge, the Pine Room greets guests warmly. The wooden beams, molding, and wainscoting are a rich brown, darker than you'd expect from this local pine. The room, as beautiful as it is cozy, offers a lovely view of the slate terrace and the recreational activities beyond.

The era when mother and children spent their summers here, with dad joining them from Philadelphia or New York on weekends, has been well preserved. Generations of families have maintained this tradition. Saturday evenings start with the Illumination Dance, which has been done for as long as anyone can remember. The winner of the Illumination Dance leads the Grand March, which starts as a two-by-two promenade, then is added to until it evolves into a hand-holding, snaking line that encourages guests to mix and mingle. Not too long ago, the manager decided to cancel the traditional festivities, thinking there was only minor interest in the activity. A distraught mother begged, "I've been threatening my children that if they didn't behave, they wouldn't be allowed to participate in the Grand March. They've been angels—you've got to have it." So the Grand March was held in customary fashion.

Skytop Lodge plays a role in shaping the table manners of the young as well. Many parents use the term *Skytop manners* to remind children of appropriate behavior when eating out. At the lodge, young and old alike get to put on their best when dining in the Windsor Room, a lovely dining room just off the main lobby. Pictures from prior decades show that this room is much as it has always been.

We enjoyed breakfast with Skytop's sales director, Robert Baldassari. The prix fixe lunch and dinner menus change daily, allowing long-term guests to stay at least a month before the same menu items are offered again. The choices are plentiful; there are several appetizers, two soups, and four entrées from which to pick. Sandwich choices also appear on the lunch menu, for those who want lighter fare. Several items caught our eye, including the Grilled Marinated Quail with Huckleberry Sauce, the Alligator Gumbo with Okra, and Skytop's famous Indian Roast Salmon on a cedar board with Lentil Fruit Relish.

As if just being at Skytop isn't special enough, the chef creates his own occasions, such as "Alice's Un-Birthday Party," held on a Saturday in April, and "An Evening with Edgar Allen Poe." We long to return to Skytop and fully experience its gracious hospitality. In any season, the lodge has much to offer.

GRILLED MEDALLIONS OF VENISON

2 pounds venison medallions
½ cup whole-grain mustard
2 tablespoons kosher salt
2 tablespoons cracked black pepper
⅞ cup virgin olive oil
2 tablespoons sesame oil
2 tablespoons fresh ginger, minced
½ bunch cilantro
2 tablespoons black sesame seeds
1 tablespoon chili pepper, crushed
salt and pepper to taste
15-ounce package soba noodles, precooked
1 stick butter, melted
¾ head Savoy cabbage, shredded fine

1 pound shiitake mushrooms, sliced
¾ cup demi-glace
⅓ cup citrus oil

Coat venison with mustard and sprinkle with kosher salt and cracked black pepper. Marinate approximately 4 hours in refrigerator.

In a food processor, combine olive oil, sesame oil, ginger, cilantro, sesame seeds, chili pepper, and salt and pepper to make ginger oil; process well. Place in a small container for further use.

Grill venison to desired doneness. Form soba noodles into 4 small patties. Heat ½ of the butter in a medium skillet and pan-fry soba patties until golden brown. In another skillet, heat remaining butter and stir-fry cabbage and mushrooms until tender. In a small saucepan, combine demi-glace and citrus oil and gently warm to make sauce.

To serve, arrange cabbage-and-mushroom mixture in a circle around outside of each of 4 plates. Spoon about ¼ cup sauce into center of circle. Place soba noodle patty in the center and surround with venison medallions. Drizzle ginger oil over all. Serves 4.

MAHI-MAHI WITH SPICY CUCUMBER SALSA

1 cucumber, peeled, cored, and cut into half-moons
½ green pepper, diced fine
½ red pepper, diced fine
½ yellow pepper, diced fine
½ medium Bermuda onion, diced fine
½ bunch scallions, sliced thin
2 plum tomatoes, seeded and diced fine
1 cup pineapple juice
⅓ cup raspberry vinegar
½ bunch fresh tarragon
1 bunch fresh cilantro
1 tablespoon jerk seasoning
1½ teaspoons fresh ginger, minced
salt and pepper to taste
6-ounce box Uncle Ben's Wild Rice Pilaf
4 7-ounce mahi-mahi steaks

¼ cup clarified butter
½ cup white wine
3 large leeks, julienned
20 sugar snap peas
1 tablespoon vegetable oil
12 slices fresh pineapple, grilled

In a bowl, thoroughly mix first 14 ingredients to make salsa. (This may be prepared a day ahead and stored in refrigerator.) Preheat oven to 400 degrees. Prepare rice according to package directions. In a large, ovenproof skillet, sear mahi-mahi on both sides in butter. Deglaze pan with wine. Place skillet in oven for 5 minutes. Stir-fry leeks and sugar snap peas in vegetable oil. To serve, place 1 mahi-mahi steak on each of 4 plates, together with ½ cup wild rice, 3 slices pineapple, and ¼ of vegetables. Place a large dollop of salsa on top of mahi-mahi. Serves 4.

WESTIN WILLIAM PENN HOTEL
530 WILLIAM PENN PLACE
PITTSBURGH, PA 15219
412-553-5235

The tradition of afternoon tea is said to have been started by Anne, Seventh Duchess of Bedford, who supposedly grew tired of the laggard feeling she experienced every afternoon around four o'clock, during the long stretch between meals. One afternoon in 1840, so the story goes, she asked that a tray of tea, bread, butter, and cake be brought to her room. She eventually got so used to this repast that a tradition was born.

The Palm Court at the Westin William Penn Hotel, located in downtown Pittsburgh, is a lovely setting for this fine tradition. The enormous chandeliers provide soft lighting for the vast lobby adjacent to the Palm Court. Mirrored Palladian windows, gilded arches, and ornate ceilings give a glimpse into the opulence of the days when the William Penn Hotel was built. In 1916, when industrialist Henry Clay Frick built the William Penn, it had a thousand rooms and was the largest hotel between New York and Chicago. Built at the height of the steel industry's glory days, it became famous not only for its elegance but also for its state-of-the-art amenities, such as electric lights and a bath in every room. When six hundred additional rooms were added in 1929, the William Penn Hotel became the second-largest hotel in the world.

During World War II, the hotel bustled with servicemen dreaming of valor or of the girl back home. The best-known bands of the day came to entertain them. During one performance, Lawrence Welk requested something to dramatize his theme song, "Bubbles in the Wine." The hotel's engineers complied by creating Welk's famous bubble machine. A vocalist with one of the bands that performed at the William Penn received her marriage proposal here—she was none other than the future Mrs. Bob Hope!

While your visit to the Westin William Penn may not be as dramatic as Dolores Hope's, it's sure to be enjoyable. We indulged in the delicious Scones and Jam during afternoon tea; Karen most definitely gave the Scones her English vote of approval. Children are welcome at tea and can order tidbits suitable to their palate from the Mad Hatter's Tea Party menu. You may also want to try lunch or dinner next door to the Palm Court in the Terrace Room. In contrast to the sparkle and shine of the Palm Court, the decor here is subdued. Richly paneled walls and deeply arched windows create a "gentlemen's club" atmosphere. All the menu items are innovative and are served with superb presentation. Treat yourself!

❦ RAISIN SCONES ❦

Scones

2 cups all-purpose flour
¾ teaspoon baking soda
1½ teaspoons cream of tartar
pinch of salt
8 tablespoons unsalted chilled butter, cut into small
   pieces
½ cup raisins
1 egg, beaten
approximately ½ cup buttermilk
glaze (see below)

Preheat oven to 425 degrees. Combine flour, baking soda, cream of tartar, and salt in a mixing bowl. Cut in the butter until the mixture resembles fine crumbs. Add raisins, egg, and enough buttermilk to make a soft dough. Knead very lightly on a floured board, handling gently to retain air needed for scones to rise. Roll out to a ½-inch thickness. Using a sharp knife, cut dough into 8 thick wedges. Place scones on 2 greased baking sheets, leaving a 1½-inch space around each scone. Brush glaze onto each scone; be careful not to drip any glaze onto pan or scones will stick. Bake for 12 to 15 minutes until golden brown. Yields 8 scones.

Glaze

1 egg yolk
1 tablespoon lukewarm water

Combine egg yolk and water in a bowl.

❦ BRONZE-SKIN SALMON ❦ WITH VEGETABLE RISOTTO IN CHARRED TOMATO BROTH

4 8-ounce portions scaled salmon, skin on
salt and pepper to taste
3 cups vegetable stock, divided
2 cups par-cooked risotto
1 cup Brunoise spring vegetables
4 plum tomatoes
4 tablespoons butter
2 tablespoons tomato concasse
1 tablespoon tomato oil
2 tablespoons chopped chives
1 cup fried shoestring sweet potatoes

Season salmon with salt and pepper and place in a hot nonstick pan with skin side down. Let salmon cook completely over medium heat, skin side remaining down so it becomes crispy.

In another pan, bring 2 cups of the vegetable stock to a simmer. Add risotto and stir with a wooden spoon. When about ½ of the liquid has been absorbed into the risotto, add spring vegetables. When remaining liquid has been absorbed, season with salt and pepper.

Roast plum tomatoes until charred. Add tomatoes to remaining vegetable stock and simmer for 15 minutes, then strain. Reduce by ½, then add butter; swirl until all butter is incorporated. Reserve.

Place salmon skin side up on risotto. Spoon tomato broth around salmon and risotto. Finish the dish with tomato concasse, tomato oil, and chives. Top with fried sweet potatoes. Serves 4.

❦   ❦   ❦   ❦   ❦   ❦

Eagles Mere Inn

MARY AVENUE
EAGLES MERE, PA 17731
570-525-3273

The town of Eagles Mere sits atop a mountain at an elevation of twenty-one hundred feet. In the center of town is a lake about a mile long. This picturesque town was started in 1794 when George Lewis spent ten thousand dollars to purchase ten thousand acres of what had formerly been Iroquois hunting ground. His dream was to build a glassworks, utilizing the white sand from the lake, which was ideal for glassmaking. He and the approximately 250 workers it took to run the business settled here by 1803. Unfortunately, after the War of 1812, foreign competition caused Lewis to go bankrupt.

However, Eagles Mere, with its lake and its fresh mountain air, was a good place for more than just glassmaking. Many people found the location therapeutic, and many more felt that Eagles Mere was a terrific place to escape the grit and grime of industrialized city life. The advent of the railroad helped to make Eagles Mere convenient for these purposes. By 1885, the area was being developed as a resort.

Just off the main drag, around the corner from the town clock, sits Eagles Mere Inn, built as the A. C. Little Boarding House in 1887. Today, the innkeepers of the charming gray structure are Peter and Susan Glaubitz. Peter grew up on Long Island in a family that loved to cook. In fact, his father once took lessons from James Beard! After a stint in advertising and a four-month gastronomic tour of Europe with Susan, he fulfilled his dream by entering the restaurant and hotel business. Eventually, the charming life of Eagles Mere called, and Peter and Susan enthusiastically took on the running of Eagles Mere Inn.

As we sat at our lace-covered table watching a ruby-throated hummingbird sip nectar from the bee balm just outside the window, it was easy to understand why visitors return to Eagles Mere to enjoy life's simple pleasures. Our five-course dinner started off with Chilled Apple and Orange Soup. It was deliciously refreshing and beautifully garnished with a Granny Smith apple wedge and an edible viola blossom. Mango Sorbet followed our salads, preparing us for the rest of the feast. Karen chose the Trout entrée, topped with Basil Cream Sauce. Light and tasty, it was very enjoyable. Debbie opted for the Cornish Game Hen, which was glazed with gingered apricots and port-soaked currants. This was served with the best stuffing either of us had ever had. We finished the meal with a fabulous Frozen Lemon Mousse, served on a chocolate cookie crust and topped with Raspberry Sauce.

DUCK HULI HULI

1 5½- to 6-pound duck
1 teaspoon fresh garlic, minced
½ teaspoon fresh thyme, minced
¼ teaspoon fresh ginger, peeled and crushed
Huli Huli Sauce (see next column)
1 scallion, julienned
1 teaspoon toasted sesame seeds
several chive flowers

Rinse duck with cold water and drain. With a chopstick or spoon handle, separate skin from meat over breasts, thighs, and legs. Combine garlic, thyme, and ginger and spread over duck meat under skin. Place duck on a rack in a large roasting pan and fill with water to top of rack. Bake in oven at 185 degrees for 17 hours, adding more water in bottom of pan as necessary. Remove duck from oven and cool at room temperature for 1 hour, then place in refrigerator for at least 1 hour. Split duck in half lengthwise and remove as much rib, back, and other bones as possible, keeping meat, skin, wing bone, and leg bone intact. Refrigerate until ready to use; serve within 3 days.

When ready to serve, preheat oven to 375 degrees. Place duck in pan and bake for 8 to 10 minutes. Top duck with 1½ tablespoons Huli Huli Sauce, then replace in oven and heat an additional 20 to 30 minutes until meat reaches serving temperature (150 degrees). Baste from time to time with sauce in pan or in reserve. Remove duck from pan and pour pan juices over duck. Sprinkle duck with scallion, sesame seeds, and chive flower pieces. Serves 2.

Huli Huli Sauce

2 tablespoons soy sauce
2 tablespoons honey
2 tablespoons fresh lime juice
¼ teaspoon brown sugar

Combine ingredients thoroughly. Yields 6 tablespoons.

CHILLED APPLE AND ORANGE SOUP

1½ tablespoons fresh lemon juice
1½ cups apple juice
1½ teaspoons sugar
1 cinnamon stick

3 Rome, Cortland, or Winesap apples, pared and
  sliced
⅜ teaspoon vanilla extract
1 cup plus 2 tablespoons orange juice
1½ cups half-and-half
8 thin, unpeeled apple slices for garnish
lemon juice
parsley leaves for garnish
edible Johnny-jump-up florets for garnish

Place lemon juice, apple juice, sugar, and cinnamon in a large cooking pot. Add Rome, Cortland, or Winesap apples and cover. Cook over medium heat until apples are tender. Remove pot from heat. Remove cinnamon stick and discard. Add vanilla. Pour into a food processor and process into a purée, then add orange juice and half-and-half. Chill immediately; keep soup chilled at all times. Serve in bowls with a slice of unpeeled apple dipped in lemon juice, a parsley leaf, and a Johnny jump-up. Serves 8.

Note: This soup will last in refrigerator for up to 2 days.

SAUSAGE AND HAZELNUT STUFFING

1 pound fresh pork sausage
½ pound skinless, boneless chicken breast
4 tablespoons unsalted butter
2 cups onions, chopped coarse
2 cups celery, chopped coarse
2 tablespoons fresh sage leaves, chopped fine
½ pound ham, diced into ¼-inch cubes
2 cups dry bread cubes, crushed fine after measuring
1 cup dry bread, diced into ¼-inch cubes

1 cup toasted hazelnuts, skinned and chopped coarse
1 cup fresh parsley, minced
1½ teaspoons salt
1½ teaspoons freshly ground black pepper
3 eggs, beaten lightly
chicken stock as required

Crumble sausage into a skillet and cook over medium heat until it is no longer pink. Remove with a slotted spoon to a large bowl and let cool. Coarsely grind chicken in a food processor, then add pork to chicken and mix to blend. Transfer all to the large bowl. Pour off sausage fat in skillet, bring skillet to a medium temperature, and add butter, onions, celery, and sage. Heat until vegetables are softened. Remove from heat and let cool in skillet, then add vegetables to sausage and chicken. Mix well and add ham, breads, hazelnuts, parsley, salt, and pepper and toss well. Add eggs. Make sure all is blended well without overmixing. If needed, add chicken stock ¼ cup at a time until desired moistness is reached. Cover and chill until it is time to stuff or to cook separately. If cooking separately, butter a casserole dish and fill with stuffing. Cover and cook to 160 degrees; uncover the dish for the final 10 minutes to toast. Serves 10 to 12.

OAK FOREST ROAD
WAYNESBURG, PA 15370
724-627-9151

Situated on eighty acres of woods and an apple orchard in the hamlet of Oak Forest, deep in Green County's Whiskey Rebellion territory, is a two-hundred-year-old farm house called Willow Inn. It was a dream come true for Ralph Wilson when he purchased the brick Colonial structure in 1974. Wilson took three years to restore it to its former beauty, filling it with period antiques. He uncovered ceiling beams, refurbished the oak plank flooring, added stenciling, and built in cupboards and shelves adorned with collectibles. During the restoration process, Wilson, a self-taught chef, opened his home to dinner guests. There were no menus, just a personal repertoire of over 140 dishes, prepared in different combinations for whatever seven-course home-style feast he served that evening. Many naysayers doubted the success of this venture, but Willow Inn's continued success has proved them wrong.

Pat Varner was Wilson's partner. Thanks to a good eye and local knowledge, he has also emerged as a well-known primitive painter. Following Ralph Wilson's death in 1998, Varner carried on the dream along side co-owners Jack and Robin Jenkins. Robin does the cooking, continuing to use Wilson's original recipes while adding many of her own.

Upon arrival, guests sip a complimentary glass of wine while settling themselves comfortably in the porch swing or nearby rocking chairs. The weather was warm the summer eve when we dined. Other guests that evening were part of a business group but readily included us in their before-dinner patter.

Guests are encouraged to tour the restored rooms, filled with many original cupboards and clocks of various styles. The walls have been painted to replicate what is thought to be original paint samples found during the renovation process. Wallpaper appropriate to the period helps re-create the environment in which the Willow Inn's first family raised thirteen children.

We were seated in the home's original kitchen, where soup and bread began our feast. All food is served family-style, and the variety and the portions are plentiful. The Tuscan Bread was delicious, and to our delight, its platter was refilled as quickly as we made each batch disappear. The creamy French Onion Soup was a tasty accompaniment to the bread, as was the Spinach Fruit Salad that followed. Robin's Orange Dressing had a refreshing citrus flavor. Two meat courses then arrived, along with two vegetables.

We were then invited to take a breather on the porch while the tables were cleared for dessert, which is served with coffee or tea. During the wait, we explored the nearby springhouse. The original stacked limestone walls, visible where chunks of plaster have fallen away, house an intimate dinner setting available by special request. Ivy playfully poked its way through the old window frame and wound its way toward the original fireplace.

After our respite, the Strawberry Mousse served for dessert was a perfect ending to a friendly and folksy evening.

❦   ❦   ❦   ❦   ❦

❦ TUSCAN BREAD ❦

1 tablespoon oil
2 cups flour, divided
½ teaspoon salt
2 tablespoons yeast
2 tablespoons sugar
1 cup water

Coat the inside of 4 small loaf pans with oil. Preheat oven to 350 degrees. In a mixing bowl, combine 1 cup of flour, salt, yeast, sugar, and water. Gradually add in the remaining 1 cup flour as needed. Lay a kitchen towel on the counter or table where you are working. Place dough on towel. Shape dough into a square and cut into fourths. Knead each piece into a round ball. Spray with oil and set in a warm place to rise. Place in pans and bake for 35 to 45 minutes. Yields 4 small loaves.

Note: If dough is too dry, it will rise slowly. If it is too moist, it will rise quickly. Robin begins the bread at 4:30 and puts it in the oven at 6:45 in order to serve it at 7:30.

❦   ❦   ❦   ❦   ❦

❦ TOMATO DUMPLING SOUP ❦

¼ cup butter
1 large onion
2 28-ounce cans tomatoes
3 cups chicken stock
½ cup sugar
1 teaspoon salt, divided
¼ teaspoon white pepper
1½ teaspoons cinnamon
1 cup flour
1 teaspoon baking powder
3 eggs
2 teaspoons oil

Melt butter in a medium sauté pan. Chop onion and sauté in butter until tender. Seed tomatoes over a strainer. Cut tomatoes into small pieces and add, along with the juice, to the onions. Transfer mixture to a stock pot or Dutch oven. Add chicken stock, sugar, ½ teaspoon of salt, white pepper, and cinnamon. Cook over low heat until well blended.

In a large mixing bowl, combine flour, baking powder, and remaining ½ teaspoon of salt. Beat in eggs and oil. Form dumplings about ½ teaspoon in size and drop onto hot soup. *Do not stir.* Cover and simmer on low for 10 to 15 minutes. Serves 6 to 8.

❦   ❦   ❦   ❦   ❦

CHAPTER 2

Back to the Barn, It's Feeding Time!

The Barn Restaurant

Barns aren't just for farm animals anymore! We've found barns that have been renovated and decked out with antique appointments in keeping with the period of the original structure. You certainly won't be eating from troughs either! These upscale restaurants have linen tablecloths, china, silver, and fresh flowers. There might be a hayseed or two in the corner, though!

Glasbern

2141 PACKHOUSE ROAD
FOGELSVILLE, PA 18051
610-285-4723

In November 1984, Al and Beth Granger discovered a run-down farm left unoccupied for thirteen years. Through renovation after renovation over the course of fourteen years, they transformed the dilapidated buildings into the haven known as Glasbern. The restaurant is located in a nineteenth-century German post-and-beam bank barn set into a hillside. "The Barn" also has rooms for overnight guests. Additional accommodations are found on the property in the Carriage House, the Farmhouse, the Gatehouse, the Garden Cottage, and the Stables. All of the delightful guest rooms combine the decor of the farm's previous era and the comforts of today.

Guests enjoying dinner in the Barn sit under a breathtaking twenty-eight-foot ceiling with exposed beams. The original stacked slate and shale walls provide an interesting backdrop to the highly polished cherry tables and the upscale menu choices. Appetizer offerings include Warm Lobster Napoleon, Smoked Salmon Terrine, and Wild Mushroom Fricassee. Further tempting the palate are entrée choices such as Atlantic Salmon with Sweet Potato Risotto and Yellowfin Tuna, served with Pepper Mango Coulis.

Debbie was dining elsewhere on the evening that I visited Glasbern. Even though I was thirty

minutes early, all was prepared. Executive chef Brian Murphy had arranged a very special meal for me, allowing me to choose only the dessert for myself. The service was impeccable, and I sat back and allowed my servers to explain each course to me. The meal began with Baby Spinach and Endive Salad, served with Gorgonzola cheese and grape tomatoes in a delicate Balsamic Vinaigrette. This was swiftly followed by a Scallop and Mushroom Napoleon, surrounded by a Carrot and Tabasco Reduction. The portabello mushrooms, spinach, and pancetta gave the dish a deliciously smoky taste, which was balanced by the sea scallops. Both the presentation and the taste were outstanding.

The entrée was Roast Pheasant with Caramelized Onion Polenta and Golden and Red Beets. The pheasant was moist and flavorful, the polenta smooth and creamy, while the vegetables were unbelievably good—so good, in fact, that I asked about them. Executive innkeeper Erik Sheetz explained to me that the grounds surrounding Glasbern have been reclaimed and developed, just like the buildings. Thus, many of the ingredients served, including the beets, are grown on the property in the organic vegetable gardens.

For dessert, I chose the Ginger-Almond Crème Brûlée, which was served with assorted fresh fruits and a Chocolate Cookie Spoon. This flavored cream with the merest wisp of caramelized sugar was very good indeed, and since Debbie wasn't there to stop me, I ate the entire dish!

It was a fabulous meal, and one I will not soon forget. As I left, I wandered down the long hallway to see the photographs of what the original buildings looked like. I lingered for just a moment to appreciate the enormity of the renovations that had been completed.

🌿 🌿 🌿 🌿 🌿 🌿

🌿 CIDER-ROASTED PHEASANT 🌿 WITH ONION GRITS AND ROOT VEGETABLES

2 2-pound pheasants, deboned
3 tablespoons olive oil, divided
4 cups apple cider, divided
4 tablespoons butter, divided
2 medium onions, chopped
4 cups cooked grits
2 medium red beets, sliced
2 medium yellow beets, sliced

Preheat oven to 350 degrees. Sear pheasants skin side down in a hot pan with 2 tablespoons of the olive oil until just brown; turn once. Add 2 cups of the cider to pan. Cover pan and bake for 10 minutes. In a saucepan, reduce the remaining 2 cups of cider by ½. Add 2 tablespoons of the butter, whisk, and set aside. In a separate pan, sauté onions in remaining olive oil until light brown. Add onions to cooked grits. Place red and yellow beets in a pan and roast with remaining butter for 12 minutes. To assemble, arrange beets around each of 2 plates and place grits in the center. Place pheasant atop grits and coat with the apple cider reduction. Serves 2.

🌿 🌿 🌿 🌿 🌿 🌿

🌿 GINGER-ALMOND CRÈME BRÛLÉE 🌿

2 cups heavy cream
½ cup sugar
4 egg yolks
½ cup almond liqueur
2 teaspoons fresh ginger, grated, or 1 teaspoon powdered ginger
fine sugar for dusting

Preheat oven to 300 degrees. Scald cream. In a bowl, whisk together sugar, egg yolks, liqueur, and ginger; continue to whisk mixture, gradually adding scalded cream. Strain mixture through a fine strainer. Place mixture in 4 6-ounce dishes. Place dishes in a large cooking pan and add water until it comes halfway up sides of dishes. Bake for 25 minutes. Remove dishes from oven. Allow to cool, then refrigerate. Prior to serving, remove from refrigerator, dust with fine sugar, and caramelize the top with a kitchen torch or place underneath a broiler; caramelization is complete when sugar takes on a caramel hue. Serves 4.

🌿 🌿 🌿 🌿 🌿 🌿

THE BARN
R E S T A U R A N T

PA 982 AND PA 31
LAURELVILLE, PA 15666
724-547-4500

In 1801, the Jacobs Creek Grist Mill stood across the street from where The Barn Restaurant is now located. The mill served this area until after the turn of the twentieth century, when it was abandoned. With an eye toward conservation, as is typical of those who work the land for a living, a local farmer decided to reuse parts of the mill. He purchased the hand-hewn beams, hauled them across the road, and put them back into service as part of a barn on his dairy farm. After the better part of another century, the dairy farm went the way of the gristmill. However, those beams still stand, an integral part of The Barn Restaurant's charm.

The rustic flavor of The Barn is softened by eleven French crystal chandeliers, artwork in gilded frames, tapestries, soothing piano music, and wonderful food. Providing good food in an enjoyable environment is part of owner Richard Gross's family heritage. Almost seventy years ago, his parents, Ben and Celia Gross, began operating The Ben Gross Restaurant on Clay Avenue in Jeanette. Although the family's longevity in the restaurant business has yet to approach the age of the beams, Richard now carries forth the tradition at The Barn.

There are plenty of opportunities for diners to experience The Barn. Lunch, dinner, Sunday champagne brunch, and dinner dances with either oldies or big-band music are designed to suit a wide range of interests and schedules. The menu is as varied as the dining opportunities. The appetizers range from a traditional Shrimp Cocktail to an unusual Stuffed Red Onion. The entrée selections include house specialties such as Blackened Salmon, Shrimp Scampi, Baby Back Pork Ribs, Pasta Rollups, and Ismael Bayeldi, a dish made from beef medallions, eggplant, tomato, croutons, and Mushroom Bordelaise Sauce.

We tried the deliciously creamy Corn Chowder, which was ladled right at the table. Debbie opted for the Cashew Chicken, a dish made interesting by serving the chicken, cashews, pea pods, and other ingredients mixed with fettuccine. Karen's Cajun Salmon was the best she'd ever eaten. Chocolate Eruption and Coconut Cream Torte were the desserts of choice. Both were extremely pleasing ways to end a delicious meal in a unique setting.

APPLE FENNEL STUFFING

1 cup onion, diced
½ cup celery, diced
4 cups Granny Smith apples, diced
2 tablespoons olive oil
2 teaspoons fennel seeds
1 large loaf bread, diced
2 cups chicken stock
½ cup butter
salt and pepper to taste

Sauté onions, celery, and apples in olive oil for 3 minutes. Add fennel seeds. Let cool for 5 minutes. Add bread, chicken stock, and butter. Add salt and pepper and mix well. Serves 6.

Note: Serve this as a side dish, or stuff 6 8-ounce chicken breasts that have been lightly pounded and dusted with paprika and parsley. Chicken should be baked uncovered at 350 degrees for 25 minutes or until it reaches 165 degrees.

ONION SOUP

3 tablespoons butter
8 cups onions, julienned
¼ cup flour
⅓ cup demi-reduction
16 cups chicken stock
pepper to taste
croutons
Parmesan cheese

Melt butter in a large pot. Add onions and cook until caramelized. Add flour and mix until smooth. Add demi-reduction and chicken stock and stir well. Simmer for 25 minutes or longer. Ladle into individual serving bowls. Add pepper and top with croutons and Parmesan. Place under a broiler until cheese is melted. Yields 16 1½-cup servings.

96 HICKORY BRIDGE ROAD
ORRTANNA, PA 17353
717-642-5261

Located just a few miles west of Gettysburg in the foothills of the Appalachian Mountains, Hickory Bridge Farm goes back to the late 1600s. Charles Carroll, father of one of the signers of the Declaration of Independence, was granted this parcel of land by the king of England. He later sold it after religious disputes with neighbors.

John Carrick settled the land where Hickory Bridge Farm is located. He and his family built the farmhouse from mud and bricks made from the property's clay soil. His sons were Revolutionary War soldiers. One of them, Samuel, became a well-known minister and teacher throughout southern Virginia and Tennessee. He founded Blount College, which later grew into the University of Tennessee.

John Carrick was nearly a hundred years old at the time of his death in 1812. The Herring family then took ownership of the farm, adding a distillery and a barn. Current owners Robert and Mary Lynn Martin have located Hickory Bridge Restaurant in that barn. Large chestnut beams support the structure, which is decorated with farm-related antiques, such as tools, implements, and kitchenware. Lanterns of all shapes, sizes, and varieties fill many of the nooks and crannies. Antique buggies and sleighs are also on display; the longest of them is used as a unique buffet for appetizers during dinner. Memorabilia from other owners—such as a photograph of the Heintzelman family and a copy of a public-sale notice—can be found on the walls.

The farm-style dinners at Hickory Bridge are extremely popular. Everything down to the piecrust is prepared on the premises, and many of the fruits and vegetables are grown on the property or on neighboring farms. The menu changes weekly, but dinner always consists of appetizers, salads, breads, vegetables, entrées, Stewed Apples, Corn Fritters, desserts, and beverages, at a fixed price. The Stewed Apples and Corn Fritters are every bit as good as Grandma's. In fact, Mary Lynn's mother, who wears an apron proudly proclaiming her status as a grandma, does a good bit of the cooking.

The guest cottages where we stayed are nestled in the woods on the bank of a creek. As the creek winds across the farm's seventy acres, it passes many interesting old structures, such as a springhouse and an outdoor oven. It eventually babbles and gurgles past the farmhouse under the bridge for which the farm is named.

STEWED APPLES

6 medium apples
1 cup water
½ cup light brown sugar
¼ cup butter or margarine
1 teaspoon lemon juice
¼ teaspoon nutmeg
1 teaspoon cinnamon

Pare, core, and cut apples into thick slices. Place in a large saucepan with water. Cook over medium heat until partially soft. Stir carefully to prevent thickening. Add brown sugar, butter, and lemon juice. Cook a few minutes more, then pour into a serving bowl. Sprinkle with nutmeg and cinnamon. Serves 4 to 6.

CORN FRITTERS

1 egg
½ cup milk
¼ cup sugar
15-ounce can cream-style corn
¼ teaspoon salt
2½ cups flour
1 tablespoon baking powder

Beat egg. Add milk, sugar, corn, and salt. Stir in flour. Fold baking powder into mixture. Fry by dropping batter with a tablespoon into 1½ inches of hot grease in a frying pan. Fry until batter is done in the center of the fritters and golden brown on the outside. Yields 1½ dozen small fritters.

FALL HARVEST BALL

14-ounce can red kidney beans, drained
1 cup cooked roast beef, chopped
¼ cup onion, chopped
¼ cup celery, chopped
1 tablespoon green pepper, chopped
1 tablespoon pimentos, chopped
2 tablespoons pickle relish
1 tablespoon prepared horseradish
½ cup mayonnaise
8-ounce package cream cheese, softened
¼ cup sour cream
½ cup sharp cheddar cheese, grated
1 teaspoon paprika
1 cup pecans, chopped
parsley
crackers

Combine first 12 ingredients in a mixing bowl. Chill mixture at least 2 hours. Shape mixture into a ball and sprinkle paprika over surface. Roll ball in pecans and place on a round serving platter. Garnish with parsley, arrange assorted crackers around edge of ball, and serve. Yields 1 ball.

Lesley's

10 MOUNTAIN VIEW LANE
DONEGAL, PA 15623
800-392-7773

Down a little country road just off US 31 sit a farmhouse and a barn surrounded by a split-rail fence. The original deed to this Westmoreland County property granted a land patent of three hundred acres to John Alexander. Two years prior to that, in 1786, the warrant for the patent had been signed by none other than Benjamin Franklin. Today, the homestead belongs to Gerard and Lesley O'Leary, who run Mountain View Bed and Breakfast, as well as Lesley's, an intimate restaurant housed in the barn on the property.

The barn, made from chestnut trees on the property, still has its rough-hewn plank floors. Wood from an old sliding door was used to create gables. The windows, gathered from salvage sites, all date to before 1840. Today, those windows offer a beautiful view of the countryside during the day and give off a warm glow from the single candles sitting on their ledges after dark. The staircase at the back of the waiting area was garnered from an old rectory in Uniontown. The mantelpieces are from the Federal period. The furnishings reflect the history of the site. The chairs and tables are an eclectic but attractive blend. Likewise, the china and silverware are mixtures of various styles that work well together.

The wine list here is fairly extensive, as are the choices of ports and other dessert beverages. The menu at Lesley's usually consists of two appetizers, two salads, and five delicious entrée choices, one of which is always Mountain View Beef Wellington. The selections change regularly—usually weekly—and are based on what is fresh and available to the chef. You might look forward to Orange Roughy with Tomato Butter Sauce and Onion Compote, Marinated Trout, or Leek Ravioli in Mushroom and Tomato Brown Sauce.

Seated at a window table, we gazed out at the lush hills of the Laurel Highlands as we mulled over our dinner choices. It was refreshing to sip a cool glass of water fresh from the farm's spring as we read. Our very knowledgeable server, Lee, brought to our attention many subtle details about the food and the menu. Karen chose an appetizer of Mussels prepared in a White Wine Sauce lightly flavored with anise. The anise was an unusual addition, but very good! Both of us opted for the Artichoke and Tomato Salad, every bite of which tasted of summer. For her entrée, Debbie chose Penne tossed with shrimp, mushrooms, asparagus, and sun-dried tomatoes. Karen chose the house specialty, Beef Wellington, served that evening with cauliflower and oven-roasted potatoes.

As tasty as our entrées were, the highlight of the evening most certainly was dessert. When presented with the menu, we simply could not choose. So we asked to sample all three desserts, and we were not disappointed. The Chocolate Splendor, made from seven different chocolates, was wonderfully moist and rich. The Cafe Latte Cheesecake was smooth, creamy, and delicious.

The third choice, a light, refreshing Orange Cake with raspberry filling, was scrumptious. Yum, yum, and again yum!

🌿 🌿 🌿 🌿 🌿 🌿

SUN-DRIED TOMATO MOZZARELLA APPETIZERS

¼ cup sun-dried tomatoes
4 ounces part-skim mozzarella cheese
2 tablespoons fresh basil leaves, chopped fine
1 clove garlic, minced
pepper
¼ cup olive oil
1 pint cherry tomatoes
salt

If using oil-packed sun-dried tomatoes, drain well, pat dry, and mince. If using dehydrated, soak in water for a few minutes, according to package directions; dry, then mince. Cut mozzarella into ¼-inch cubes. Combine cheese, basil, garlic, sun-dried tomatoes, and pepper in a small bowl. Add olive oil and blend well. Cover and refrigerate 1 hour to blend flavors. Just before serving, prepare cherry tomatoes by removing the stem ends and cutting a thin slice from bottoms of tomatoes to keep them sitting straight. Remove center from tomatoes with melon baller or small spoon. Sprinkle inside of tomatoes very lightly with salt and invert on paper towels to drain briefly. Stuff tomatoes with cheese mixture, garnish with extra basil, and serve immediately. Yields approximately 2 dozen appetizers.

🌿 🌿 🌿 🌿 🌿 🌿

SALADE NICOISE

6 tablespoons olive oil
6 tablespoons vegetable oil
2 tablespoons wine vinegar
2 teaspoons Dijon mustard
1 teaspoon salt
1 teaspoon fresh thyme, chopped
2 cloves garlic, crushed
pinch of black pepper
2 pounds fresh green beans, snipped
1 pound new potatoes
8 sole fillets, boned and skinned
12 to 14 cups romaine lettuce, washed and torn
29-ounce can artichoke hearts, drained
½ pound mushroom buttons, sliced and sautéed
1 pint cherry tomatoes
16 Greek olives
16 stuffed olives
2 red onions, diced or shredded
2-ounce can anchovies
⅓ cup parsley, minced
2 tablespoons sweet basil, chopped
6 hard-boiled eggs, quartered

Combine first 8 ingredients to make vinaigrette; reserve. Cut green beans into 1½-inch pieces and boil in salted water until al dente. Wash potatoes, boil to al dente, chill, peel, and slice thin. Poach sole and chill. Arrange lettuce, artichoke hearts, mushrooms, green beans, potatoes, cherry tomatoes, olives, onions, sole, and anchovies on chilled salad plates. Sprinkle with parsley. Dress with vinaigrette and garnish with basil and eggs. Serves 8.

🌿 🌿 🌿 🌿 🌿 🌿

1005 HORSHAM ROAD
NORTH WALES, PA 19454
215-362-7500

Joseph Ambler was the skilled wheelwright who built this fieldstone home in 1734. Surviving from those early days—and providing an impressive collection of early architecture on one estate—are the tenant cottage and the stone bank barn. It is in the barn that Joseph Ambler's delectable restaurant is housed.

Random-width wood floors, handcrafted cherry tables, Windsor chairs, and exposed stone walls contribute an atmosphere worthy of the food that is served. The still-intact stable doors provide an interesting ambiance to both the exterior and interior. Above, the large window that replaced the doors of the hayloft washes the interior with the dappled sunlight that makes its way through the trees. Miniature quilts hang on the walls, and area rugs warm the wood floors, providing colonial color to the interior, while wrought-iron accessories remind guests of the structure's early days. The bar, located just to the right of the entrance, is a warm setting full of richly polished wood. Two of the dining rooms are intimate, seating about twenty people each.

The third dining room, in the back of the barn, is slightly larger.

Rack of Lamb, the house specialty, is prepared several different ways. It may be pan-seared and served with Pink Peppercorn Sauce, accompanied by Smoked Tomato and Herb Risotto. Or guests might find the lamb brushed with Dijon mustard, then coated with seasoned breadcrumbs and a mild Garlic Sauce. An equally appealing option is the Rack of Lamb smoked in Moroccan spices and served with Apricot Sauce.

The rest of the menu is just as deliciously tempting. The unusual appetizers include Lobster and Chicken Sausage, Thai Beef, and the Joseph Ambler Inn Sampler, which allows those of us tempted by more than one of the tasty starters not to miss a morsel. The list of entrées provides selections such as Tilapia with Horseradish Sauce, Blackberry-Barbecued Leg of Duck, and Roast Pheasant Stuffed with Mozzarella and Sautéed Spinach. Even something as traditional as Surf-'N'-Turf gets an updated twist! Here, it's a petite filet encased by Lobster Française and served with sautéed Swiss chard, Napa cabbage, and Pear William Ginger Sauce—truly innovative and truly delicious.

We got the full effect of the Joseph Ambler Inn, as we spent the night in the Penn Suite, located in the original farmhouse. The estate's schoolroom, located on the first floor of this building, now functions as a parlor for all the guests. The room's fireplace is enormous. The fireplace in our room was also large, located in the rustic sitting area of the suite. Up a tiny set of curving stairs was the bedroom area, comfortably appointed with period furniture. It was easy to imagine a time when climbing out of bed and heading for the barn was done a lot earlier than we made the trek, and for a more difficult purpose than a filling farm breakfast.

THREE-TIERED TROUT WITH LEMON CAPER BUTTER

6 tablespoons smoked salmon, chopped fine
2 3-ounce packages cream cheese
2 teaspoons cracked black peppercorns
2 8-ounce rainbow trout, deboned, heads removed
4 tablespoons jumbo lump crabmeat
1 Idaho potato, peeled and grated
2 tablespoons fresh herbs, chopped
salt to taste
2 tablespoons extra-virgin olive oil
4 tablespoons Lemon Caper Butter (see next column)

Place salmon, cream cheese, and pepper in a standard mixer with a whip attachment. Whip on high speed approximately 1 minute until ingredients are well blended. Remove from mixer

and place in a piping bag with a large star tip. Place trout on a baking sheet or other flat surface skin side down. Pipe salmon mixture down both sides of trout. Place crab on top of salmon. Mix potato with herbs and salt and place a generous portion over crab. Heat olive oil in a medium sauté pan over medium-high heat. Place fish in pan potato side down. Be careful not to flip fish before potato has turned golden brown. When potato reaches that point (after about 3 minutes), the trout is almost done; flip trout and cook approximately 2 minutes on skin side. Finish trout in a preheated 350-degree oven for 8 to 10 minutes. Remove from oven and place on 2 plates. Top with Lemon Caper Butter and serve. Serves 2.

LEMON CAPER BUTTER

juice of 1 lemon
½ cup white wine
pinch of minced shallots
1 tablespoon roasted red pepper, chopped
1 teaspoon capers
2 tablespoons butter, sliced
salt and pepper to taste

Over high heat in a medium sauté pan, reduce juice, wine, and shallot by ½. Remove pan from heat and whip in remaining ingredients. Keep in a warm area until ready to serve. Yields about 4 tablespoons.

SAUTÉED SEA SCALLOPS WITH SPINACH PESTO AND SUN-DRIED TOMATO CREAM SAUCE

Spinach Pesto

½ bag spinach, cleaned and picked over
8 fresh basil leaves
¼ cup pine nuts
¼ cup Parmesan cheese
1½ cloves fresh garlic, minced
½ cup extra-virgin olive oil

Purée all ingredients but oil in a food processor. Continue to blend while slowly adding oil until mixture is thick. Set aside.

Sun-Dried Tomato Cream Sauce

½ cup white wine
1 tablespoon shallots, chopped
2 tablespoons sun-dried tomatoes, chopped
1 bay leaf
½ pint heavy cream
salt and pepper to taste

Over high heat in a medium sauté pan, reduce wine, shallots, tomatoes, and bay leaf by ½. Add cream and reduce until thick. Remove bay leaf and discard. Add salt and pepper as desired.

Scallops

20 jumbo sea scallops
1 tablespoon olive oil
fresh basil for garnish

In a thick skillet or saucepan on high heat, sauté scallops in oil until golden brown. Pull from heat and top with pesto mixture. Put scallops on a cookie sheet. Place under broiler for 1 to 2 minutes to heat pesto. Serve over Sun-Dried Tomato Cream Sauce and garnish with basil. Serves 2.

GLEN MILLS AND THORNTON ROADS
THORNTON, PA 19373
610-459-3702

Prominent Whig Party member George Gray operated a ferry across the Schuykill River. During the Revolutionary War, Gray felt that his family would be safer at his summer home, called the Yellow House, which was located in the heart of the Brandywine Valley. However, to counter the movements of the British army, Washington and his troops advanced to nearby Chadds Ford, which meant that the Yellow House was within earshot of the fighting. During the Battle of Brandywine, wounded soldiers were brought to the home, where Gray's wife and daughters helped care for them. The effort put forth by these women has been remembered through the centuries, as hospital volunteers around the country are frequently called "Gray ladies."

Since British muskets had a very short range, many of the soldiers they shot received injuries from the knees down. Hence, the area around the home-turned-hospital became known as Shintown. At other times, the area was known as Thorntonville or Yellow House, so named in honor of Gray's large, two-story structure,

complete with a wide porch perfect for swings and rocking chairs.

After the war, Thomas Carlton took over the building and set up hand looms in its spacious interior. The looms were used to manufacture towels and linens. When a general store was established on the Gray property around 1830, the name of the area was changed to Thornton. Today, it remains fairly close to what it was then, an unobtrusive intersection with a few houses, a store, and what is reputed to be the longest continuously operating post office in the United States.

Ted Pace converted the old barn on the Gray property into a restaurant after he purchased the estate in 1978. Originally from Pittsburgh, where his family has a long tradition in the food industry, he has used his expertise to create Pace One's dining experience. Hand-hewn beams and walls from the 1740s stone barn are part of the charming decor, as are pierced-tin lighting fixtures and simple furniture. Guests enter through the bar area, where braided rugs are scattered on the plank floor and an old feed bin has been turned into a cozy window seat. At the other end of the bar sits an old feed bucket, now used to chill bottles of wine. A huge cast-iron pot hangs in the front dining room against an original stone wall. Pictures of structures similar to Pace One decorate the walls of the larger dining room.

The menu at Pace One is in keeping with the history of the building. Sparkling Apple Cider is featured on the beverage list, while New England Pudding is listed as one of the desserts. As we scanned the menu, our server brought us a heaping plate of Pumpernickel Bread, served with Feta, Cream Cheese, and Butter Spread. To go along with the bread, we had the Butternut Squash and Apple Bisque. It was fabulous—definitely one of the best soups we'd ever tasted. Light and creamy, with bits of various squash for texture, it had a flavor that was overtly apple, with a light touch of butternut. Debbie ordered the evening's pork selection, served with Southwestern Compound Butter and Raspberry Reduction. It was accompanied by Red Cabbage Slaw and a delicious side dish of White Cheddar Grits. Karen opted for the more traditional Lobster, Shrimp, and Crab Casserole. Served piping hot, this rich, creamy casserole was full of seafood. Ted Pace shared the recipe with us, so everyone can have a taste of Pace One's tradition.

NEW ENGLAND PUDDING

2 15-ounce cans pineapple chunks
6½ cups apples, pared, cored, and cubed
1½ cups walnuts, chopped
1 cup brown sugar
4 eggs
2 cups sugar
2 cups flour
1½ cups butter, melted
ice cream

Drain pineapple completely. Place pineapple and apples in the bottom of a 12-by-9-inch pan. Spread walnuts and brown sugar over fruit. Whip eggs in a mixer. Add sugar and blend. Add flour and melted butter alternately until mix is smooth. Spread mixture over fruit, concentrating on the center of the pan, away from the edges. Bake in oven about 1 hour until golden brown. Poke crust with a finger; if it is still runny underneath, continue baking until firm. Serve warm with ice cream. Serves 12.

LOBSTER, SHRIMP, AND CRAB CASSEROLE

3 pounds lobster meat
1½ pound shrimp
6 cups mayonnaise
6 eggs
2¼ tablespoons garlic powder
2¼ tablespoons Old Bay seasoning
½ loaf fresh white bread
2 pounds lump crabmeat, cleaned

Drain lobster and shrimp, squeezing out excess water. Combine mayonnaise, eggs, garlic powder, and Old Bay. Mix thoroughly. Remove crust of bread, then cube. Add to mayonnaise mixture. Cut lobster into 1-ounce portions. Mix lobster, shrimp, and crabmeat into mayonnaise-and-bread mixture. Divide mixture among 10 individual casseroles. Bake at 350 degrees for 30 minutes until heated through. Serves 10.

1 PINE BARN PLACE
DANVILLE, PA 17821
570-275-2071

This typical German bank barn was built during the early nineteenth century on property deeded by William Penn. After the death of the original farmer who owned the property, the acreage was divided equally among his five sons. About that same time, Abigail Geisinger saw the need to build a quality medical facility in Danville. Three of the brothers sold their acreage to allow for expansion of the Geisinger Medical Center during the 1920s. At that time, part of the barn was turned into a stable. The barn was located just down the hill from the hospital. It was convenient to have horses close by, so they could be used for transportation when making house calls. Once the automobile came into fashion, the barn was turned into a riding stable for local residents.

During World War II, an eccentric citizen converted the barn into his residence. He boasted that it was the first all-electric house in the state. He even installed a circular platform on which he could park his car. At the push of a button, the platform would rotate 180 degrees. By using this contraption, this gentleman never had to back his car in or out of the barn!

It was in 1950 that an entrepreneur first saw potential in creating a first-rate restaurant from this multipurpose barn. Martin Walzer purchased the property in 1967. Over the years, Pine Barn Inn has developed into one of the finest restaurants and lodgings in the area.

The building's history as a barn is evident in the main dining room, where the original stone walls have been whitewashed. The crossbeams and support beams are there, too, draped with pine boughs to add a festive touch. Along one wall sits an old feed bin, adding charm to the decor. The bar area of the restaurant was once the stable. Dried flowers and baskets hang alongside farm implements and an old doctor's bag. The focal point of this room is the stone fireplace, still in working order and blackened from smoke.

While we dined in the Garden Room, the staff prepared for the weekly Thursday-night cookout. We opted for light summer fare, choosing the Pine Barn Salad, a delicious combination of iceberg lettuce, spring greens, mandarin oranges, grapes, red onions, and sliced almonds. Topped off with Fruit Vinaigrette Dressing, it was deliciously different. Our other choice was the day's special, White Albacore Tuna Salad on a French Roll, topped with shredded carrots, alfalfa sprouts, and white American cheese.

Our server told us to save room for "Polly's pies," and we took her at her word. Every morning around six o'clock, Polly, age seventy-something, comes in and bakes pies, pies, and more pies. Not wishing to disappoint her, we chose the pie of the day, Lemon Sponge. It proved a light, fluffy end to a delicious meal.

That was the end of lunch, but not the end of

our Pine Barn experience. Following an afternoon of research, we stopped back at the dining room for our second round of sweets. The Florentina Cone, a brown, sugary Austrian-style dessert edged in white chocolate and filled with whipped cream and fruit, was just enough for an afternoon bite. Karen's fondness for English meringues prompted her to have the Vacherin, two meringues filled with low-fat strawberry yogurt and topped with cream and Strawberry Sauce. There were several others we wanted to try, but at last, we rediscovered our restraint.

CHICKEN SCIUTTO

½ cup butter
4 6-ounce skinless, boneless chicken breasts, cut into strips
seasoned flour
1 cup Chardonnay
2 cups mushrooms, sliced
2 cups scallions, chopped
2 cups tomatoes, diced
½ pound prosciutto, cut into strips
2 tablespoons fresh parsley, chopped
1 tablespoon garlic, chopped
1 tablespoon Italian seasoning
½ tablespoon lemon juice
2 pounds mozzarella, grated

Melt butter in a large skillet. Dredge chicken in seasoned flour. Place chicken in hot skillet and cook until golden brown. Deglaze skillet with wine and add mushrooms, scallions, tomatoes, prosciutto, parsley, garlic, Italian seasoning, and lemon juice. Cook on low heat for 5 minutes. Place on heat-proof plates, top with mozzarella, and melt cheese under broiler. Serve immediately. Serves 6 to 8.

FRUIT VINAIGRETTE DRESSING

¼ cup cider vinegar
¾ cup salad oil
¼ cup strawberry jelly
¼ cup cherry-pineapple jelly
¾ teaspoon onion powder
¾ teaspoon garlic powder
¾ teaspoon salt
¼ teaspoon black pepper
1 teaspoon sugar

Combine all ingredients in a blender and mix well. Yields 1½ cups.

at the Gables

900 SOUTH MAIN STREET
LEWISTOWN, PA 17044
717-248-4242

Lewistown was originally the site of the Ohesson Indian village. A mural painted on wood by Ken Wilson in 1958 depicts this history. Today, the mural hangs in the main dining room of the restaurant called At the Gables. When it was commissioned, it hung in the Ohesson Room of the Green Gables Hotel, the pride of Lewistown, known for miles around. In addition to the Indian village, the mural shows the location of many other early sites, such as Freedom Forge, the Stone Arch Bridge, and First Church, built in 1776.

Fifty-five years after the church was established, the first building was constructed on this property. Built in 1831, that barn housed carriage horses and served as a stagecoach stop. The heavy, hand-hewn beams still visible in the dining room are breathtaking in their enormity. Rosalee Dodson, the owner of At the Gables, told us that two men lost their lives trying to get those beams down the river, up the bank, and into position for the barn.

Deeds to the property have been traced as far back as 1864, when owner Joseph B. Ard conveyed the land to David Woods. In 1908, the O'Meara family purchased the 180 acres for the sum of $20,000. In the process, the O'Mearas created the largest dairy farm in Mifflin County. A recent dinner guest at the restaurant told the staff that his father used to milk cows in the very room in which he now ate.

Today, it's a welcoming room with a large stone fireplace and plaster walls. Coach lights provide warm lighting from their perches on the columns and along the walls. An interesting terrazzo floor at one end serves as a stage when local artists such as the group Blackwater perform. At that same end of the room is an unusual mosaic archway. It had been covered up for quite some time when a workman inadvertently discovered it. It turns out that it was a fountain during the barn's tenure as the Green Gables Hotel.

As we sat and browsed through two scrapbooks about the building's history, we were taken by the pride that prompted so many residents to assist in its renovation. Even the local firemen got involved, contributing their equipment to help in the painting of the highest peaks as the structure was converted from the Green Gables Hotel to the Inn at the Gables.

It was late when we arrived, so we opted for dessert before relaxing for the evening. Taking a quick look at the dinner menu, we noted that it has traditional favorites for everyone. Porkchops, Veal Parmesan, Sirloin Steak, and Butterflied Shrimp are some of the choices available.

Breakfast the following morning was enjoyable. We chatted with Rosalee Dodson at a table beside the fire. Starting the morning with a Vegetarian Omelet and Apple-Banana French Toast with Strawberry Syrup, we felt replenished to start our day.

❧ BAKED CORN ❧

7 eggs, beaten
¼ cup cornstarch
¼ cup sugar
1½ teaspoons butter-flavored oil
1½ teaspoons salt
8 cups creamed corn
4 cups milk

Preheat oven to 350 degrees. Combine all ingredients and place in a large casserole. Bake in a water bath approximately 2½ hours until set. Serves 10.

❧ ❧ ❧ ❧ ❧ ❧

❧ SWEET AND SOUR DRESSING ❧

2½ cups sugar
¾ cup vinegar
1½ teaspoons celery seed
½ cup Miracle Whip
¼ cup mustard
½ teaspoon salt
1½ teaspoons black pepper
2 tablespoons onions, chopped
1½ cups salad oil

Combine all ingredients except oil. Gradually add oil while continuing to beat mixture. Store in the refrigerator in an airtight container. Yields 4 cups.

Note: This dressing will keep for up to 60 days.

❧ ❧ ❧ ❧ ❧ ❧

CHAPTER 3

In Days Gone By

The Towne House Inn

The statement "The more things change, the more they stay the same" certainly applies to the establishments in this chapter, all of which served as homes in times past. Today, although each functions as a restaurant, the homey atmosphere has been maintained through original floor plans, appointments such as fireplaces and windows, and domestic touches such as period furnishings, wallpaper, and window treatments. So visit and enjoy a new home away from home.

Sunnyledge

5124 FIFTH AVENUE
PITTSBURGH, PA 15232
412-683-5014

As we entered the sweeping brick driveway and pulled the car up to the front door, we both began to smile, because we knew that we were in for a treat. As the valet whisked away the automobile and we entered the main hall, we were enveloped in the luxurious atmosphere of Sunnyledge. Built in 1886 as the home and office of Dr. James H. McClelland, it is now a Boutique Hotel and restaurant and a National Historic Landmark.

Straight ahead is the original gleaming, wood-paneled Victorian staircase carpeted in taupe floral, which leads upstairs to the eight lavish guest rooms complete with Egyptian linens and marble bathrooms. Downstairs, on the main floor, what was once Dr. McClelland's office is now the library, complete with original oak paneling, bookshelves, and fireplace. An antique phonograph sits in the corner of the cozy room, which has stuffed chairs, a pedestal table, and vases of fresh flowers. Crossing the hall, guests enter the original living room, which now serves as the Tea Room, or main dining room. Blue silk draperies with deep fringe pockets swag the

windows, and the faux-tile ceiling reminds visitors of Sunnyledge's earlier era. Victorian-style chairs provide much of the seating. Next door, Dr. McClelland's dining room now houses a sweeping, tile-topped oak bar and matching tables. This room is particularly popular when young neighborhood professionals stop in after work.

The restaurant serves breakfast, lunch, tea, and Sunday brunch. Dinner is offered Wednesday through Saturday. The lunch menu is innovative, the choices ranging from Fire-Roasted Vegetable Salad to Spinach and Feta Cheese Strudel. The dinner menu is upscale traditional. The choices there include Veal Marsala, Confetti Fettuccine, and New York Strip au Poivre.

After ordering, each table is served a spread accompanied by Toast Rounds. By the time our server came back to identify what it was, the Toast Rounds were gone and our ramekin was conspicuously empty! Our spread happened to be a fabulous Red Pepper and Broccoli combination, but the selection varies from day to day. The appetizer selections included such delectable choices as Spring Rolls, Cheddar Fritters, and Lobster Croquettes. We were both extremely pleased with our meal choices. Karen *mmm*ed and *aah*ed her way through the Lobster Salad, served on a bed of field greens in a creamy dressing, garnished with shrimp puffs, and topped with black caviar. It was truly delicious. Fettuccine in Green Pepper Vodka Sauce with tomatoes, onion, and Parmesan cheese was Debbie's choice. The serving was plentiful and the flavor absolutely wonderful. A definite winner!

The service at Sunnyledge is equal to the surroundings and the food. We left the dining room and took one last, longing look around the beautifully restored home. As we turned to leave, the valet was there, keys in hand, and our car was at the front door, ready to go. True service at its best.

❦ ❦ ❦ ❦ ❦ ❦

VICTORIAN CHOCOLATE

2 cups heavy whipping cream
1/3 cup sugar
1 tablespoon Karo syrup
8 ounces semisweet chocolate

Combine cream, sugar, and syrup in a sauce pot. Bring to a boil, remove from heat, and add chocolate. Stir with a wooden spoon (to prevent bubbles) until chocolate is completely melted. Pour into 8 to 10 4-inch ramekins and cover immediately with plastic wrap on the surface of the chocolate until mixture cools and sets; putting plastic wrap on the surface keeps the chocolate from drying out. Yields 8 to 10 desserts.

❦ ❦ ❦ ❦ ❦ ❦

CONFETTI FETTUCCINE

Fettuccine

2 to 3 tablespoons olive oil
10 shrimp
2 tablespoons garlic, chopped fine
1/2 cup onion, chopped
1 cup sun-dried tomatoes, sliced in half
2 teaspoons red pepper flakes
salt and pepper to taste
1 cup Fried Capers (see below)
1 pound fettuccine, cooked
1/4 cup chopped parsley for garnish

In a nonstick frying pan, heat olive oil and cook shrimp halfway. Add garlic, onions, tomatoes, and red pepper flakes. Sauté until shrimp is cooked through. Season with salt and pepper. Add Fried Capers. Heat cooked fettuccine in microwave. Toss pasta with shrimp mixture and sprinkle with parsley. Serves 2.

Fried Capers

vegetable oil or olive oil
1 cup capers

In a small pot, heat enough oil to cover capers. Fry capers until crispy; this may take up to 15 minutes. Drain capers. Save the oil; it is now a caper oil and may be used for cooking.

❦ ❦ ❦ ❦ ❦ ❦

1844 RESTAURANT

PA 66 NORTH
LEECHBURG, PA 15656
724-845-1844

Two years of restoration in the 1970s created the 1844 Dining and Keeping Room from an early-American homestead built by James and Robert Coulter. Although the grant for the property can be traced back to 1756, the land was not cultivated until this farmhouse—consisting of a root cellar, a kitchen, a dining room, two front parlors, and four bedrooms—was constructed. Though the year of construction is unknown, the first recorded date related to the property was a tax assessment in 1844.

The farm was sold to Hiram Hill, who eventually sold it in 1893 to his son-in-law, Anthony Wayne Smith. After settling his family on the farm, Smith became successful in the fruit business. He and his son, Herman Hill Smith, also developed quite a reputation for raising standard-bred horses. During that time, the property was called Pleasant Valley Stock Farm. It was home to Hyland Barron, a stud, and Katrina Belle Sire, a harness-racing mare, both well-known horses of their time. Herman Hill Smith was an active farmer until his death in 1961. His wife, Marie, continued living on the property until the early 1970s.

Each of the original rooms had a fireplace in it. The restoration maintained those fireplaces as the focal point of each room. The root cellar has fieldstone walls. It now functions as the bar and casual dining room, called The Keeping Room. The stone fireplace there crackled cheerily the night we visited. Upstairs, antiques such as cast-iron cooking pots and copper tubs decorate the early-American dining rooms, as do antique photographs on the walls. The service mirrors the tradition of the old farmhouse. Folksy and friendly, the wait staff provides excellent, efficient service while still finding time to chat.

The food is anything but old-fashioned, however. The menu says that the restaurant specializes in Prime Rib (which even appears on the lengthy appetizer menu), but the seafood selections are definite winners as well. The Buffalo Shrimp, a seafood version of wings, were delicious—not too tangy, not too spicy. Debbie's salad of spring greens was topped by a balsamic vinaigrette with pesto mixed in, a creative and tasty touch. The Blackened Tuna in Gingered Buerre Blanc Sauce, available as an appetizer or an entrée, was wonderful. Equally enjoyable was the sampler of Grilled Chicken, Grilled Tuna, and Grilled Swordfish, each served in its own sauce— Teriyaki, Gingered Buerre Blanc, and Shiitake Peppercorn Cream, respectively. Believe it or not, we saved room for dessert, trying the Chocolate Mousse Cake, sinfully good and not as rich as expected, and the Raspberry Cheesecake Parfait. The light, refreshing parfait consisted of a scoop of vanilla ice cream topped by cheesecake pieces, fresh Raspberry Sauce, and whipped cream. It was certainly one of the most deliciously innovative desserts we've encountered.

TUNA TATAKI WITH PONZO SAUCE

1 pound sashimi-quality tuna
2 lemons
2 limes
2 oranges
dash of soy sauce
2 teaspoons Shichimi (Japanese seven spice)
1 bunch scallions, cut thin
1 thumb ginger, peeled and grated

Heat skillet to 500 degrees. Sear outside of tuna for 2 minutes on each side. Place in freezer for approximately 10 minutes or until cool. Slice paper-thin and place on 4 appetizer dishes. Squeeze juice of lemons, limes, and oranges into a bowl. Add soy sauce and Shichimi; mix. Add scallions and ginger to sauce; mix again. Serve atop tuna. Serves 4.

SHRIMP CHRISTINE

2 large red peppers
½ cup roasted almond slivers
3 teaspoons olive oil
16 large shrimp, peeled, deveined, and washed
2 teaspoons Cajun spice
4 cloves garlic, peeled and chopped
1 bunch fresh basil, chopped

Roast peppers over an open flame until completely black. Place in an ice bath and peel. Cut into julienne slices and set aside. Roast almonds under broiler and set aside. Heat olive oil in a large sauté pan. Dust shrimp in Cajun spice and cook approximately 2 minutes on medium heat; add roasted pepper, garlic, and almonds. Flip shrimp, reduce heat to simmer, and continue cooking until pink. Add basil just before serving. Serves 4 as an appetizer or 2 as an entrée.

A Bed & Breakfast Inn

PA 601
SOMERSET, PA 15501
814-443-1043

After reading a magazine article about opportunities for young men, farm boy D. B. Zimmerman left his North Dakota home, headed farther west, and bought his first cattle in 1877. Soon, cattle bearing the "Z" brand grazed on acreage stretching from the Dakotas to California. It has been said that Zimmerman's ranches shipped at least forty thousand cattle to market each year.

Twenty years after starting his cattle venture, Zimmerman was at the forefront of Pennsylvania's coal-mining industry, developing mines at Goodtown and company towns called Wilson Creek, Ralphton, and Zimmerman within Somerset County. By age forty-five, he was the county's largest independent coal operator. By age fifty, he was the largest independent cattle dealer in the United States.

The wealthy Zimmerman built what many called "Somerset's most pretentious home," where he lived with his wife, Lizzie; his son, Ralph; and his daughter, Sally. Since Mrs. Zimmerman was a homebody, Sally frequently served as hostess for her father's parties and as his traveling companion when he visited his many holdings. Zimmerman died in 1928. Sally, who never wed, continued to live in the mansion until 1944, when she sold it to a local coal operator. Just five years later, the house was sold for $30,500 at a sheriff's auction.

Vacant for many years, the mansion was restored to its original grandeur and opened as a bed-and-breakfast in 1993. It is paneled with native wood and decorated with brass and silver wall fixtures. We were impressed by the crystal and gold-leaf chandeliers, the elegant moldings, and the nine fireplaces. Opening the oversized front door and entering the marble entrance hall, guests step into an atmosphere of elegance known to the wealthy at the turn of the century.

Through the hall is the main dining room, with its herringbone-pattern parquet floor. Here, guests look out over the portico and Lake Somerset beyond. Down the hall to the right is the library/sitting room, which is beautifully decorated in period reproductions. The atmosphere is so welcoming that, on the day of our visit, a luncheon guest sat down at the grand piano and serenaded us while we waited. Just off the sitting room is the sunroom, where we were seated. It is a bright, airy room with terrazzo floors, French doors, and filigreed shutters.

We enjoyed tea while savoring our panoramic view. A plate of sandwiches—Toasted Triangles with Mushroom Spread, Banana Nut Bread with Cream Cheese Filling, Salmon Pâté, Cucumber on Marbled Rye, and Tomato Basil on Pumpernickel—was served to each of us. Although it was difficult to choose, our favorite was the Smoked Chicken with Lingonberries on a Mini-Croissant. The sandwiches were followed by Scones and cream and jam, which were then followed by Apple Strudel.

Jon Knaupp, who operates The Inn at Georgian Place, is a delightful individual who truly cares about the home's preservation. As we toured the upstairs guest rooms after tea, he accepted our praise in humble fashion. Although he spoke of his disappointment that the grounds of the original estate had been sold, we are very glad that the manor house was saved and is now under his expert care.

ROASTED POBLANO CHILI SOUP

10 Poblano chilis
1 large onion, chopped
1 teaspoon garlic, minced
2 tablespoons butter
3 14½-ounce cans chicken broth
2 cups half-and-half
¼ teaspoon ground cumin
kosher salt to taste
ground white pepper to taste
crème fraîche

Blacken outer skin of chilis. Place chilis in a bowl and cover with plastic wrap. Let sit for 15 minutes to loosen skin. Peel, seed, and chop chilis. Sauté onion and garlic in butter until soft and golden. Add chopped chilis. Purée in a food processor, then pour into a medium saucepan. Add chicken broth, half-and-half, and cumin. Add kosher salt and white pepper. Cook until desired thickness. To serve, garnish with crème fraîche. Serves 4.

MUSHROOM SPREAD FOR TEA SANDWICHES

1 cup shallots
6 pounds mushrooms
½ cup butter
2 teaspoons thyme
2 teaspoons savory
2 teaspoons ground rosemary
2 teaspoons salt
dash of ground white pepper
¼ cup sherry
3 8-ounce packages cream cheese
loaf of sliced white bread

Chop shallots and mushrooms in a food processor. Place butter in a saucepan and sauté shallots and mushrooms until dry. Add spices and sherry and simmer for a few minutes. Turn off heat and add cream cheese. Mix well and allow to cool completely. Spread one slice of bread with mushroom mixture and place another slice over the top; repeat until you have as many sandwiches as desired. Grill sandwiches on both sides. Trim crusts and cut into quarters. Yields approximately 40 tea sandwiches.

Historic
DILWORTHTOWN *Inn*
Established 1758

1390 OLD WILMINGTON PIKE
WEST CHESTER, PA 19382
610-399-1390

From the middle of the eighteenth century until the early twentieth century, Dilworthtown was a thriving village. Local businesses included a general store, a blacksmith's shop, a wheelwright's shop, a harness and saddlery shop, a cheese factory, a millinery, and a shingle- and stave-cutting operation. There was also a powder keg manufacturer who was so successful that in 1849, he produced a thousand powder kegs and twenty thousand flour barrels.

This thriving hamlet began when James Dilworth built the first log cabin here. In need of additional space to shelter his family of eleven children, he built a new home behind the cabin in 1754. After his death in 1770, his son Charles applied for a tavern license, thus beginning the history of Dilworthtown Inn. The inn has been known by many names through the years, including Sign of the Pennsylvania Farmer, The Black Horse Tavern, Sign of the Rising Sun, and Cross Keys.

The inn was occupied by British troops during and after the Battle of Brandywine. Charles Dilworth, a well-known Whig, found it necessary to submit a damage claim for losses totaling 820 pounds, 15 shillings, 3 pence. He claimed that the soldiers had broken doors and a staircase and had even "pulled down an oven." He also listed the loss of livestock and of a servant, age fourteen, who decided to join the British army.

Although the damage was great, the inn continued in operation, assuming its current name in 1821. Through most of the twentieth century, the dwelling served as a private residence and boardinghouse. Extensive renovation began in 1969 and continued through 1972, when the inn was once again opened for dining.

Guests enjoy the elegant simplicity of the inn's many dining rooms, each of which is unique. Colonial colors and decor are prevalent throughout. Attractive stenciling adorns the walls in each room. Likewise, each room has a fireplace.

We each started with soup, a cup of the Shrimp and Fennel Bisque for Karen and the evening's special, Yukon Gold Potato Soup, for Debbie. Both were creamy and delicious. During the salad course, we both opted for the Toasted Sesame Salad Dressing, the house specialty. As we raved about its unusual flavor to our waiter, he explained that the recipe had been introduced by the Korean chef who worked at the inn many years ago.

This fact helped us start a conversation with the delightful couple with whom we shared the small dining room. We all proceeded through our tasty entrées, our choices being the Grilled Ostrich Tenderloin and the Pan-Roasted Breast of Chicken. The presentation was lovely and the flavor equal to the food's appearance. When it came time for dessert, what the waiter gave us wasn't really a listing of the choices, but more of a recitation! The list was lengthy, and everything on it was appealingly unusual. Karen chose the Three-Layered Chocolate Mousse, served in a graham crust. The Tropical Bombe caught

Debbie's fancy. It was light and had layers of Almond Meringue and Mango and Coconut Sorbet separated by a thin, white cake.

When the couple ordered their desserts, they told the waiter that they had listened intently, so he didn't have to go through the breathtaking list again. Thanks to their warm conversation, the evening was truly delightful. Good company and wonderful food in lovely surroundings are always a perfect recipe.

MARYLAND CRAB AND SWEET CORN CHOWNER

6 large ears sweet corn
1 teaspoon corn oil
2 medium onions, diced
2 cloves garlic, chopped
3 cups chicken stock
2 cups heavy cream
salt and white pepper to taste
1 pound jumbo lump crabmeat
1 medium baking potato, peeled and diced medium
¼ red bell pepper, seeded and diced small, membranes removed
¼ yellow bell pepper, seeded and diced small, membranes removed
1 tablespoon parsley, chopped fine

Shuck corn, remove silk, and cut kernels from cob. Set aside ¾ cup of corn. Heat oil in a heavy saucepan over medium heat. Stir in remaining corn and onions. Sauté vegetables until soft; do not brown. Add garlic and chicken stock and bring to a boil. Reduce heat and simmer for 20 minutes. Stir in cream and simmer for 5 to 10 minutes until slightly reduced. Remove soup from heat and blend until very smooth. Season with salt and white pepper. Set aside and keep warm. Add crabmeat. Fill a large pot with boiling water. Add potato and cook for 2 minutes. Add ¾ cup of corn kernels set aside earlier, along with bell peppers. Drain vegetables and immediately add to soup. Garnish with chopped parsley. Serves 6.

PAN-SEARED SHRIMP WITH JULIENNED VEGETABLES AND PERNOD CREAM SAUCE

Vegetables

1 tablespoon olive oil
1 bunch asparagus, bias-cut
1 bulb fennel, julienned
1 red pepper, julienned
1 tablespoon shallots, minced
1 teaspoon garlic, minced
salt and pepper to taste
1 tablespoon parsley, chopped
1 tablespoon basil, cut into fine strips

Place olive oil, asparagus, fennel, and red pepper in a warm sauté pan. Sweat for about 2 minutes. Add shallots and garlic and sweat for about 30 seconds. Season with salt and pepper and toss in fresh herbs. Cook until vegetables are tender.

Shrimp and Pernod Cream Sauce

15 jumbo shrimp
salt and pepper to taste
1 tablespoon olive oil
1 tablespoon shallots, minced
1 teaspoon garlic, minced
¾ cup Pernod
1 cup heavy cream
1 tablespoon chives, chopped fine
1 tablespoon parsley, chopped
additional fresh herbs for garnish

Season shrimp with salt and pepper. Place shrimp and oil into a warm sauté pan. In about 1 minute, shrimp will start to curl. Flip them over and toss in shallots and garlic. Sweat for about 30 seconds, then add Pernod. Reduce by ⅔. Add cream and reduce. Toss in chives and parsley. When shrimp are fully cooked, take them out and finish reducing the sauce until it coats the back of a spoon.

To serve, place julienned vegetables in the center of 3 large plates. Place 5 shrimp on top of each serving of vegetables. Top with sauce and garnish with fresh herbs. Serves 3.

THE GARDEN
R E S T A U R A N T

1617 SPRUCE STREET
PHILADELPHIA, PA 19002
215-546-4455

The green awning of The Garden Restaurant stretches over the marble stairs to greet guests at the sidewalk. In the vestibule, lovely ivy wallpaper and green trim begin guests' illusion that they are stepping into a garden. The floral walls in the entry hall and the main dining room continue the springtime feeling. And in the back of this Center City restaurant is an outdoor garden dining area complete with wisteria and climbing roses wending their way around the property.

Built in 1860 as a private home, this townhouse was soon converted into the Philadelphia Music Academy. That school's marble sign, complete with lyre and laurel-leaf insignia, still hangs outside the restaurant. Up a winding set of wooden stairs on the third floor of the restaurant is the room that once served as the performance area. The stage is still there, as is the Victorian wallpaper with a gilded palm-tree pattern. How students got their instruments up there is something that the restaurant's owner, Kathleen Mulhern, has a hard time visualizing. Other remnants of the musical academy to be found at The Garden include restaurant patrons who like to reminisce about their lessons there.

The configuration of the dining room reflects the building's history. Long and thin, the room has lovely mirrors along one wall. Opposite them are several short walls interspersed with open areas. These are the doorways and support walls for what used to be the academy's practice rooms.

The lovely classical music playing in the background, a tribute to what transpired here for nearly a hundred years, provided a perfect backdrop to a perfect meal. The wait staff was superb—professional and unobtrusive. Recommendations for the meal were made by Cheryl Cotton, the restaurant manager, who has worked for Ms. Mulhern for twenty-five years. Her suggestions were excellent. We started with Baby Arugula served on Grilled Toast Points, a wonderful alternative to a traditional salad. That was followed by the most delicious Fillet of Dover Sole we've ever eaten; the light Hollandaise Sauce perfectly complemented the entrée. To end this delightful midday meal, we were served a tender Profiterole filled with vanilla ice cream and topped with hot fudge.

As we strolled down the street past the delightful rows of townhouses, each with its own personality, we came across a violin maker and an antique store specializing in vintage instruments. The shops made us smile, thinking of the musical history we'd just left behind and the wonderful legacy that The Garden Restaurant has carried forward.

ROAST GAME HENS STUFFED WITH WILD MUSHROOMS

¾ pound wild mushrooms
2 tablespoons olive oil
⅓ cup onion, chopped
1 clove garlic, minced
salt and freshly ground black pepper to taste
⅓ cup white wine
¼ teaspoon thyme leaves, chopped
¼ pound fresh goat cheese, crumbled
2 tablespoons fresh parsley
4 tablespoons dried breadcrumbs, divided
4 Cornish game hens
4 tablespoons unsalted butter, room temperature

Clean mushrooms and slice into ¾-inch pieces. Heat oil in a large skillet over medium heat and add mushrooms, onions, and garlic. Season with salt and pepper. Cook 10 to 12 minutes, stirring frequently, until mushrooms have released all their liquid and are lightly browned. Add wine and thyme and cook until wine evaporates. Remove from heat. Transfer mushrooms to a bowl. When mushrooms are cool, stir in cheese, parsley, and 3 tablespoons of the breadcrumbs. Preheat oven to 350 degrees. Rinse hens well and pat dry. Fill cavities of the hens with mushroom stuffing. Place stuffed birds in roasting pans. Dot each bird with 1 tablespoon of butter and sprinkle with salt and pepper and remaining breadcrumbs. Roast 1 hour, basting occasionally until golden brown; legs should move easily. Remove pan from oven. Place hens on a cutting board and let rest for 5 minutes before carving. Serves 4.

Whisk eggs, lemon juice, zest, sugar, and baking powder together. Pour into cooled crust. Bake at 350 degrees for 20 minutes until light brown and firm. Cool. Dust top of tart with powdered sugar. Serve with Blueberry Sauce. Yields 24 tarts.

❦ LEMON TART ❦
WITH BLUEBERRY SAUCE

Crust

2 cups flour
½ cup confectioners' sugar
2 sticks butter, cut into chunks
pinch of salt

Combine all ingredients and pulse in a food processor until mixture resembles peas. Press into a 16-by-11-inch pan with fingers and bake at 350 degrees about 10 minutes until very lightly browned. Allow to cool.

Filling

8 eggs
¾ cup lemon juice
zest of 2 lemons
4 cups sugar
1 teaspoon baking powder
powdered sugar
Blueberry Sauce (see next column)

Blueberry Sauce

6 cups blueberries, divided
juice of 1 lemon
juice of 1 orange
½ cup sugar

Combine 2 pints of the blueberries, lemon juice, orange juice, and sugar in a medium saucepan. Simmer for 20 to 30 minutes on low heat. Remove from heat and add remaining pint of blueberries. Cool. Yields enough sauce for 24 tarts.

❦ ❦ ❦ ❦ ❦ ❦

La Bonne Auberge

VILLAGE 2
NEW HOPE, PA 18938
215-862-2462

Serving classic French cuisine since 1972, La Bonne Auberge is located in what was formerly the Joshua Ely House, built in the late 1700s. Situated on a ridge adjacent to William Penn's Manor of the Highlands, it overlooks the hamlet of New Hope and neighboring New Jersey just across the Delaware River. The Lenni-Lenape Indians and early settlers cultivated orchards on these hills. Some of the orchards remain in cultivation today.

The elevated location is strategic as well as scenic. This area was the site of a redoubt constructed by Continental soldiers between December 8 and December 25, 1776. The fortification allowed colonial soldiers to be well apprised of approaching British troops.

A vision of beauty, the stone house is nestled among wooden walkways and landscaped gardens. Guests will not be disappointed by the inside either, where stone walls and wood paneling mingle with linen table appointments and tapestry-rich seating. The fresh flowers on each table and the one-of-a-kind plates adorning the wall give this farmhouse a true feeling of the country. There is a large bar to one side of the room, where entering guests get a glimpse of the dessert pleasures to come.

We were seated at a corner table. To our left was a window looking out on the gardens. To our right was the old stone wall of the original Joshua Ely House. La Bonne Auberge serves classic French cuisine. Every selection on the à la carte menu was so tempting that we opted for the full-course table d'hôte menu. We began with a glass of champagne and awaited what was to be one of the best meals we've ever eaten.

It began with Watercress Soup, which arrived steaming hot and accompanied by warm, freshly baked Rolls. The flavorful soup was swiftly followed by Asparagus Salad—long stems of steamed asparagus with mixed cress, spring greens, and House Vinaigrette Dressing on the side. The vinaigrette was smooth and creamy and the whole salad delightful in its simplicity. As our hostess, Rozanne Caronello, sweetly wished us *bon appétit*, our entrée was served—a Sirloin of Beef done to perfection, served with a Purée of Watercress, Spinach, and New Potatoes. Each delicious portion here is ample but restrained, allowing guests to sample a full array of courses and yet be prepared for more.

We paused as the table was cleared, the crumbs removed, the water replenished, and the cutlery replaced. The next course was Apricot Sorbet and Strawberry Sorbet, which were tangy and not too sweet. Then a trio of desserts awaited our pleasure: an open-faced Raspberry Tart with a bed of almond paste and sweet pastry, a Blueberry Tart, and a layered Genoise and Mocha Cream confection called Chocolat Opéra. Each mouthful was more delectable than the last.

What more could anyone want than exquisite food and swift and unobtrusive service in beautiful surroundings? We regretfully departed from La Bonne Auberge, sated and happy, visions of return visits dancing in our heads.

❦ ❦ ❦ ❦ ❦ ❦

LOBSTER MARTINIQUAISE

4 12-ounce cold-water lobster tails
2 cups water
1 teaspoon salt
½ teaspoon pepper
1 tablespoon wine vinegar
¼ teaspoon thyme
1 bay leaf
½ teaspoon parsley
¼ cup butter
¼ cup flour
2 cups milk
1 large Spanish onion, chopped
½ pound fresh mushrooms, chopped
2 tablespoons pimentos, chopped
salt and pepper to taste
cayenne pepper to taste
1 generous tablespoon Parmesan cheese, grated
4 teaspoons butter

Cook lobsters in water, salt, pepper, wine vinegar, thyme, bay leaf, and parsley. Allow to cool, then split tails and remove flesh, ensuring that shells are not damaged. Cut up lobster meat, then refrigerate both shells and meat. To make a roux, melt butter and whisk in flour until it ribbons; cook lightly and allow to cool. Boil milk and slowly add to roux until texture is smooth. Sauté onions, mushrooms, and pimentos and cook until dry. Add to sauce and adjust seasonings. Add lobster pieces and grated cheese. Mix well. Fill lobster shells, sprinkle with additional Parmesan, and bake with 1 teaspoon butter on top of each lobster for 10 minutes in a 500-degree oven. Garnish with lemon and parsley. Serves 4.

❦ ❦ ❦ ❦ ❦ ❦

FILET DE VEAU ROTI JARDINIERE

12-ounce veal fillet
salt and pepper to taste
½ cup pesto
½ cup mushroom duxelle
1 teaspoon butter
1 tablespoon shallots, chopped
2 tablespoons white wine
1 teaspoon Dijon mustard
½ cup veal or chicken stock

Cut fillet lengthwise and season with salt and pepper. Fill the cut with pesto and mushroom duxelle. Tie fillet with a fine string and season on outside with salt and pepper. Top fillet with butter and bake for 30 minutes at 500 degrees. Remove from pan and set aside. Place shallots, wine, Dijon, and stock in same pan. Reduce by ⅓. Slice the fillet and arrange in a semicircular pattern on a serving plate. Garnish with vegetables of your choice, such as glazed carrots and snow peas. Pour sauce over veal and serve. Serves 2.

❦ ❦ ❦ ❦ ❦ ❦

NORTH MAIN STREET
JERSEY SHORE, PA 17740
717-398-1981

From the outside, the Gamble Farm Inn is a picture to behold. The single tapers shining from each window and the dozens of mums in flower boxes enhance the brick-red exterior and tan and slate-blue trim. You might feel inclined to sit in a rocking chair on the wide front porch and watch the west branch of the Susquehanna River drift lazily by.

The house was built around 1850 by Judge Gamble, a prominent civil-law judge in Lycoming County. As was traditional with houses of this kind, in the twenty-five years that followed, four or five additions were wrapped around the original structure. After the good judge passed away, the structure served as a home for several clubs and a nice restaurant named The Cedars, whose good reputation is recalled by many local guests.

In 1949, the George Porters bought it as a private residence. Mrs. Gladys Porter was the daughter of Prince Farrington, a well-known bootlegger on the East Coast. The Porters were nothing if not enterprising. Over the years that they lived in the house, they tried their hand at various businesses, beginning with a Studebaker car lot, which progressed to an antique shop in the late 1950s and 1960s. In the 1970s, they procured a liquor license and opened a bar. In 1986, the Knarr family bought the house and began to restore it for the purpose of turning it into a fine-dining establishment.

The main dining room and bar are enchanting. They have wide-plank floors and plain white walls and are decorated in early-American primitive furnishings and lit with white twinkling lights. The wealth of knickknacks on the shelves had us craning our necks to see more. Sitting with Jean Knarr in the turquoise room just off the bar area, we saw that a lot of love had gone into the making of this business. She told us the histories of the handmade quilts that adorn the walls, and how most of the stained-glass lamps had been made. Jean even hand-writes all the menus for the restaurant.

We allowed ourselves to be guided by Jean in our choice of food—and extremely good choices they were. The Sherried Crab Spread with Seafood Toasties was very tasty. It was quickly followed by the delicious Cream of Brie and Sausage Soup. The Grilled Tuna Steak Teriyaki with Pineapple Sauce sounded most appetizing, as did the Grilled Lamb Chops with Portabello Mushroom Stuffing. However, we chose the Pork Tenderloin Medallions with Sweet and Sour Bacon Sauce. The tenderloins melted in the mouth, and the sauce was fabulous. Debbie pronounced her dessert—Angel Food Cake layered with Chambord and Frangelico and topped with Bailey's Ganache Icing—to be delectable, and Karen's Death by Chocolate was indeed "to die for." All in all, it was a very enjoyable evening of splendid food and good company. As we departed, we discovered that the main dining room was absolutely full. It was hardly surprising!

CREAM OF BRIE AND SAUSAGE SOUP

1 pound ground sausage
2 tablespoons butter
1 cup celery, diced fine
½ cup onion, diced fine
½ cup flour
1 cup cream
3 or more cups chicken stock
4 ounces Brie, cubed
salt and pepper to taste

Crumble sausage and sauté until cooked. Remove from pan and reserve. Drain most of fat from pan and discard. Add butter, celery, and onions to the pan and sauté until vegetables are cooked. Whisk in flour a little at a time, incorporating thoroughly. Whisk in the cream, incorporating thoroughly. Let mixture thicken. Whisk in 3 cups of chicken stock and Brie and let thicken; add more stock if needed. When Brie has melted, purée mixture and return it to the stove. Simmer to reduce to desired thickness. Add reserved sausage meat and season with salt and pepper. Serves 6.

SHERRIED CRAB SPREAD

2 tablespoons cream cheese
1 tablespoon mayonnaise
1 teaspoon sour cream
2 teaspoons sugar
2 tablespoons sherry
1 tablespoon fresh chives, chopped
1 tablespoon roasted red pepper, chopped
8-ounce can crabmeat
Seafood Toasties (see below)

Combine first 7 ingredients with a hand mixer until thoroughly blended. Fold crabmeat into mixture very gently, so as not to break up the chunks of crab. Place mixture in an ovenproof dish and bake at 400 degrees until bubbly and lightly browned on top. Serve with Seafood Toasties. Yields 4 appetizer servings.

Seafood Toasties

4 stale rolls
6 tablespoons butter, softened
1 teaspoon Old Bay seasoning

Preheat oven to 350 degrees. Cut rolls into slices. Lay slices on a cookie sheet. Dab each slice generously with butter and sprinkle with Old Bay. Bake 10 to 15 minutes until bread is crisp.

GABRIEL'S RESTAURANT AT

321 MARKET STREET
NEW BERLIN, PA 17855
570-966-0321

John Showers, once a state representative, forged one of his most successful campaigns as he and his wife, Nancy, undertook a loving restoration of New Berlin's Jacob Schoch House. The home was built in 1906 as a summer residence for a wealthy Philadelphia merchant who had relatives in the area. It was constructed during a gentler time when hospitality was an art, when time spent in a swing on the front porch was not considered wasted.

Frequently referred to as Victorian, the home technically falls under the Colonial Revival style. As guests enter the front door, their attention is immediately drawn to the lovely wooden staircase, embellished with intricate wreaths and garlands. The stained-glass windows and archways throughout the home speak to its craftsmanship.

The dining room to the left of the hall has an original fireplace surrounded by marble tiles. Nearby sits a marble-topped sideboard. The wooden folding doors that separate this room from the next have etched-glass panels that add a soft touch. This dining area has two built-in cupboards, each with a large golden angel at the top. They represent the angel Gabriel—hence the restaurant's name. The myriad angels in various nooks and crannies throughout the room are a delight to the eye.

We were seated in the intimate dining room to the right of the entry hall. Several small tables were clustered near a beautiful grand piano, against a backdrop of lace curtains and navy wallpaper. As we gazed at the menu, we knew we were in for a treat. The luncheon menu at Gabriel's is appetizingly unique. Brunch items are listed alongside salads and entrées. Guests are certain to find many things to please their palate, from Peach Pancakes to an Asparagus and Brie Omelet to a Wild Mushroom Frittata. Choices such as Spinach and Citrus Salad and Grilled Duck Salad are also tempting. Karen thoroughly enjoyed her Smoked Salmon Salad, which included artichokes, fennel, tomato, walnuts, and chives. Debbie savored every bite of her Sesame-Crusted Sea Bass.

As we toured the grounds, we discovered that many of the ingredients served at Gabriel's are grown right on the property. The aroma of herbs enveloped us. It's easy to allow yourself to be carried away by both the scents and the surroundings here.

Overnight guests are seen to in the greatest detail. Gift baskets full of goodies are waiting for them upon their arrival, and teddy bears are lovingly placed atop each bed. John and Nancy have expanded their inn beyond the Schoch House to include three other historic homes. They've also added a carriage house near where John's ancestors once operated New Berlin's original country store. In chatting with John and Nancy and their personable hostess, Lisa, it was easy to see that their boundless enthusiasm is the not-so-secret ingredient that makes Gabriel's and The Inn at Olde New Berlin everything anyone could imagine.

CHAMBORD ROASTED DUCKLING

1 cup blackberry preserves
⅔ cup granulated sugar
3 tablespoons cider vinegar
⅔ cup Chambord liqueur
½ cup chicken stock
4 ducklings halves
flour
water

Preheat oven to 350 degrees. Combine first 5 ingredients in a heavy saucepan on medium heat. Heat until mixture reaches a boil, then simmer for 5 to 10 minutes on low heat, stirring constantly to avoid scorching. Place ducklings in a baking dish breast side up. Coat each duckling half with 2 tablespoons sauce. Bake 25 to 30 minutes until ducklings are crispy. Thicken remaining sauce with equal portions of flour and water until it coats the back of a spoon; use 1 tablespoon flour

to 1 tablespoon water for each 1 cup of sauce. Pour thickened sauce over ducklings and serve. Serves 4.

WALNUT AND PECAN CARAMELIZED BRIE

⅔ cup brown sugar, packed
⅓ cup water
½ cup heavy cream
⅛ teaspoon nutmeg
⅛ teaspoon cinnamon
5 tablespoons butter
¼ cup pecan halves
¼ cup walnut halves
8-inch wheel Brie, top rind removed
1 Granny Smith apple, cored and sliced
8 Nejaime's Lavasch crackers
4 ounces red seedless grapes

Combine sugar and water in a heavy saucepan and bring to a boil. Cook over medium heat for approximately 4 minutes from the time mixture comes to a boil. Let cool slightly, then stir in cream, nutmeg, and cinnamon. Boil 3 to 4 minutes until slightly thickened and glossy. Remove from heat and stir in butter, pecans, and walnuts. Place Brie on a 12-inch round serving plate and surround it with apples slices, crackers, and grapes. Pour caramel evenly over top of Brie until it just begins to run over the sides. Use a spoon to evenly distribute pecans and walnuts. Serves 8.

201 EAST STATE STREET
KENNETT SQUARE, PA 19348
610-444-5688

The town of Kennett Square, settled by William Penn's Quakers, boasts a rich historic past. During the Battle of Brandywine in 1777, Lord Howe moved his troops from Maryland to Kennett Square. His troops—encompassing Hessians under the command of Knyphausen and British under the command of Cornwallis—made a two-pronged attack against Washington. The battle was a decisive victory for the British, and Washington was forced to retreat to Valley Forge during the winter of 1777–78.

John Love built a residence on this historic site in 1835. During the Victorian era, houses began to spring up all around the area. The Love house continued to be used as a residence by many successive owners until 1927. At that time, during Prohibition, it was renovated and renamed The Green Gate Tea Room. Perhaps visitors to Kennett Square imbibed something a little stronger than tea in the back rooms!

In 1976, the inn was restored with great care. It now houses a formal dining room and colonial tavern. As we drove past the inn on a warm summer day, it was a picture. A profusion of hanging floral baskets decorated the front of the building. The taupe-and-white-striped awning over the stone terrace invited us to stay awhile.

We peeked into the dining room on our way to lunch in the more casual tavern. The dining room was decorated in the Federal style, with wooden tables and chairs surrounding the original fireplace. The room was graced with fresh flowers and taupe linens, and the walls were covered with pictures of wild game and various views of the Battle of Brandywine. Beyond the main room was a smaller room for more intimate dining. We were seated in the tavern at the sunny corner window overlooking the bustling town. The hardwood floors, cherry tables, and wooden bar created a relaxed, cheery atmosphere. We sipped homemade Lemonade as we examined the town's first wooden telephone kiosk and its built-in wooden seat, located in a corner of the room.

The specials of the day included Grilled Swordfish with Roasted Corn, Mushrooms, and Green Chilis and Fried Oysters over Spinach with Blue Cheese Dressing. We opted for the Eggplant Garlic Soup, which had a smooth, creamy texture and a mushroom base. This last was hardly surprising, since Kennett Square is known as the "Mushroom Capital of the World." Guided by Joyce, our server, we chose the Jumbo Lump Crab Cake Sandwich, which was reputed to be "all lump meat, no fillers, and broiled not fried." The Crab Cake duly arrived, surrounded by tomatoes and lettuce on a toasted muffin, complete with homemade Tartar Sauce and House Fries. It certainly lived up to its reputation.

In the evening, the Kennett Square Inn offers such entrées as Rosemary Dijon–Encrusted Rack of New Zealand Lamb, Honey Orange–Glazed Duck Breast, served over wild rice, and Sautéed Chicken Roille, which is an egg-battered chicken breast with Roasted Red Pepper Sauce, served over spinach. The extremely tempting desserts range from the "Killer Chocolate" to the "Nutmeg Vanilla from Grenada." We mused over the choices, smiling as we contemplated our next visit to Kennett Square.

SHRIMP LE JON

12 large shrimp
6 teaspoons horseradish
12 slices bacon
La Maise Sauce (see next column)

Preheat oven to 450 degrees. Peel and devein shrimp. Fill the vein pocket of each shrimp with ½ teaspoon of horseradish. Wrap each shrimp in 1 slice of bacon. Place shrimp in a pan and bake for 5 to 7 minutes until bacon is done. Serve with La Maise Sauce. Serves 4 as an appetizer.

La Maise Sauce

1 cup mayonnaise
3 tablespoons ketchup
1 tablespoon dill
2 tablespoons horseradish
1 teaspoon garlic

Combine all ingredients. Chill until ready to serve. Yields approximately 1 cup.

TORTELLINI AND SHIITAKE

16-ounce package cheese tortellini
16 to 20 shiitake mushrooms
2 tablespoons olive oil
2 cloves garlic, minced
¼ cup white wine
1 cup heavy cream
2 tablespoons fresh parsley, chopped

Par-boil tortellini; drain and set aside. Stem and julienne mushrooms. Heat oil in a sauté pan and add garlic and mushrooms; cook until mushrooms look a little soft. Add wine and flame. Add cream and stir to make sauce. Reduce heat to simmer. Continue cooking until sauce is reduced to desired consistency; it should coat the back of a spoon. Add tortellini and stir gently until heated through. Fold parsley into mixture to evenly distribute. Serves 2.

THE TOWNE HOUSE INN

138 CENTER STREET
ST. MARYS, PA 15857
814-781-1556

St. Marys was one of Pennsylvania's early German settlements. The first settlers arrived on December 8, 1842. The name St. Marys came from the fact that the day they arrived was the Feast of the Immaculate Conception. Being devout Catholics, they felt they should honor the Virgin Mary in naming the town.

Slightly off the beaten path today, St. Marys boasts many examples of the opulent lifestyle of the early 1900s. Several luxurious homes built during that time are part of The Towne House Inn property. The Towne House Inn joined forces with The Willows and The Carriage House in 1992. Great care was taken to maintain the historic integrity of these properties. The Towne House Inn and The Willows were named to the National Register of Historic Landmarks in 1994.

The Towne House Inn was built by Dr. Eben J. Russ, a prominent local businessman and physicist. He purchased the land in 1899 and took up residence after the home was completed in July 1907. Many of the exquisite materials used in the home were imported from Europe.

In the expansive front hall, guests are quick to notice the stained-glass window just behind the first landing of the staircase. The window was part of the home's original decor. The grand oak stairway is magnificent. The enormous pocket doors, still in working order, triggered Debbie's childhood fascination with the much-loved pocket doors in her grandmother's house.

Just inside the front door are two murals painted during the construction of the house. Originally, many such murals—mostly of famous musicians—were located throughout the first floor. Mrs. Russ, a musician before her marriage, enjoyed performing in the room to the left of the hallway. Specially invited guests teetered on fragile gilt chairs during her weekly musicales. Today, the grand piano is gone, and the music room is used as an intimate dining room. The decor is predominantly taupe, and the original mantelpiece is painted to match. Just across the hall is the parlor, decorated in tones of mauve, in which guests can also partake of a meal. The original dining room has mahogany woodwork and a wooden mantelpiece with intricate carvings. The built-in, curved mahogany breakfront with leaded-glass doors defies description.

The Towne House Inn serves breakfast, lunch, and dinner, so there are ample opportunities to enjoy the unique atmosphere in each of the three dining rooms. Omelets, French Toast, and Pancakes are typical of the breakfast fare; the lunch menu is comparably traditional. The innovative dinner menu has selections to suit everyone's appetite.

❧ SALMON GERG ❧

Salmon Marinade

½ cup pineapple juice
½ cup cranberry juice
½ cup apple juice
½ cup orange juice
juice of 1 lemon
juice of 2 oranges
1 tablespoon honey
¼ cup poppy seeds, crushed
pinch of nutmeg
¼ cup brown sugar
dash of white pepper
1 cup poppy seeds, whole
2 8-ounce salmon fillets
Honey Dijon Mustard (see below)

Combine first 11 ingredients to make marinade; reserve 1 tablespoon for later use. Place salmon in marinade for 2 to 4 hours. Remove salmon from marinade and coat with whole poppy seeds. Heat a sauté pan until slightly warmed. Put fillets in pan and toast for 45 to 60 seconds on each side to release flavor from poppy seeds, then bake in a 400-degree oven for 5 to 7 minutes until flaky. Serve with Honey Dijon Mustard. Serves 2.

Honey Dijon Mustard

½ cup Dijon mustard
1 teaspoon balsamic vinegar
1 tablespoon Salmon Marinade (see above)
pinch of black pepper
½ teaspoon garlic salt
1 teaspoon dry mustard

2 tablespoons honey
1 teaspoon brown sugar

Combine all ingredients and serve over salmon. Yields ⅔ cup.

❧ GREEK CHICKEN ❧

2 6-ounce chicken breasts
2 tablespoons butter
2 tablespoons Chablis
1 tablespoon juice from black olives
1 tablespoon juice from green olives
1 tablespoon juice from feta cheese
6 black olives, sliced in half
6 green olives, sliced in half
4 pepperocini, sliced in half
capers, if desired
1 tablespoon fresh oregano
1 tablespoon fresh basil
1 tablespoon garlic, chopped
4 to 6 anchovy fillets, if desired
2 vine-ripened Roma tomatoes, quartered
12 ounces penne pasta, cooked al dente
¼ cup feta cheese, crumbled
salt and pepper to taste

Cut chicken into 1-inch strips. Melt butter in skillet and add Chablis, olive juices, and feta cheese juice. Sauté chicken in juices. When chicken starts to turn white, add olives, pepperocini, and capers. Toss with the herbs, anchovies, and tomatoes. Return to stove over low heat. Toss with penne and feta cheese until feta has melted. Season with salt and pepper and serve immediately. Serves 2.

US 19
VENANGO, PA 16440
814-398-4330

This area of Pennsylvania was rife with Indian hostilities when Thomas Campbell and Christopher Silverling first visited in 1794. Two years later, the conflicts quieted, and the two men returned with their families to settle along the river called Wenango by the Seneca tribe, which in their dialect means "mink." The river was later renamed French Creek by George Washington, in reference to the many French settlements he encountered as he traveled north to Fort LeBoeuf by this route.

Silverling purchased 180 acres from the Holland Land Company in 1821. That acreage was subsequently bought by John Kleckner in 1833. Kleckner surveyed a village plot that he named Klecknerville. Around that time, he also opened the town's first tavern. Several years later, he began building what the tax records call "a two-story, 14 room brick mansion." Kleckner constructed the home in the Federal style with bricks made by his son Matthias, who owned a kiln in Cussewago township.

Perhaps the wealthiest of the home's residents were the Tarrs, who originally owned property in nearby Oil Creek Valley. After discovering a large oil well on their Oil Creek Valley land, they sold the property for a cool five million dollars in the mid-1860s and moved to Venango. Following the deaths of the Tarrs, the property changed hands numerous times until 1929. It was then that Gideon Sundback, inventor of the first hookless fastener for clothing, known as the "Talon zipper," purchased the property. He called the home the Venango Valley Inn and opened it to friends and business associates from all over the world.

In 1968, the land was again sold, this time to a Mr. Kemp and a Mr. Erath, most noted as the builders of Arnold Palmer's Laurel Valley Golf Course. Those gentlemen turned much of the property into a quality eighteen-hole golf course. Originally known as the Canadian-American, it is called the Venango Valley Golf Course today. The home that John Kleckner built graces the grounds of the course and provides guests with delicious meals.

Lunch is served in the new addition, which is festively adorned with golf pictures and prints of rural scenes done by local artist Leslie Blake. Dinner is served in the home's original rooms, where property deeds, antique photos, and other memorabilia adorn the walls. To the left of the front hall is a lovely room with deep raspberry walls, white and burgundy linens, and Federal-style draperies. Across the hall are two more casual dining rooms with original fireplaces and cast-iron insets.

The varied menu reflects the Italian heritage of previous owners Joe and Mary Petrucelli. In honor of their contribution to the cuisine, Debbie chose Spaghetti with Italian Sausage. According to the menu, the homemade sauce simmers all day. The Spaghetti was delicious, as was the Herbed Parmesan Bread that accompanied it. The Foccacia Chicken that Karen sampled was equally appealing. These choices were not arrived at lightly, however, as our waitress had to come back three times to see if we were finally ready. We hesitated over selections such as Roast Beef and Gravy, Pesto al Pasta, and homemade Cannelloni, filled with meat, spinach, and cheese.

Whether you're a duffer or an accomplished golfer, Venango Valley Inn is an enjoyable experience. We encourage you to work up an appetite on the links or to go for the dining pleasure alone.

APPLE DUMPLINGS

2 cups flour
2 teaspoons baking powder
1 teaspoon salt
¾ cup Crisco
½ cup milk

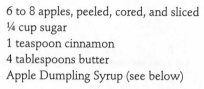

6 to 8 apples, peeled, cored, and sliced
¼ cup sugar
1 teaspoon cinnamon
4 tablespoons butter
Apple Dumpling Syrup (see below)

Combine flour, baking powder, and salt. Cut in Crisco. Add milk and mix to form a soft dough. Roll out and cut into 8 squares. Divide apple slices equally among dough squares. Sprinkle apples with sugar and cinnamon and dot with butter. Fold edges of dough into the center and seal. Place dumplings in a 9-by-13-inch baking pan. Pour Apple Dumpling Syrup over dumplings and bake at 350 degrees for 30 to 40 minutes. Serves 8.

Apple Dumpling Syrup

2 cups sugar
¼ teaspoon cinnamon
2 cups water
¼ teaspoon nutmeg
¼ cup butter

Place all ingredients in a small saucepan and heat until sugar dissolves. Yields 2 cups.

CANNELLONI

3 eggs
3¼ cups milk, divided
½ stick margarine, melted
2 cups flour
dash of salt
dash of nutmeg
dash of white pepper
¼ cup powdered sugar
cooking spray
2½ pounds ground beef
2½ 10-ounce packages frozen chopped spinach,
   thawed and squeezed dry
12-ounce container ricotta cheese
1 cup Parmesan cheese, grated
salt and pepper to taste
1 tablespoon granulated garlic powder

In a large bowl, whip together eggs, 3 cups of milk, and margarine. Add dry ingredients and continue to beat. Add enough milk to make a thin pancake batter. Spray a 6-cup skillet with cooking spray. To make crepes, spread ¼ cup of mixture in bottom of pan and cook both sides over medium heat; repeat until mixture is used up. Crepes may be stacked between sheets of waxed paper to cool.

Sauté ground beef in a skillet. Remove from heat, add next 5 ingredients, and mix well. Divide mixture equally among crepes and roll up. Serve immediately. Serves 10.

407 WEST FOURTH STREET
WILLIAMSPORT, PA 17101
717-322-0165

The soft rose exterior of The Peter Herdic House invites the gaze to linger on the Italian villa–style structure. Built in 1854 as the home of Williamsport lumber baron Peter Herdic, it was one of many such homes on Fourth Street, known as "Millionaire's Row."

Even though it changed hands several times, it remained a private dwelling until the late 1950s. At that time, it was converted into apartments. An unsightly addition built on the front housed a television repair shop. A 1977 fire destroyed portions of the house and caused it to remain empty for seven years. Fortunately, a group of citizens created Millionaire's Row Historical Homes, Inc. They began to purchase and refurbish properties in order to bring them to saleable condition. The Peter Herdic House was one such property. By the mid-1980s, its future was promising once again.

Ten months in the making, the extensive renovations were well worth the wait. When Gloria and Marcia Miele opened their restaurant in The Peter Herdic House in late 1984, the Bureau of Historic Preservation recognized it as the top project for that year.

As guests step through the enormous front doors, the reasons that the award was bestowed are quite obvious. The interior elegance is enveloping. Rose walls, darker than the exterior, provide a quiet, welcoming atmosphere. The elaborate plaster molding has been painstakingly painted in hues of burgundy, dark teal, and gray. Lace curtains soften the large, narrow windows, where single candles stand.

I was sorry that Karen was not there to enjoy the tour Marcia Miele gave me. In the comfortably appointed waiting area, Marcia brought my attention to old menus from the Herdic House, one of Williamsport's finest railroad hotels, also owned by Peter Herdic. Beyond the waiting area was the bar, interestingly crafted using the witness stand from the town's old courthouse. As we made our way toward the second and third floors, Marcia pointed upward. To one side of the elaborate chandelier was the open stairwell of keyhole design. It was breathtaking to look up three floors and imagine being a child in this home and peering over such a lovely banister.

Before I finished my tour, my food was ready. I opted for the Venison and Lamb Chili, served with a dollop of sour cream. Game is not always on the menu, but Marcia indicated that the restaurant likes to offer game specials during the autumn months. Having found it difficult to decide on a starter, hemming and hawing over the Crispy Won Ton Ravioli and the Shrimp and Crab Roll, I was delighted with the Chili and its blend of flavors. In an autumnal mood myself, I opted for the Salmon entrée, which was served with Apples and Caramelized Walnuts in an Apple Cider Reduction. It was delicious, as were the Steamed Vegetables and the Mashed Red Potatoes that came with it. Full, I had to pass on the Ganache Torte with Pecan Crust and Caramel Sauce, the Apple Cinnamon Bread Pudding, the Crème Brûlée, and the Frangelico Cheesecake. Another time, I told myself, because one visit to The Peter Herdic House is not enough.

CHICKEN BREASTS IN CHAMPAGNE CREAM

4 whole chicken breasts, skinned, deboned, and halved
¼ cup all-purpose flour
1 teaspoon salt
½ teaspoon freshly ground white pepper
¾ pound mushrooms

9 tablespoons butter, divided
2 tablespoons vegetable oil
1 cup heavy cream
¼ cup champagne
1 teaspoon lemon juice
1 tablespoon parsley, chopped fine

Place breast halves between 2 pieces of wax paper or plastic wrap and flatten slightly with a mallet. Put flour, salt, and white pepper in a paper bag and toss the chicken inside the bag to coat. Remove chicken from bag, shaking off excess flour mixture. Clean mushrooms and discard stems. Reserve 8 large mushrooms for garnish and cut the rest into quarters. Melt 8 tablespoons of the butter in a large skillet. Add oil. Brown the floured chicken lightly on both sides. Add mushroom quarters. Cover, reduce heat, and simmer for 10 minutes. Uncover pan and remove excess butter with a spoon. Add cream and champagne and continue to simmer uncovered for 5 to 7 minutes. Remove from heat. Flute the reserved mushroom caps and sauté them slowly in the remaining 1 tablespoon of butter. While cooking, sprinkle lemon juice over them.

To serve, remove chicken breasts to a warm serving platter. Taste the sauce; if it has become too thick, thin with a little milk or cream. Spoon sauce over each chicken piece, top with a sautéed mushroom cap, and sprinkle lightly with parsley. Serves 4 generously.

GANACHE TORTE WITH PECAN CRUST AND CARAMEL SAUCE

3½ cups pecans
2¼ cups sugar, divided
7 tablespoons unsalted butter, melted and cooled
1 pound fine-quality bittersweet chocolate, chopped
1 egg yolk
3 cups heavy cream
½ cup unsalted butter
16 pecans, toasted lightly

Preheat oven to 350 degrees. In a food processor, blend 3½ cups pecans and 1¼ cups of the sugar. With motor running, add 7 tablespoons butter in a stream. Blend until well combined. Press mixture into the bottom and 1 inch up the side of a 10-inch springform pan, making the sides ⅜-inch thick and the bottom ⅛-inch thick. Bake crust for about 30 minutes until lightly browned. Let cool in the pan on a wire rack.

To make ganache, melt chocolate in the top of a double boiler set over barely simmering water. Whisk in yolk and 2 cups of the cream; whisk until mixture is just combined. Pour ganache into crust and chill for at least 2 hours and up to 24 hours.

To make sauce, melt ½ cup butter in a heavy skillet over moderate heat. Stir in remaining sugar and cook mixture, stirring constantly with a fork; continue stirring until mixture is a dark golden caramel. Remove skillet from heat. Add remaining cream carefully, stirring. Continue stirring until sauce is smooth.

Before serving, arrange 16 pecans on top of torte. Serve with Caramel Sauce drizzled over torte or on the side. Serves 12 to 16.

650 PINKERTON ROAD
MOUNT JOY, PA 17552
717-653-2048

Groff's Farm Restaurant is located in a yellow and pale gray stone house built for the McFarland family back in 1756. It is considered by many to be the home of the best Pennsylvania Dutch cooking. The Groff family has entertained guests for lunch and dinner for more than four decades, and after visiting the restaurant for myself, I can well understand why. Most of the original rooms in the farmhouse have been transformed into cozy dining areas, each with its own collection of antiques, wall coverings, and decorative woodwork. The original fireplaces have been restored, and the wooden floorboards, which are typical of the period, are intact.

I sat in the only carpeted area in the farmhouse, the elegant addition, which overlooks a beautiful golf course. The room was light and airy. White and peach linens adorned the tables, and fresh flowers enhanced the pewter accouterments. The view from the wraparound windows was delightful; there were ducks on the small pond next to the original springhouse, and the trees were wearing their autumn colors.

All the food here is prepared on the premises and can be served family-style or à la carte. Even though Debbie was dining elsewhere, I opted for the family-style menu and began with the Seafood Chowder, which was piping hot and spicy. My friendly server then brought me a selection of relishes and desserts. She explained that Mrs. Groff serves desserts with the relishes because she thinks that dessert should come first, before you are full from the main course. Knowing what was to come, I sampled only a little from each of the dishes brought to the table: Coleslaw, creamy and sweet; Cracker Pudding, stuffed full of coconut; Chocolate Cake with Butter Cream Frosting; Pickled Cucumbers; and home-baked Bread with Whipped Butter.

For my entrée, I could have chosen the Home-Cured Ham or the Prime Rib of Beef, both of which are specialties of the house, but I opted for the Chicken Stolzfus. Groff's Farm Restaurant is world-famous for this recipe, which includes chunks of roasted chicken smothered in Betty Groff's own Cream Sauce and served on a bed of flaky, diamond-shaped butter pastry. The chicken was outstanding, served with seasoned, lightly steamed Broccoli, Carrots, and Red Bliss Potatoes. I completed my meal with a Crème de Menthe Parfait, which was yummy. The family-style servings here are enormous, giving guests unbelievable value for their money.

After my meal, I chatted with Betty Groff about her Mennonite childhood and how the family's restaurant business began. She told me that she started the restaurant as a hobby. Preparing authentic Pennsylvania Dutch cuisine in a real farm setting for small groups of visitors to Lancaster County was something she very much enjoyed. Encouraged by her husband, Abe, she began with weekend cooking ventures, then transformed the living and dining rooms of the farmhouse into a tiny restaurant and started entertaining visitors from all over the world. Today, Betty and Abe have been joined by their son Charlie and his wife, Cindy, making the restaurant a real family affair. Charlie, now the executive chef, has added the popular à la carte menu. Still, the Groffs and their staff emphasize that the family-style menu hasn't changed since Betty welcomed her first guests. I hope it never does.

BAKED CABBAGE

1 medium head cabbage
2 tablespoons flour
1 teaspoon salt
freshly ground pepper to taste
½ teaspoon chives
1 teaspoon chervil
2 tablespoons sugar
3 tablespoons butter
1 cup hot milk
½ cup cheese, grated

Cut cabbage into wedges ¼ inch thick and boil in water for 10 minutes. Drain well and place in a buttered casserole. Sprinkle cabbage with flour, salt, pepper, chives, chervil, and sugar. Dot with butter. Pour hot milk over cabbage and sprinkle cheese over the top. Bake in a preheated 350-degree oven for 35 minutes. Serves 6 to 8.

CRACKER PUDDING

Pudding

4 cups milk
2 eggs, separated
⅔ cup granulated sugar
2 cups saltine crackers, broken
1 cup coconut, grated
1 teaspoon vanilla

Heat milk in a medium saucepan. Beat egg yolks and sugar in a bowl until frothy and light. Add to hot milk. Stir in crackers and coconut. Cook over medium heat, stirring frequently until thick. Remove from heat. In a separate bowl, beat egg whites until stiff, then fold in vanilla. Fold egg whites into cracker mixture and pour into a casserole dish. Place in refrigerator to set.

Meringue

3 eggs whites
¼ teaspoon cream of tartar
4 tablespoons sugar

Beat egg whites with cream of tartar until soft peaks form. Gradually beat in sugar; continue beating until stiff and glossy. Pile meringue lightly over Cracker Pudding and bake in a 350-degree oven until meringue is golden brown. Serves 8 to 12.

643 PITTSBURGH STREET
SPRINGDALE, PA 15144
724-274-5022

The gabled house on the main drag of Springdale is pink. Not pastel pink, but bright pink with white window boxes, dental molding, and gingerbread trim. Greeting guests as they pull into the parking lot is a large Berliner bear statue. Such statues are typically black, but this one is painted white either to alarm the guests less or to match the house—you decide. The house was inherited by Chuck Spix, who now resides upstairs while providing a culinary treat on the first floor at Kleiner Deutschmann.

Chuck's grandparents, Barbara and Winnand Spix, emigrated from Aachen, Germany, and entered the United States via Ellis Island. They purchased the home in the late 1800s and operated Springdale's bakery for many, many years. Chuck was born in this house and lived here as a child. However, he left Pennsylvania for New York in 1957 and worked in the restaurant business there during his thirty-year stay. When his aunt passed away in the 1980s and the house was left to him, he decided to return to Springdale. Rather than raze the house, he opted to restore it and open his own restaurant. He invited co-owner Dick Tetreault, a waiter with whom he'd worked in New York, to embark on the project. In 1986, Kleiner Deutschmann was born.

Its cuisine is distinctly German. Chuck does much of the cooking himself. From German Pancakes to Sauerbraten to Schnitzel, the choices are all there. Soups are the house specialty, the Kleiner Deutschmann Cream Soup being a favorite. To further heighten the German experience, the wait staff is attired in folk dress while German music tinkles in the background. Even Chuck wears a pair of Bavarian suspenders over his kitchen whites!

Don't expect a bier-hall atmosphere, though. The setting here is intimate. The cream color of the small, lace-covered tables is set off against forest-green carpeting and seating, accented by lilac wallpaper chosen in honor of Chuck's mother. Original wood can be found throughout, from the lovely staircase in the entrance hall to the Victorian mantelpiece in the center dining room, once the home's living room. The original dining room features a built-in china cabinet. The third seating area, the sun porch, boasts an authentic stained-glass insert in the doorway transom.

Chuck is a collector, and his pieces are shown throughout the restaurant. Steins—all of them German, some given by regular patrons—line the walls. A curio cabinet in the main dining room houses porcelain birds, while the waiting area has an étagère filled with Hummel figurines. Kleiner Deutschmann has so much to look at and so much to offer that one trip will certainly not be enough!

RED CABBAGE (ROTKRAUT)

2 pounds red cabbage, shredded
2 tart apples, shredded
1½ bay leaves
1 teaspoon salt
6 whole cloves
½ cup red wine vinegar
1½ tablespoons butter or shortening
1½ cups water
1 to 2 tablespoons sugar
salt and pepper to taste

Place cabbage, apples, bay leaves, 1 teaspoon salt, and cloves in a large, deep bowl. Pour vinegar over cabbage mixture and mix well. Cover and let sit over night. The next day, melt butter or shortening in a large pan. Add cabbage mixture, 1 cup of water, and 1 tablespoon of sugar. Cook until tender, adding additional ½ cup water as needed. Add remaining sugar and salt and pepper. Serves 4.

APPLE PANCAKES
(APFEL PFANNENKUCKEN)

1 cup flour
2 large eggs
1 cup milk
dash of salt
½ teaspoon vanilla
1½ cups sugar
2 or 3 large cooking apples
2 tablespoons butter or shortening
⅓ cup sugar
1 tablespoon cinnamon
¼ cup powdered sugar

Stir flour, eggs, milk, and salt together until smooth; add vanilla and 1½ cups sugar. Peel apples and slice thin. In a large skillet, fry apples in butter or shortening until tender. Leave apples in skillet. Pour batter over apple slices. Let batter cook for a few minutes until set. Remove from skillet, place on a baking sheet, and heat in oven until golden brown. Combine ⅓ cup sugar and cinnamon in a small bowl. To serve, sprinkle pancake with cinnamon sugar and then powdered sugar. Serves 4.

CHAPTER 4

Bottoms Up!

Penn Brewery

The fun thing about "Bottoms up!" is that you say it only with a drink in your hand. The establishments in this chapter, regardless of their previous history, are now all great places to imbibe. The specialty in all of these restaurants is the beer, which has been incorporated into many of the delicious menu items and is micro-brewed on the premises, in full view of dinner guests.

3525 LIBERTY AVENUE
PITTSBURGH, PA 15201
412-688-8200

Hand-painted cypress beams on the high, vaulted ceiling and intricate European-style stained-glass windows are just two of the decorative details of The Church Brew Works, housed in the former St. John the Baptist Church. The building's stained-glass rose window is a backdrop for the turn-of-the-century pipe organ in the church's balcony. The designers of the church, Louis and Michael Beezer and John Combs, employed the finest craftsmen when the church was built in 1902 in the historic Pittsburgh neighborhood of Lawrenceville.

St. John the Baptist served as the spiritual home of many Carnegie Steel and Black Diamond Steel workers and their families. During the steel industry's boom, the community and the church grew; a convent, a school, and a rectory were added to the church property. However, like many other urban neighborhoods, Lawrenceville went through a decline during the 1970s and 1980s. One of the results was that the St. John the Baptist parish was merged with St. Augustine's, a church begun by the founders of Iron City Beer. Then, in an official ceremony that took away the religious status of the structure, St. John the Baptist Church was suppressed in October 1993.

Respect for the building's craftsmanship motivated its transformation from church to restaurant. Attention to detail and reuse of existing fixtures helped to create a spectacular atmosphere. The kitchen now occupies the former rectory. Original pews have been revitalized to provide dining-room seating. Additional pews were transformed to create the wooden bar. The eight carefully restored lanterns in the center aisle occupy their original location. Steel and copper brew tanks are located where the altar previously stood; celestial blue is used as a backdrop color out of respect for this sacred area of the church. Added in the summer of 1997, the European courtyard reuses old bricks from the original structures. In recognition that the building's beauty has been maintained and interior changes have been minimized, The Church Brew Works received an Award for Merit from the Pittsburgh History and Landmarks Foundation for reuse of the property.

The uniqueness of the setting is matched by the taste of the beer and the originality of the menu. The menu, which reflects the varied culinary styles throughout the country and the diversity of Pittsburgh itself, will appeal to both the most traditional and the most adventuresome of diners. Try the Pierogies, an unusual twist on a local staple!

CRAB CAKES WITH GOURMET SPROUT AND SEAWEED SALAD

Crab Cakes

2 pounds crabmeat
1 jumbo egg
½ cup mayonnaise
1½ teaspoons dry mustard
1½ teaspoons seafood seasoning
¼ cup red pepper, diced and blanched
¼ cup green pepper, diced and blanched
½ teaspoon Tabasco sauce
2 teaspoons Worcestershire sauce
¾ teaspoon salt
pinch of white pepper
2 teaspoons parsley
½ cup cracker crumbs
roasted red pepper strips
fried egg roll strips

Remove shells from crabmeat. In a large bowl, combine next 11 ingredients and mix well. Form into 5 patties. Coat with cracker crumbs. Lightly sauté until golden brown. Serve atop Gourmet Sprout and Seaweed Salad. Garnish with roasted red pepper strips and fried egg roll strips. Serves 5.

Gourmet Sprout and Seaweed Salad

4 heads frisee
1½ cups broccoli florets
2 cups Mung bean sprouts
1½ cups radish sprouts
1½ cups seaweed, blanched

Clean vegetables. Mix ingredients until evenly blended. Drizzle with Black Sesame Vinaigrette. Serves 5.

Black Sesame Vinaigrette

½ cup olive oil
½ cup sesame oil
½ cup vegetable oil
½ cup red wine vinegar
1 tablespoon soy sauce
½ tablespoon black sesame seeds
½ tablespoon white sesame seeds
3 tablespoons tomato, seeded, peeled, and minced

Whisk together all ingredients in a large bowl. Drizzle over Gourmet Sprout and Seaweed Salad. Yields approximately 2 cups.

GRILLED TURKEY AND WATERCRESS SALAD

1½ to 2 cups baby greens
½ cup watercress
¼ cup sun-dried cranberries
¼ cup pistachios
¼ cup cranberry vinaigrette
5-ounce turkey fillet, grilled and julienned
½ cup sweet potato curls

Place baby greens in a bowl among the watercress. Disperse cranberries and pistachios over the top of the salad. Ladle vinaigrette over top. Place turkey strips on salad, top with sweet potato curls, and serve. Serves 1.

50 NORTH CAMERON STREET
HARRISBURG, PA 17101
717-221-1080

Appalachian Brewing Co., located in a building originally owned by the Harrisburg Passenger Railway, is one of the largest brewpubs in the country. The oldest part of the structure dates to 1890. The Auchenbach Printing Company was housed here during the 1920s and 1930s, until fire practically destroyed it. Printing machines from that era are on display in the entry area.

During the 1940s, it was used as an office building for the Works Progress Administration, as verified by a WPA certificate found in the wall. When the United States became involved in World War II, aircraft parts were made and warehoused here while aircraft mechanics were trained next door.

The building later fell into disrepair. A fire in March 1993 rendered it practically useless. Restoration began on July 4, 1995. Fire and smoke damage was removed, along with years of paint covering the original brick walls, the massive beams, and the hardwood floors. Miles of electrical wiring and plumbing, some of it dating to the 1920s, were removed. It took two years of hard work by the owners and their friends, known as "Friends of the Brewery," to renovate the first floor and parts of the second floor and to build the brewery operation.

The result of their vision and elbow grease is Appalachian Brewing Co., which recaptures the area's brewing tradition. As far back as the 1700s, the Harrisburg area produced much of the beer for this region. Now, stained-glass doors depicting the city's portion of the Susquehanna River invite guests to enter the brewpub. Inside, the brewery operations are visible from the dining room. The history of each of the brews made here can be found on a placard at every table. Jolly Scot Scottish Ale, now produced here, was once a famed local beer made by R. H. Graupners Brewery, which was located just a block from where Appalachian Brewing Co. stands today. Graupners survived Prohibition but closed on May 14, 1951, exactly forty-six years before Appalachian Brewing Co. opened.

Many menu items feature beer in their preparation, including the Trail Stew, made with Riverside Red Ale. We tried the Appalachian Asparagus Rolls, which were as unusual an appetizer as we've encountered, and very tasty. We shared a Spinach and Artichoke Pizza, which was thoroughly enjoyable. The crust was thin and flavorful, and the toppings were in just the right proportions. Salads and sandwiches also appear on the menu and are popular with many lunch guests. However, we agreed that one of the gourmet pizzas would be our choice every time.

ARTICHOKE SPREAD

1 tablespoon Water Gap Wheat or light ale
1 cup pistachios, shelled and grated fine
⅔ cup artichoke hearts, diced
¾ teaspoon white pepper
generous ¼ teaspoon cayenne pepper
1 tablespoon dried chives
2 8-ounce packages cream cheese, softened
⅔ cup artichoke hearts, chopped
1 loaf French bread, sliced thin
olive oil
oregano
garlic
lettuce

Combine ale, pistachios, diced artichokes, white pepper, cayenne, and chives in a food processor and blend thoroughly. Slowly add cream cheese until well blended. Remove from food processor and place in a mixing bowl. Gently fold in artichoke chunks. Refrigerate until ready to serve. Place bread slices on a sheet pan. Sprinkle with olive oil and season with oregano and garlic. Toast until golden brown. Prior to serving, microwave spread until warm. Place 1½ to 2 cups of the mixture atop a bed of lettuce in the center of a large platter. Place toast rounds around the spread and serve. Yields 4 cups.

APPALACHIAN ASPARAGUS ROLLS

2 large eggplants
2 tablespoons water
1 egg
1 cup flour
1 teaspoon salt, divided
1 teaspoon white pepper, divided
1 tablespoon vegetable oil
1 bunch asparagus
12-ounce bottle Purist pale ale
4 8-ounce packages cream cheese
2 pounds ricotta cheese
4 teaspoons lemon pepper
2 teaspoons black pepper
2 teaspoons Bavarian mustard
2 cups tomato sauce
½ teaspoon oregano
spring greens

Peel eggplants and slice them thinly lengthwise; slices should be about ⅛-inch thick. Blend water and egg in a mixing bowl. In another mixing bowl, combine flour, ½ teaspoon salt, and ½ teaspoon white pepper. Place eggplant slices in flour mixture, then dip in egg wash, then back in flour mixture; remove excess breading. Heat vegetable oil in a saucepan on medium-hot. Fry each side of eggplant until golden brown. Place eggplant on draining rack, then refrigerate until cold.

Preheat oven to 350 degrees. Place asparagus in a single layer on a sheet pan. Cover with ale and bake for 10 minutes, then chill immediately on sheet pan.

Blend cream cheese, ricotta, lemon pepper, black pepper, and mustard in a medium mixing bowl. Chill for 30 minutes.

Mix tomato sauce with the remaining salt, the remaining white pepper, and oregano. Place in a small saucepan on low heat until warmed through.

Lay eggplant on a large sheet pan in a preheated 350-degree oven. Spread cheese mixture on eggplant, place asparagus across eggplant, and gently roll eggplant from end to end; the asparagus should stick out of the roll. Bake for 15 minutes. Remove from oven, cover with warm tomato sauce, and serve atop a bed of spring greens. Yields 16 to 20 appetizers.

101 STATION PLACE
GREENSBURG, PA 15601
724-850-7245

Housed in Greensburg's train station, Red Star Brewery & Grille has a history and a future that are closely intertwined. When the station was built in 1910, the city was home to two breweries. Ten years later, after the onset of Prohibition, those breweries were forced to close. They were unable to reopen when Prohibition was repealed in 1933. Today, more than sixty-five years later, Greensburg again has a brewery to call its own. Red Star strives to combine the brewing tradition of the early Greensburg operations with those of the area's Bavarian forefathers.

In fact, the name of this perky little restaurant emerged from that Bavarian background. At the turn of the century, many small Bavarian towns had breweries that also functioned as restaurants or taverns. In those days, it was a special occasion when an establishment's brew was ready for consumption. The accepted method for advertising that fact was for the tavern owner to hang a red star outside the door for the town to see. Now, at the turn of a new century, Red Star

Brewery & Grille, by virtue of its name, continues the tradition right here in Pennsylvania.

Its brewery operation is front and center. You pass the tanks, housed behind glass windows, before actually entering the restaurant. And upon opening the doors, you can't miss the large copper brew tanks located behind the bar.

Much of the interior remains as it was in the early 1900s. The marble water fountains are still in place, though they are now used as planters. Wainscoting and other embellishments are found throughout. The tongue-and-groove ceiling and the arched beams speak of craftsmanship from a time long ago. The expansive benches, having provided a respite for many travelers, now provide seating in the center of the restaurant. Oversized postcards, all with a Greensburg postmark, hang above.

The eclectic menu offers options from a variety of cuisines. Many incorporate beer in the preparation, such as Salmon poached in a beer fume and French Fries blanched in beer and garlic before being fried. For sausage lovers, Red Star offers four house-made varieties. You can order these as an appetizer or in a sandwich served on Pumpernickel Bread. We tried a sandwich and found it delicious and filling. And if you're in the mood for home brew, you might want to try Red Star's Sampler—each of the brewery's four house beers served in five-ounce glasses. There is certainly something for everyone here.

GINGERBREAD STOUT CAKE

2½ cups all-purpose flour
2 teaspoons powdered ginger
2 teaspoons ground cinnamon
2 teaspoons baking soda
½ teaspoon ground cloves
1 cup unsalted butter, softened
1¼ cups brown sugar
3 large eggs
1 cup molasses
¾ cup stout beer, room temperature
vanilla ice cream
chocolate sauce

Preheat oven to 350 degrees. Grease and flour a 12-cup fluted pan or Bundt pan. Sift dry ingredients together. Beat butter and sugar until light in texture. Beat in the eggs 1 at a time. Add molasses; batter will look curdled. Beat in flour mixture at low speed ⅓ at a time. Beat in beer. Pour into pan and bake 45 to 55 minutes until a toothpick inserted in the center of the cake comes out clean. Serve warm with vanilla ice cream and chocolate sauce. Yields 1 cake.

BEER-STEAMED MUSSELS

1 pound black mussels
1 tablespoon garlic, minced
1 tablespoon shallots, minced
1 tomato, diced
1 tablespoon fresh herbs (such as parsley, basil, or cilantro), chopped
¾ cup fresh beer

Place all ingredients into a sauté pan and cover with lid. Cook on high for 3 to 4 minutes until mussels open up all the way. Serve steaming hot in a serving bowl with the lid on. When you lift the lid, your guests will be greeted by an aroma of herbs, seafood, and beer. Serves 2 to 4.

800 VINIAL STREET
PITTSBURGH, PA 15212
412-237-9402

Tom Pastorius and his wife, Mary Beth, lived in Germany for many years before coming back to Pennsylvania in the mid-1980s to raise their two sons. Upon returning, they missed many things about German life, including the simple foods and the good beer. However, the family's inspiration to establish a brewery and open a restaurant in Pittsburgh went back much farther than that—more than three hundred years, in fact. It all started on October 6, 1683, when Franz Daniel Pastorius, Tom's great-great-great-great-great-great-great-grandfather, founded the first German settlement in America. A scholar, Franz Daniel wrote the first schoolbook in Pennsylvania and one of the first medical books in the United States. He was also a true German who was passionate about beer. A friend of William Penn, he frequently enjoyed the products of Penn's home brewery.

Tom Pastorius used this same passion to rescue the abandoned Eberhardt & Ober Brewery, built in the 1800s in the Deutschtown section of Pittsburgh. He created the Pennsylvania Brewing Company in 1986 and added Penn Brewery in 1989. While Tom sees to the brewery, Mary Beth sees to the restaurant.

The restaurant is a fun, festive experience that begins as soon as you leave your car. After walking down the steps, you enter a cobblestone courtyard that exudes Old World charm; this courtyard is used as a *biergarten* in the warm months. Large flags from foreign countries hang above the family-style dining hall, from which guests can view the brewery operations.

The menu is traditional German. According to Mary Beth, Germans, just like Americans, are eating lighter, and their cooking today reflects that trend. Penn Brewery's Vegetable Strudel is an example of that evolution. We threw caution to the wind, choosing appetizers of Potato Pancakes and Kasespatzle, which consists of German noodles with melted Jarlsberg cheese and onions; the delicious Kasespatzle could be a meal in and of itself. Since deciding on an entrée was difficult, we had a sampler platter of Sauerbraten, Schweinbraten (roasted pork loin), Braised Red Cabbage, Sauerkraut, Mashed Potatoes, and Hot Potato Salad. The meats were so tender the we cut them with a fork. Debbie happens to love sauerkraut and voted this some of the best she'd ever eaten. The service was fabulous—both friendly and attentive. In hiring wait staff, Mary Beth looks for people who have not only the skills to get the job done but also the personality to interact with guests in the bier-hall atmosphere.

Penn Brewery is the site of many special events throughout the year. Oktoberfest, of course, is a popular time. The Microbrewery Festival is always the first Saturday in June. Or patrons can try their hand at their "Cooking with Beer" contest. A previous first-prize winner, "Chicken Cordon Brew," is now a feature on the regular menu! *Guten Appetit*!

VEGETABLE STRUDEL

1 cup butter
1½ cups mushrooms, sliced
1 pound yellow squash, sliced
1 pound zucchini, diced
12-ounce bag spinach, stemmed
2 cups breadcrumbs
2 tablespoons salt substitute
2½ cups muenster cheese, grated
2 9-inch sheets puff pastry
3 egg yolks

Melt butter in large saucepan and sauté vegetables. Let cool. Add breadcrumbs, seasoning, and cheese. Mix thoroughly and set aside. Roll puff pastry to ⅛-inch thickness. Divide mixture evenly between the 2 pieces of pastry. Spread vegetables to within 1 inch of pastry edges. Roll; tuck in the ends. Place folded side down on a baking sheet and brush with egg yolks. Bake for 45 minutes at 350 degrees. Yields 2 8-inch strudels.

PENN BREWERY SAUCE

½ cup butter
1½ cups flour
4 cups milk
4 cups cheddar cheese, shredded
¾ cup Penn Pilsner beer
2 tablespoons whole-grain mustard

Melt butter in a saucepan. Add flour and whisk until smooth. Set aside. Heat milk but *do not boil.*

Add cheese and stir constantly until cheese is melted and mixture is smooth. Add beer and mustard. Use flour and butter mix to thicken mixture to desired consistency. Yields approximately 4 cups.

Note: At Penn Brewery, this is served with Chicken Berlin, a boneless chicken breast stuffed with sharp cheddar cheese, onions, and whole-grain mustard.

KASESPATZLE

2 eggs
½ cup water
1½ cups flour
1 teaspoon salt
pinch of nutmeg
1 cup Jarlsberg cheese, grated
1 cup extra-sharp cheddar cheese, grated
4 ounces cream cheese
1 cup onion, chopped coarse and sautéed

Combine eggs and water in a large mixing bowl, then whip. Add flour, salt, and nutmeg. Place dough in a colander over 2 to 3 gallons of boiling, salted water. Force dough through the colander. While cooking, stir frequently so the dough will not stick. When spatzle is soft to the touch, remove from heat, strain, and rinse with cold water. Reheat as needed.

Combine Jarlsberg, cheddar, and cream cheese with a mixer. Stir spatzle into cheese mixture by hand. Place in 4 individual baking dishes and top with small amount of onions. Microwave or heat in oven until hot. Serves 4.

Pub & Brewery

248 HUNTERSTOWN ROAD
GETTYSBURG, PA 17325
717-337-1001

I had so many plates and glasses in front of me that the gentleman at the next table felt compelled to ask, "Did you try it all?" I had sampled four of the special brews, soup, two entrées, and a pie, two bites of which were still on the plate, waiting for Karen to taste when she picked me up after her dinner appointment. The gentleman had just been seated, so he hadn't seen the process, just the aftermath.

Earlier, as I'd contemplated my choices, owner Paul Lemley started me off with a sample of Red Sled, an easy red lager. Paul is passionate about his creations. He uses no rice, corn syrup, or preservatives. Because of this, you can get his brews only on-site. He next brought over the Milk Stout, which had none of the aftertaste of typical dark beers. He explained that the yeast in the beer couldn't break down even the small amount of milk used, allowing the milk sugar to combat the bitterness. A quick lesson in biochemistry! I also sampled the Orange Cream Soda and the Root Beer, which are brewed on the premises. They contain no caffeine and 20 percent less sugar than commercial brands—and taste much better!

As if I hadn't enjoyed enough beer, I tried the Beer Cheese Soup, which was thick and steamy and had chunks of ham. I ordered the Chicken Piegga Sandwich with Horseradish Sauce, in order to sample the topping for which Lemley gets so many recipe requests. It was very flavorful without being overpowering. The sandwich was large, and I was just beginning to wonder how I might finish it when the chef, Heinz, delivered a miniature version of the wonderful Shrimp Foccacia. The bread was delicately crisp on the edges and nice and soft in the center. Topped with shrimp and a sauce that has a little zing of its own, then finished off with freshly grated Parmesan cheese, it, too, was scrumptious.

The fare here is simple. The items in each menu category are all delicious and very well prepared. The atmosphere is appealingly simple as well. The restaurant and brewery are located in the barn of the historic Montfort Farm. Built in 1862, a year after the farmhouse was constructed, the barn is one of only about forty Pennsylvania Dutch brick-end barns still standing. The brick has intricate open hour-glass patterns. The uneven plank flooring and rough-hewn beams are still in place, as are two of the ladders once used to access the hayloft.

A family letter written on July 8, 1863, documents the farm's involvement in the Battle of Gettysburg. As troops were evacuated from nearby Culp's Hill, the farm was converted into a Confederate field hospital. Over thirteen hundred Confederate soldiers were placed in the house and barn, making it one of the largest field hospitals during the war. Soldiers who were not severely injured took up a significant amount of space on the ground around the two structures.

As the Confederates retreated from Gettysburg, they left 446 soldiers at the farm.

Those men recuperated here for approximately a month before being consolidated with other wounded at Camp Letterman on Hospital Hill. Forty-seven men died during that time and were buried on the farm. Not surprisingly, the Montfort family lost considerable crops, livestock, furniture, clothing, and linens, all of which were used to meet the needs of the wounded. They were not compensated for their troubles until twenty years later.

Today, the farm is used for reenactments of those events. Proud of the educational value this provides, Lemley brings the learning experience into the brewery as well. As I chatted with him between his phone calls and brewmaster duties, I discovered that he is as energetic in his approach to life as he is in the making of his beer. He's a purist committed to education, historic preservation, and the supreme quality of his product. GETTYSBREW is an All-American restaurant run by an All-American guy!

HORSERADISH SAUCE

1 cup prepared horseradish
2 cups mayonnaise

Thoroughly combine ingredients. Let sit in refrigerator overnight. Yields 3 cups.

Note: This simple, easy-to-make sauce adds an exciting finish to many foods. GETTYSBREW tops a chicken breast with Horseradish Sauce and a four-cheese blend, then bakes it to make one of its most popular sandwiches.

SHRIMP FOCCACIA

2 cups frozen salad shrimp
1 teaspoon Mrs. Dash salt-free seasoning
¼ teaspoon paprika
cayenne pepper to taste
1 cup celery, diced
1 cup sweet pepper, diced
8-ounce package cream cheese
½ cup sour cream
1 tablespoon A-1 sauce
½ teaspoon cornstarch
12 slices foccacia bread
3 cups cheese, shredded

Thaw, rinse, and drain shrimp. Mix in dry seasonings, celery, and sweet pepper. In a separate bowl, combine cream cheese, sour cream, A-1, and cornstarch. Combine shrimp and cream cheese mixtures. Top each slice of bread with ¼ cup of mixture, then with ¼ cup shredded cheese. Bake in oven at 350 degrees until cheese melts and turns golden brown. Enjoy! Serves 12.

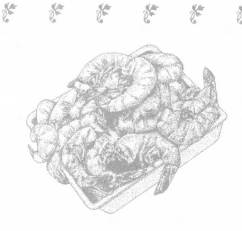

102 NORTH MARKET STREET
MOUNT JOY, PA 17552
717-653-2056

A young brewing apprentice by the name of Alois Bube emigrated from Germany to the United States in the early 1870s. In 1876, he bought a small brewery in Mount Joy. Alois Bube worked hard and expanded his brewery several times to keep up with the demand for his lager beer. A very successful businessman, he eventually built a large Victorian hotel right next to the brewery to serve his beer and accommodate overnight guests.

In 1908, at the age of fifty-seven, Bube suddenly died, leaving the business to be run by members of his family. He left a considerable fortune. Even though the brewery closed just before Prohibition began in 1920, his family continued to live in the hotel. The family did not move any of the brewery's equipment or tools and did little or nothing to the buildings.

In the late 1800s, breweries such as this one were extremely common. However, this is the only "lager era" brewery in the United States that remains almost completely intact today. Restoration of this registered historic building began in 1968 and still continues, as new owner Sam Allen prepares to begin brewing again, using the original recipes of Alois Bube.

This huge brewery is divided into several unusual dining areas. Sam took me on an extended tour of the buildings while Debbie was dining in nearby Reading. After passing through the Brewery Gallery, which features local artists, I found myself in the Alois Restaurant, located in the old Victorian hotel. I visited the original tavern and the card room, which remain much as they were when the hotel was built. Meals are served in the original parlor and dining room.

At the Alois Restaurant, you have the opportunity to taste everything on the menu. Beginning in the parlor, you can try the Cajun Artichoke Hearts with Remoulade Sauce and the Crabmeat-Stuffed Mushroom Caps. You then continue your meal in the dining room, where you may sample the Roasted Beef Tenderloin with Fennel and Mustard Seed Rub, the Chicken Skewers marinated in Red Chili Vinaigrette, and perhaps even the Dijon Swiss Pizza with Prosciutto and Mushrooms. And remember to save room for the homemade desserts.

Next, I descended forty-three feet below ground to the cellars of Bube's Brewery. Here, in the Catacombs Restaurant, you can partake of a delicious dinner most nights of the week. The specialty is the Medieval Feast, which takes place each Sunday. It features inspired cooking and entertainment provided by minstrels, beggars, and wenches.

Sam guided me through the Cooper's Shed, a museum and brewery store. I was astounded to view such a large collection of antique cooper's tools, most of which were discovered on the premises. I even tried my hand at cooperage in the barrel-producing area.

I decided to eat in the Bottling Works, a

pleasant, casual restaurant and tavern located in what was the original bottling plant. I opted for the Seafood Quiche with Fresh Fruit and took a quick stroll around the outdoor *biergarten* while my selection was made to order. Right in the center of the brick paths are the original boiler and smokestack, once used to create the steam power required to run the brewery. They now provide a focal point for conversations and an interesting backdrop for the live jazz performed here on Sunday evenings. When I returned to my quiche—hot from the oven and surrounded by an enormous serving of melons and berries—it was easy to see why Bube's Brewery is so popular with locals and tourists alike. There is something here for everyone.

BROILED SALMON WITH LEMON BEURRE BLANC

½ cup heavy cream
2 tablespoons shallots, minced
½ cup Chardonnay
juice of 1 lemon
2 tablespoons vinegar (white balsamic, if available)
2 sticks butter, softened
1 tablespoon lemon zest
4 8-ounce salmon fillets

Bring cream to a boil in a small saucepan and reduce by ½. In a separate saucepan, combine shallots, wine, lemon juice, and vinegar; reduce until nearly dry. Stir in reduced cream and continue to reduce. Whisk in butter, remove from heat, and mix in lemon zest. Broil salmon for 10 to 15 minutes to desired doneness; fish should be firm but not flaky. Place salmon on each of 4 plates and top with Lemon Beurre Blanc. Serves 4.

CAPPUCCINO CHEESECAKE

1½ cups Oreo cookie crumbs
¼ cup 10X sugar, sifted
6 tablespoons butter, melted
4 8-ounce packages cream cheese
3¼ cups sugar, divided
1 teaspoon pure vanilla extract
3 tablespoons instant coffee moistened with 2 tablespoons water, divided
4 eggs
1½ teaspoons cinnamon, divided
2 cups sour cream

Preheat oven to 325 degrees. In a bowl, combine cookie crumbs, 10X sugar, and butter. Press mixture into the bottom of a 9½-inch springform pan. Place cream cheese, 1¾ cups of the sugar, vanilla, ½ of the coffee mixture, eggs, and 1 teaspoon of the cinnamon into the bowl of a food processor; process until smooth. Pour into pan on top of cookie crumb base. Bake for 1 hour until center of cheesecake is set. Leave cheesecake in pan and set aside to cool for at least 1 hour.

In a small bowl, whisk together sour cream and the remaining sugar, coffee mixture, and cinnamon. Turn cheesecake out of pan and top with sour cream mixture. Serves 8.

CHAPTER 5

On the Waterfront

Golden Pheasant Inn

Water has long provided us with access to places, people, and things far away. Because of this, the acreage beside it is often the first to be developed and is considered highly valuable. The establishments in this chapter, which now derive their livelihood from the restaurant trade, once relied heavily on the water flowing nearby to ensure the success of their endeavors.

River's Edge Cafe

203 YOUGH STREET
CONFLUENCE, PA 15424
814-395-5059

The history of this area can be traced to explorer Christopher Gist, who arrived in 1751. He crossed the Youghiogheny River at the point where it combines waters with the Casselman River and Laurel Hill Creek. He called the area "Three Forks" and "Turkeyfoot." Three years later, another notable visitor, George Washington, came to this site. "Tarried there for some time to examine the place, which we found very suitable for the erection of a fort . . . because it was at the mouth of three branches," he wrote. No such fort was built. All in all, it isn't difficult to see how this area came by its name, Confluence.

As you might surmise, this large, two-story, clapboard, Williamsburg-style home, built about 1890, is situated near the water. It overlooks the Youghiogheny River, locally called the "Yough," as it flows between Mount Davis and Sugarloaf Mountain, Pennsylvania's two highest peaks. The home has been restored and filled with antiques, even down to the restrooms. The ladies' room houses a collection of hats and dress collars; an old bathing suit hangs on the wall, surrounded by photos of turn-of-the-century bathers. The interior of the restaurant is filled with bric-a-brac. Each turn of your head will bring yet another interesting and unexpected item into view. Dried flowers hang from the soffit in the back dining room. Framed photographs—including old aerial pictures of the area—emphasize the history in which River's Edge Cafe is steeped. The whole atmosphere—oak tables and chairs, lace curtains, subtle wallpaper—will remind you of going to Great-Aunt Lucille's for cookies warm out of the oven.

On the beautiful, sunny day when we visited, we were given a table on the porch, overlooking the river. The water level was low, so the river gurgled and splashed its way over the rocks as it meandered by. The grounds of River's Edge are beautifully landscaped. Enormous hostas and lovely day lilies grew along the brick walk, and a rambling rose climbed the trellis beside our table. The cafe was busy, as many guests arrived by bicycle, ready for a tasty respite after a morning of touring the surrounding countryside.

We sipped Lemonade and contemplated the menu, finally choosing Black Bean Hummus (served with tortilla chips) and Pesto Di Pomodoro (toast rounds topped with Sun-Ripened Tomato Pesto) as appetizers. We then had a Veggie Hoagie and a Chicken Salad Sandwich made with apples, raisins, and walnuts. Our dessert selections were White Chocolate Cheesecake in a chocolate crust and Carrot Cake, unusual in that its middle layer was a brown sugar-nut paste. The menu items were every bit as appealing as the atmosphere.

We'd like to go back sometime, not only to dine but also to poke around in the River's Edge antique store before enjoying an overnight stay in the bed-and-breakfast. Just thinking about the experience puts smiles on our faces!

❧ WALNUT POULET ❧

12 6-ounce boneless, skinless chicken breasts
2 tablespoons dried parsley, divided
2 tablespoons dried basil, divided
2 tablespoons oregano, divided
2 teaspoons pepper, divided
4 sticks butter, softened (do not substitute)
½ cup walnuts, lightly crushed
⅛ cup garlic, crushed

Lightly season chicken breasts with a tablespoon each of parsley, basil, and oregano and a teaspoon of pepper. Grill breasts until done. In a medium saucepan, combine remaining ingredients over low heat; do not overheat. Pour over chicken breasts and serve two breasts per person. Serves 6.

❧   ❧   ❧   ❧   ❧   ❧

❧ SMOKED PORK DIJON ❧

Pork

12 4-ounce smoked porkchops with bones
½ to 1 cup Honey Mustard Sauce (see below)
24 thin slices smoked turkey
12 slices Swiss cheese

Grill porkchops 2 to 3 minutes on each side. Pour Honey Mustard Sauce in the center of each porkchop. Roll up turkey slices and place 2 on each porkchop, then place 1 slice of cheese on each chop. Cover with a lid or place in broiler to melt cheese. Serves 6.

Honey Mustard Sauce

¼ cup honey
¼ cup brown mustard
1 cup commercial ranch dressing

Gently fold honey and mustard into dressing. Yields 1½ cups.

❧   ❧   ❧   ❧   ❧   ❧

3660 SOUTH RIVER DRIVE
YORK, PA 17406
717-252-1521

Accomac Inn's future began in late March 1722, when the tract of land on which it sits was first surveyed. Ten years later, Maryland granted a patent for the two-hundred-acre parcel to partners Philip Syng and Thomas Brown. The land was part of an ongoing controversy between Maryland and Pennsylvania, as authorities argued over lands west of the Susquehanna River.

But for the Susquehanna, Accomac Inn would never have existed. European settlers began to cross the river at this point as early as 1725. James Anderson, who owned land adjoining that of Syng and Brown, began operating a ferry here around 1730. By 1775, a stone structure known as Anderson's Ferry Inn had been built and was granted a tavern license. During the American Revolution, many notable military figures were guests at the inn, including the Marquis de Lafayette and Continental Army general Horatio Gates.

In the early 1800s, flat-bottomed boats ferried passengers, cargo, and animals. John Elgar, a local machinist, designed the first iron steamboat in America. Propelled by two paddle wheels, it could manage an unheard-of seven miles per hour in calm water, significantly reducing travel time at what was then called Keesey's Ferry.

During the Civil War, John Coyle purchased the property. His ownership was marked by a romantic tragedy. Coyle's not particularly bright son Johnny was repeatedly spurned by a hired girl named Emily. In a fit of rage one day, Johnny shot Emily, creating a sensation that spread through several counties.

Exactly when Coyle's Ferry became known as Accomac Inn is unclear, although advertising from the 1890s refers to the inn by its current name. The name comes from the local Nanticoke tribe and means "across the water." After the invention of the automobile, however, it was no longer necessary for travelers to cross by ferry and stay at the inn. Instead, families could travel to and from the inn in one day. Thus began the restaurant business here.

In the spring of 1915, Norman T. Pickle assumed proprietorship of the inn and updated and modernized the structure. On May 16, 1935, the building caught fire and burned. Mr. Pickle then reconstructed it using original stone from the inn and additional stone from the old Whitmer Bridge.

Since that time, several owners have come and gone. Under the helm of H. Douglas Campbell, the menu has been expanded and updated. The restaurant no longer serves chicken and waffles, as it did for many years. It now boasts menu items such as New Zealand Rack of Lamb, Salmon au Citron, and Pistachio-Crusted Trout. We ordered Salad Ann, which was delicious and unusual. We followed that with entrées of Cashew-Crusted

Sea Bass and the salmon special, which was topped with a potato crust. Everything was superb, from the presentation to the flavor. Dining by candlelight, seated at a table with a panoramic view of the river, it was easy to imagine waiting on the bank for that special someone to arrive.

SALAD ANN

Salad

1½ cups mesclun lettuce
¼ Granny Smith apple, julienned
¼ cup sun-dried cranberries
½ teaspoon walnuts, toasted and chopped
2 tablespoons walnut oil
¼ cup plus 1 tablespoon Maple Berry Vinaigrette (see next column), divided
1 crown fenelles de brick

Toss mesclun, apples, cranberries, ½ of the walnuts, ½ of the walnut oil, and ¼ cup of the vinaigrette. Place mixture in fenelles de brick. Surround with remaining walnuts, walnut oil, and 1 tablespoon vinaigrette. Serves 1.

Maple Berry Vinaigrette

2 pints strawberries
2 pints blueberries
1 pint raspberries
1 cup maple syrup
12-ounce bottle raspberry vinegar

Wash and stem berries. Place in a saucepan and bring to a boil. Add syrup. Bring to a simmer and reduce by ¼. Add raspberry vinegar and reduce by ¼. Strain through a berry cup or fine sieve. Yields 7 cups.

RED SNAPPER IN PARCHMENT

½ cup macadamia nuts, ground
1 cup all-purpose flour
½ teaspoon salt
¼ teaspoon freshly ground black pepper
¼ cup vegetable oil
4 6-ounce red snapper fillets, deboned and skinned
1 leek, greens removed
¾ cup sweet butter
2 tablespoons port wine
¼ cup Roquefort cheese
1 green onion, chopped fine
2 sheets 16-by-24-inch parchment paper
¼ cup melted butter

Process nuts, flour, salt, and pepper in a food processor until combined. Pour oil into a large, heavy skillet and heat on medium-high. Lightly coat fillets with flour mixture and sear both sides quickly in skillet. Remove fish and allow to cool. Clean pan. Cut leek in half lengthwise and rinse thoroughly in cold water. Mince leek and sauté in 2 tablespoons of the butter. Add port and simmer until liquid evaporates but leeks are still moist. Whip remaining 6 ounces of butter. When smooth, add Roquefort and green onion. Roll into a log shape in wax paper or plastic film. Chill butter mixture. Cut each parchment paper in half across the width. Fold each parchment piece in half and cut to form a heart shape when unfolded. Open hearts and brush both sides with melted butter. Place ¼ of leek mixture in center of right side of 1 heart. Place snapper fillet on the leeks and top with ¼ of butter mixture. Fold other side of heart around fish and make an overlapping fold around the border; fold the point under. Repeat with remaining fillets. Bake at 450 degrees for 15 minutes. Serves 4.

735 COLUMBUS BOULEVARD
PHILADELPHIA, PA 19147
215-923-2500

Displacement of 3,116 gross tons, draft of 12 feet, and overall length of 394 feet: the vital statistics of the *Moshulu* are impressive. Reputed to be the world's oldest and largest four-masted sailing ship, she was built for G. J. H. Siemers & Co. of Hamburg, Germany, by Wm. Hamilton Shipyard, Port Glasgow, Scotland. Launched in 1904 under the name *Kurt*, she spent most of her first ten years as a supply ship for a copper mine in Santa Rosalia, Mexico.

In 1914, the *Kurt* docked in Astoria, Oregon, to pick up grain. She was still in port when World War I broke out. The owners, concerned about their investment, decided to keep her there. Three years later, when the United States entered the war, the government confiscated the ship. The *Kurt* was renamed the *Dreadnaught* and was placed in service to make voyages across the Pacific to Australia and the Philippines. However, before she could put to sea, First Lady Edith Wilson renamed her. Mrs. Wilson selected the name Moshulu (which means the same as dreadnaught) to honor the Seneca tribe of Native Americans.

In 1921, Charles Nelson Company of San Francisco purchased the *Moshulu* from the government to haul lumber along the West Coast. Eventually, steamers took over most of the lumber trade. The *Moshulu* was laid up near Seattle for six years until Gustave Ericson, a Finnish grain merchant, expressed his interest in putting her back into service. She voyaged between Australia and Europe, rounding Cape Horn fifty-four times between 1934 and 1939. An informal race was held among the grain carriers to see which vessel could make the fastest time from Australia to Europe. Of course, the *Moshulu* won, but it was to be the last of such races because of the start of World War II.

The *Moshulu* made one more commercial run, to Argentina, but upon her return to Norway, the Germans confiscated her. For most of the war and until 1970, she was used as a floating warehouse in various parts of Scandinavia. In 1970, Raymond E. Wallace, who had been commissioned to find a ship to convert into a restaurant, brought the *Moshulu* back to the United States.

HMS Ventures, Inc., the current owner, has transformed the *Moshulu* into a dining, entertainment, and tourist attraction. She now serves the public in the style of a grand turn-of-the-century luxury liner. As a gold-braided member of the staff guided us to our table overlooking the Delaware River, we admired the etched Victorian glass, the Honduran mahogany paneling, and the sparkling chandeliers. The elegant atmosphere was enhanced by the ivory table linens and silver oil lamps. We perused the menu and discovered that, in keeping with the *Moshulu*'s many ports of call, the choice of items was truly global. The *Moshulu* has a well-deserved reputation for good food, and we looked forward to a delicious meal.

We started with the chunky and extremely tasty Blackened Chicken and Sweet Corn Chowder with Polenta Croutons. Debbie then opted for the Seared Filet Mignon with Gorgonzola Potato Gratin, Roasted Vegetables, and Morel-Bordeaux Sauce, while Karen chose the Onion-Crusted Mahi-Mahi with Plantain and Corn Strudel, Baby Spinach, and Ancho Chili Sauce. Both entrées were beautifully presented and tasted wonderful. We swapped dishes about halfway through the meal and still could not decide on a favorite. For dessert, we shared a Chocolate Tasting Plate, which consisted of a Chocolate and Banana Sacher Torte, Chocolate Flan topped with a Truffle and Caramelized Sugar, a Flourless Chocolate Pecan Bar topped with Raspberry Sorbet, and, last but definitely not least, a chocolate-filled Beggar's Purse. Each dessert could have easily stood alone, but blessed with no will power whatsoever, we loosened our belts another notch and ate the lot!

PAN-ROASTED GROUPER WITH SPICY LOBSTER BROTH

salt and pepper to taste
2 8-ounce grouper fillets
2 tablespoons canola oil
½ cup white wine
1 cup lobster stock
2 teaspoons ginger, minced
2 teaspoons onion, minced
2 teaspoons garlic, minced
2 teaspoons butter, softened

Preheat oven to 375 degrees. Season fillets. Heat oil in a medium ovenproof sauté pan. Add fillets to pan and sear on both sides. Remove pan from stovetop and place in oven for 3 to 5 minutes. Remove from oven and deglaze with white wine. Remove fish from pan and set aside. Return pan to heat and add lobster stock and all other ingredients except butter. Reduce liquids by ½. Stir in butter. Add fish back to pan and heat thoroughly. Place fish in 2 shallow bowls and pour sauce over top. Serves 2.

❦ SEAFOOD PAPPILLOTTE ❦

2 sheets parchment paper
2 5-ounce snapper, striped bass, or halibut fillets
6 littleneck clams
4 jumbo shrimp, peeled and deveined
4 fresh mussels
2 sprigs thyme
2 teaspoons chives, chopped
½ cup white wine
½ leek, julienned
½ carrot, julienned
2 shallots, minced
salt and pepper to taste

Fold each piece of parchment paper in half lengthwise. Place equal amounts of fish and shellfish in center of each paper. Top with remaining ingredients. Bring together top and bottom edges of parchment and fold edges together, keeping fish in center; twist edges tightly together. Place on sheet pan and bake at 400 degrees for about 25 minutes until fish is cooked through and shellfish are open. To serve, cut paper open in an **X** shape with scissors. Fold back edges of cut, place on plate, and garnish as desired. Serves 2.

❦   ❦   ❦   ❦   ❦   ❦

Centre Bridge Inn

2998 NORTH RIVER ROAD
NEW HOPE, PA 18938
215-862-9139

As early as 1700, passengers and cargo were being transported across the Delaware River near what is now New Hope. An inn was constructed here in 1705 to accommodate the growing number of passengers. In 1765, Joseph Mitchell became the latest in a long line of owners. His son William ran the ferry. William was also involved in the construction of Centre Bridge, which eventually put the ferry out of business. Completed in 1814, the bridge was operated by John Abel. Funeral processions and families on their way to church services were allowed to cross for free, but everyone else had to pay a toll. It wasn't long before the inn was renamed Centre Bridge. Extensive improvements were made to the property, including the addition of an icehouse and a blacksmith's shop.

By 1832, the Delaware Division Canal had been constructed alongside the river next to the inn. It was possible to sit on the back porch of Centre Bridge Inn and watch mule-drawn barges pass by on their way to Philadelphia. The canal is now a National Historic Landmark, and its towpath is used for cycling and walking.

Today, Centre Bridge Inn is noted for its rich history, its creative cuisine, and its magnificent panorama of the Delaware River. In summer, guests enjoy the romantic atmosphere of the brick terrace, located just a few feet from the canal and the river. The five-tiered waterfall and the large, overhanging, ivy-covered sycamore trees give this arbor a feeling of seclusion and peace. It's a perfect spot to sit awhile with a glass of one of the fine wines available. In spring and fall, the conservatory running the entire length of the inn is a popular spot. Guests can relax in comfort away from the elements and still enjoy a fabulous view of the spring blossoms or the fall foliage. When winter comes around, it is time for the cozy Old World Restaurant, where a low-beamed ceiling, flickering candlelight, and an enormous walk-in fireplace create an intimate atmosphere. Guests enjoy the numerous historical artifacts tucked away in each nook and cranny.

The inn's continental cuisine is inspired by fresh ingredients available seasonally. We began with Cream of Carrot Soup. It was fragrant and delicate and had the merest hint of cumin and mint. As we awaited our salads, our host, Stephen Dugan, insisted we try the Shrimp Appetizer. Four large shrimp served in a Vol-au-Vent Shell with a sauce of hazelnut and fresh dill, the appetizer was as sweet and delicious as it was beautiful. After a crisp, tangy salad, we enjoyed an unbelievably good entrée of Grilled Pork Tenderloin topped with Black Currant Brandy and served with a profusion of Seasonal Vegetables and Potato Galette. We sat back in our chairs and listened to the piano playing in the background as we tried to decide among such desserts as Coconut Pie and Hazelnut Torte. We reluctantly decided that we were just too full to eat another mouthful.

Whatever season you visit, you won't be disappointed by the view or the food or the gentle, unhurried service that matches the flow of the Delaware. This is truly an inn for all seasons!

SAUTEED CALAMARI IN SAFFRON SHRIMP BROTH

1 teaspoon garlic, minced
½ cup red onion, diced fine
1 tablespoon olive oil
3 cups tomatoes, skinned, seeded, and diced
1 cup Chardonnay
¼ bulb fresh fennel
2 tablespoons fresh basil, chopped
1½ teaspoons sugar
pinch of saffron
3 cups shrimp stock
1 tablespoon sweet butter
½ teaspoon cracked black pepper
salt to taste
1 pound calamari

Sauté garlic and onions in olive oil until onions are translucent. Add tomatoes, deglaze with Chardonnay, and reduce by ½. Add fennel, basil, sugar, saffron, and shrimp stock. Simmer for 30 minutes. Discard fennel. Swirl in butter and bring sauce to a simmer again. Season with pepper and salt. Poach calamari approximately 5 minutes until tender. Drain and add to sauce. Serve over your favorite pasta. Serves 4 to 6.

PORTABELLO MUSHROOMS STUFFED WITH ARTICHOKE MOUSSE

14-ounce can artichokes, drained
½ teaspoon fresh garlic, minced
2 scallions (white ends only)
pinch of parsley
pinch of fresh dill
¼ cup Chardonnay
¼ cup sour cream
¼ cup mayonnaise
¼ teaspoon fresh lemon juice
2 tablespoons fresh Parmesan cheese, grated
salt and pepper to taste
5 large portabello mushrooms
4 tablespoons olive oil
¼ cup seasoned breadcrumbs, moistened with olive oil

Place artichokes, garlic, scallions, parsley, and dill into a food processor; mix. Transfer mixture to a stainless-steel bowl and add Chardonnay, sour cream, mayonnaise, lemon juice, Parmesan, and salt and pepper; fold together. Chill to allow mixture to thicken. Sauté or grill mushrooms in olive oil. Pipe mousse into center of mushrooms and garnish with breadcrumbs. Serves 5.

Cuttalossa Inn

RIVER ROAD (PA 32)
LUMBERVILLE, PA 18933
215-297-5082

The name of the Cuttalossa Inn was derived from the Delaware Indians, who inhabited the Cuttalossa Valley during the last century. Legend has it that the word (pronounced Cut-a-lah-sa) once inspired a poet to write about an Indian maiden with that imagined name.

The inn is at the south end of Lumberville, a quaint village with two rows of beautifully maintained homes, a country store, two inns, and a lumberyard. It sits on the site where Colonel Joseph Wall built one of his two sawmills around 1785. The area was called Wall's Landing until 1814, when two businessmen, Messrs. Heed and Hartley, renamed it Lumberville to attract business. Lumbering and quarrying were the area's main industries. Although diminished, they still exist today.

The Cuttalossa Inn utilizes the ruins of the old mill in a unique way. Guests can cross the babbling brook by way of a narrow footbridge that is a smaller version of those over the nearby canal. Wisteria winds its way around the top of the stone building. A waterfall that comes off Coppernose Ridge feeds the creek and provides a lovely backdrop for Cuttalossa's terrace seating. Diners bask in the serenity of an Old World setting. Guests are seated in iron chairs at black-iron tables made from old Singer sewing tables, still with their treadles. Red-and-white cotton tablecloths add a touch of color. During inclement weather and in the winter months, guests dine in the main building, which was built in 1758 and served as a stagecoach stop on the route between New York and Philadelphia.

Seated on the terrace, we were mesmerized by the waterfall as we perused the menu. The Cuttalossa Inn offers a lunch/brunch menu with quiches and omelets, including a Brie and asparagus choice that sounded delicious. We opted for the soup of the day, Santa Fe Seafood Stew, which had just a touch of spice, and the quesadilla of the day, which featured albacore tuna and pineapple topped off by pepper jack cheese and attractively garnished with diced red, green, and yellow bell peppers. It was appealingly different and very tasty. Trying to watch our calorie intake, we decided not to have dessert, although we were tempted toward the Lemon Madness Dessert in a Lemon Crust and the Dreamsicle, which consists of an orange purée blended into vanilla ice cream. Maybe next time.

POACHED SALMON WITH GRANNY SMITH HORSERADISH SAUCE

Salmon

2 cups water
1 teaspoon salt
½ teaspoon pepper
1 tablespoon wine vinegar
¼ teaspoon thyme
1 bay leaf
½ teaspoon parsley
8 5-ounce salmon fillets
Granny Smith Horseradish Sauce (see below)

Combine first 7 ingredients in a large saucepan. Heat until simmering. Poach salmon carefully. Lift fish out and set aside. Spoon Granny Smith Horseradish Sauce over salmon and serve warm, or refrigerate salmon for 1 hour and serve chilled. Serves 8.

Granny Smith Horseradish Sauce

1½ Granny Smith apples, peeled and chopped
1 Granny Smith apple, peeled and puréed
1 cup apple cider
½ cup apple brandy
½ teaspoon cinnamon
½ teaspoon cloves
2 tablespoons horseradish
1 pint nonfat vanilla yogurt

Combine first 6 ingredients in a large saucepan and place over medium heat. Bring to a simmer and continue to cook until juice is gone. Remove from heat and stir in horseradish. Let cool. Fold mixture carefully into yogurt.

CHICKEN CAPRICE

½ cup red onions, chopped fine
1½ teaspoons garlic, minced
½ cup pitted calamata olives, cut into strips
½ cup oil-packed whole sun-dried tomatoes, drained
¼ pound feta cheese, crumbled
1 teaspoon dried marjoram
olive oil
6 chicken breasts with skin on

Combine first 6 ingredients in a medium mixing bowl. Use just enough olive oil to bind mixture. Using the back of a spoon or a chopstick, separate the center of the skin from the chicken breasts. Carefully spoon ⅓ cup of the mixture between the meat and the skin of each breast. Bake at 350 degrees for 30 to 40 minutes. Serves 6.

763 RIVER ROAD
ERWINNA, PA 18920
610-294-9595

This fieldstone structure, built in 1857 on the eastern boundary of Tinicum township, is literally steps away from a canal. It was built as a stop-off for the bargemen who made their way up and down the waterway on their runs from Easton to Bristol. The inn was built on land originally purchased from the London Company by William Penn in 1699. Just across the road is the Delaware River. Guests staying overnight at the inn have a lovely view of that waterway as well.

The proprietors of the Golden Pheasant Inn, Barbara and Michel Faure, follow a family tradition established across the Atlantic in the French provinces. The inn has three restored dining rooms, one of which is a greenhouse overlooking the canal. The Blaise Room, tucked between the entry hall and the greenhouse, is a lovely setting for small parties and intimate dining. We dined in the Tavern Room, which has a lovely natural pine mantel, rough beams, and exposed stone walls. Much of the woodwork, including the window sills and the built-in cupboards, is painted a holly green, which is beautifully accented by the copper cookware displayed throughout the dining room. White linen on the tables and simple green-and-white chair pads round out the French Country decor.

Our meal was served on dishes from Barbara's lovely collection of Quimper pottery, made in France. Other pieces are displayed in various nooks and crannies in several eye-catching groupings. After ordering, we browsed the family photos lining the window sills before sitting down again to enjoy Crostini and a Vegetable Spread made of cream cheese, green olives, and pimentos. Soon afterward came a flavorful, refreshing Salad of fresh greens, sliced tomatoes, fresh mozzarella, and fresh basil. The Shrimp in Creole Sauce was tantalizingly spicy. The Grilled Salmon Provençal was delectable, and the Grilled Vegetables that accompanied it were equally enjoyable. We couldn't pass on a wee bit of dessert, choosing the Chocolate Mousse and the Cassis Sorbet, so as not to feel too guilty.

After dinner, we chatted with Michel, who obviously loves cooking and enjoys sharing it with others. His cooking classes, extremely popular in the area, are ones we'd certainly participate in if we lived closer. Since we were the last dinner guests that evening, the dining room took on additional coziness as the rest of the family and the staff gathered around the bar to relax and chat. It felt like a Sunday evening at home.

TUSCAN SAUTÉED CHICKEN WITH OLIVES

6 tablespoons extra-virgin olive oil
4 cloves garlic, minced
2 4-pound chickens, quartered
2 tablespoons fennel seed
zest of 2 oranges, minced
salt and freshly ground black pepper to taste
2 cups dry white wine
1½ cups black Gaeta olives, pitted

In a heavy, 8-quart pot, warm olive oil and garlic over medium heat. Add chicken and cook about 10 minutes until golden; turn chicken occasionally. Add fennel seed, orange zest, and salt and pepper. Pour in white wine and cover. Cook over low heat for 45 minutes; add more wine if pan becomes dry. Add olives and cook 10 minutes. Arrange chicken on a warm platter and serve. Serves 8.

ST. ANNA BEANS

4 tablespoons extra-virgin olive oil
4 cloves garlic, chopped
3 pounds runner beans (St. Anna, if available), trimmed
2 cups plum tomatoes, diced
salt and freshly ground black pepper to taste

Warm olive oil in a large skillet over low heat. Add garlic and cook about 5 minutes until translucent. Add beans and tomatoes and season with salt and pepper. Lower heat and cook beans until tender. Transfer to a warm dish and serve. Serves 8.

ORANGE GINGER ICE CREAM

1 cup water
1 cup sugar
3 egg yolks
pinch of salt
3 tablespoons frozen orange juice concentrate
1 teaspoon vanilla
2 cups heavy cream
3 tablespoons candied ginger, minced

Bring water and sugar to a boil; boil for 5 minutes to form a syrup. In the top of a double boiler, whisk egg yolks and salt. Gradually add boiling syrup. Cook over boiling water for 3 minutes, beating constantly. Place top of double boiler in a bowl of ice and water and beat until cold. Add orange juice concentrate, vanilla, cream, and ginger. Pour into a container, cover, and freeze for at least 6 hours. Serves 6.

The Inn at Starlight Lake

P.O. BOX 27
STARLIGHT, PA 18461
570-798-2519

As the Delaware River winds toward Philadelphia from its headwaters at Hancock, New York, it passes through the hamlet of Starlight, Pennsylvania. Tucked away not far from the river, visitors can find an inn sitting on the banks of Starlight Lake, which is one of the many such beautiful lakes left behind after glaciers passed this way. The inn, named for the lake, opened in 1909 as a summer boardinghouse near a depot of the New York, Ontario, and Western Scranton Railroad. The tracks were removed long ago, and the railroad bed is now used for hiking, cycling, and snowmobiling.

The Inn at Starlight Lake is the last of the numerous inns and boardinghouses that once provided respite for travelers in this picturesque part of the state. The quaint, turn-of-the-century atmosphere still exists here. Canoeing, rowing, and sailing are some of the favorite activities in springtime, while a dip in the lake is quite popular during the summer. The foliage colors are splendid from mid-September through mid-October, until the first snow brings out the cross-country skiers for the winter.

It was a delightfully cool summer day when we visited. We lounged in the rocking chairs on the front porch while waiting for our reservation to be called. As we watched guests sitting in Adirondack chairs and diving off the wooden jetty into the waters of the lake, we felt ourselves slow down to a time before computers and car phones.

The dining room offers a wonderful view of the lake. On the day of our visit, a gentle breeze drifted through the lace curtains. The tables adorned with crisp linens, the garden flowers nestled in porcelain teapots, and the many hanging baskets with trailing greenery all served to make us feel like we were in a garden. The highlight of Debbie's meal was the Cornmeal-Crusted Catfish, which reminded her of summer meals at her grandmother's. Deliciously mild and flaky, it was served with Pepper Hash and Sage Tartar Sauce. Karen opted for the Veal Chop with Shiitake Mushroom Sauce and Potato Leek Gratin, an unusual but scrumptious combination. The flavorful, homemade Maple and Walnut Ice Cream rounded off a relaxing evening in this quiet corner of the state.

SOUR CREAM APPLE PIE

Crust

2 cups flour
½ teaspoon baking powder
1 scant teaspoon salt
½ cup lard
½ cup butter
6 tablespoons cold water

Combine ingredients. Turn onto floured board and knead gently for a few seconds. Roll out to make 2 9-inch piecrusts. Place crusts in 2 9-inch pie pans and prick with a fork.

Filling

2 tablespoons flour
⅛ teaspoon salt
⅔ cup sugar
1 egg
1 cup sour cream
1 teaspoon vanilla
¼ teaspoon nutmeg
3 medium apples, peeled and diced

Combine flour, salt, and sugar. Add egg, sour cream, vanilla, and nutmeg. Beat to form a smooth, thin batter. Stir in apples. Pour filling evenly between the 2 pie pans. Bake in a 400-degree oven for 15 minutes, then reduce heat to 350 degrees for 30 minutes.

Topping

⅓ cup brown sugar
⅓ cup flour
1 teaspoon cinnamon
½ cup butter

Combine topping ingredients in a medium bowl. Remove pies from oven and sprinkle topping over filling. Increase oven temperature to 400 degrees. Return pies to oven for an additional 10 minutes. Cool to serve. Yields 2 pies.

PORK JAEGER SCHNITZEL

4 thick pork loin cutlets
½ cup flour
1 egg
1½ cups heavy cream
1½ cups seasoned breadcrumbs
1¾ cups brown sauce
2 Polish dill pickles, chopped
2 teaspoons Dijon mustard

Butterfly the cutlets. Pound with a mallet. Dip cutlets in flour, then in mixture of egg and cream, then in breadcrumbs. In a heated sauté pan, cook cutlets over medium heat approximately 5 minutes on each side until thoroughly done. Add remaining ingredients and simmer for 1 minute. Place cutlets on plates, pour sauce on top, and serve. Serves 4.

PA 532 AND PA 32 (RIVER ROAD)
WASHINGTON CROSSING, PA 18977
215-493-3634

Christmas night in 1776 saw George Washington and his troops assembled at McConkey's Ferry Inn, waiting to cross the Delaware River. It has been said that General Washington supped here before going into battle, and that Hessian soldiers captured during the fray were imprisoned here after the Continental Army's victory.

During the next year, the Taylor family settled in the area and purchased almost all of the land surrounding the inn. Consequently, the area became known as Taylorsville. Bernard Taylor built his home on land adjacent to where Washington and his troops spent much of their fateful night.

The commonwealth of Pennsylvania subsequently purchased much of Taylorsville, preserving many of the original buildings and protecting the surrounding area from development. To commemorate Washington's victory and its significance in changing the course of the American Revolution, the name of the hamlet was changed to Washington Crossing.

Today, Taylor's home has been incorporated into Washington Crossing Inn as the "Hearth Room." The charred fireplace, in use for so many years, is the focal point of this dining room. A front porch added in 1817 can be enjoyed today as the inn's Covered Bridge Room. Plaster murals on the walls depict scenes from earlier days, including an aqueduct, the village of Taylorsville, Neely's Mill, and Canal New Hope.

Like the building, the menu is appealingly traditional. It offers soups such as Maryland Cream of Crab and Homemade Snapper. The entrées range from New York Strip to Veal Chops to Rack of Lamb, and the pasta choices include Linguine and Clams and Rigatoni Di Pomodoro. Seafood and poultry also appear on the lengthy list of choices. The Chicken Carcioffi, sautéed with artichoke hearts, shallots, and garlic, all in a light Tomato Wine Sauce, was delicious. Fresh, perfectly tender Green Beans and a Baked Potato accompanied it. When the dessert tray came around, the choices were all appealing—Chocolate Mousse Cake, White Chocolate Cake with Raspberry Mousse filling, Lemon Zinger Cake, and Hazelnut Bonbon Cake.

Touring the grounds after dinner, one gets a sense of walking where Washington walked. The lawn is truly lovely at today's inn. Flowers, window boxes, and hanging baskets are everywhere, and soft coach lights illuminate the pathways. A visit to Washington Crossing Inn is truly a step back in time.

GRILLED WHOLE STRIPED BASS

¼ cup plus 1 tablespoon virgin olive oil, divided
¼ cup parsley, chopped fine
3 cloves garlic, chopped
salt and pepper to taste
4-pound whole striped bass
juice of ½ fresh lemon

Prepare a hot charcoal fire or preheat a gas grill for 15 minutes. Combine ¼ cup of the olive oil, parsley, garlic, and salt and pepper. Dip both sides of fish in oil mixture. Place fish on hot grill and cook, turning once, until most of the skin is blackened on both sides and fish is no longer mushy to touch. This will take about 10 minutes per inch of thickness. You can also check doneness by pulling on 1 of the backbone fins; if it nearly comes off with little effort, the fish is done. Place cooked fish on a large platter. Drizzle remaining olive oil and lemon juice over fish. Debone fish when ready to serve. Serves 4.

PORKCHOPS OREGANATO

1 cup olive oil
6 cloves garlic, chopped
1 medium onion, chopped
¼ cup oregano, chopped fine
¼ cup fresh rosemary
salt and pepper to taste
8 12-ounce center-cut porkchops
8 slices lemon for garnish
8 sprigs rosemary for garnish

To make marinade, combine first 6 ingredients in a shallow dish. Dip both sides of chops in marinade; marinate in refrigerator for 4 to 5 hours, turning several times.

Remove chops from refrigerator 15 minutes before grilling. Prepare a medium-hot fire on grill. Place porkchops on charcoal fire until they reach desired doneness, turning once. Place chops on a serving plate and garnish with lemon slices and rosemary sprigs. Serves 8.

❦ STUFFED ARTICHOKES NAPOLITANO ❦

12 large artichokes
½ can black olives, pitted
4 cloves garlic, minced
juice of ½ fresh lemon
1 bunch fresh parsley
10 capers, minced
½ cup white wine
3 cups Italian breadcrumbs
¼ cup Parmesan cheese
½ cup olive oil
salt and pepper to taste
1 tablespoon paprika

Remove outside lower leaves and cut stems from artichokes; set aside stems. Slice off pointed tops of leaves and cut across top of artichokes to open top level; bang open side of artichokes on the table to open up the leaves. Using a fork, clean out the middle of the featherlike choke in center of leaves. Rinse out artichokes and open leaves for stuffing. Add an olive to each artichoke center.

Clean and rinse stems. Boil stems in salted water for 10 minutes. Remove from water and mince. Sauté garlic, minced stems, remaining olives, lemon juice, parsley, and capers. Add wine and reduce by ½. Remove from heat. Add breadcrumbs and Parmesan. Allow to cool, then stuff artichokes with mixture.

Place stuffed artichokes in a roasting pan with ½ inch of water in bottom. Drizzle olive oil over each artichoke and top with salt and pepper and a sprinkle of paprika. Cover pan and bake in a preheated 375-degree oven for 1½ hours. At each ½ hour, check level of water in pan, adding more as required. Check leaves for tenderness; additional baking may be needed to reach desired tenderness. Remove lid and brown artichokes. Serve hot. Serves 12.

Ever May
On The Delaware

RIVER ROAD
P.O. BOX 60
ERWINNA, PA 18920
610-294-9100

Nestled among the trees in the Bucks County hamlet of Erwinna is a jewel of an inn. The area is named for Arthur Erwin, a colonel in Washington's Continental Army. The inn's name is intriguing. We surmised that EverMay reflects the passion of innkeepers Bill and Danielle Moffly for flowers, particularly roses. The parlor is frequently full of them—in vases, adorning knickknacks, and as the subject matter of many of the room's gorgeous books.

The mansion was built in the 1700s and enlarged and remodeled in 1871. While the parlor reflects the interests of the current owners, the guest rooms show the character of previous Bucks County property owners. For example, the Pearl Buck Room is a large, airy bedroom with three pairs of windows overlooking the Delaware River. A portrait of Ms. Buck, a copy of her book *The Good Earth*, and Chinese artwork all pay homage to the author. Other rooms highlight notables such as Oscar Hammerstein, Dorothy Parker, and James Michener.

Dinner in this lovely setting is served promptly at seven-thirty on Friday and Saturday evenings. The menu is a six-course prix fixe that changes constantly. The apéritifs and hors d'oeuvres that begin the feast are served in the lovely gardens when the weather allows. The soup of the evening may be Cream of Tomato with fried basil or perhaps a Duck Consommé with chanterelles. The appetizer that follows could be a Shrimp Cake on Sweet Corn Risotto or Sautéed Shrimp and Herbed Gnocchi. Even the salads are unusual, with offerings such as Field Greens and Blueberries, served with Lemon Thyme Vinaigrette. Dinner guests can choose one of two entrées. The tempting options might include Grilled Glazed Quail on Saffron Couscous or Veal Tenderloin wrapped in mustard greens and prosciutto. A selection of cheeses, red grapes, and pears always follows the entrée. Last but not least come desserts such as Blueberry and Banana Tarts or Apricot and Blueberry Tarts with Brandied Blackberry Sauce.

On the night we dined, the weather was lovely for late September. Usually very talkative, we sat quietly and took in the immaculate patio gardens. Guests were gradually invited in to dinner, which started with a Stuffed Grape Leaf. Just a bite or two in size, it was very tasty. The Cream of Asparagus Soup that followed was very nice, as was the appetizer of Marinated Scallops served on Horseradish Potato Timbale. The Fresh Citrus Vinaigrette, served on a bed of field greens, was very lemony and good. For our entrées, Karen had the Seared Salmon on Sweet Corn with Wild Rice Relish, while Debbie tried the Grilled Petite Filet. Both were enjoyable. A selection of four cheeses from around the world followed. As expected, the dessert was a tart, on this occasion a Candied Pear Tartlet with Blueberry Purée and Almond Cream. Not too sweet, it was the ideal ending for our elegant evening.

and run a knife around inside edge of springform pan to loosen. Cool to room temperature, then refrigerate for several hours before serving. Serves 8.

PEAR ALMOND CHEESECAKE

2 cups toasted almonds
1¼ cups plus 1 tablespoon granulated sugar, divided
3 tablespoons unsalted butter, melted
4 8-ounce packages cream cheese
1 cup pear purée
2 large eggs
pinch of salt
1 teaspoon freshly squeezed lemon juice
⅛ teaspoon cloves, ground
¼ teaspoon nutmeg, grated

Preheat oven to 325 degrees. Wrap the bottom of a 9-inch springform pan tightly in aluminum foil. In a food processor, grind almonds with 1 tablespoon of the sugar. In a mixing bowl, stir together almond mixture and butter. Press this mixture into the bottom of the springform pan. Bake 10 to 15 minutes until dry. Cool crust to room temperature.

Combine cream cheese, pear purée, and remaining sugar; beat until smooth. Add eggs, salt, lemon juice, cloves, and nutmeg; mix until well combined. Spread filling over crust in springform pan. Place cheesecake in a large baking pan on rack in middle of oven. Fill baking pan with water until it comes halfway up sides. Bake 45 to 55 minutes until all but center of cheesecake is set. Remove cheesecake from larger baking pan

GOLDEN POTATO BISQUE

1 leek, white part only
6 cloves garlic, minced
½ teaspoon celery seed
1 teaspoon oil
2 tablespoons celery leaves, chopped
3 medium Yukon Gold potatoes, peeled and diced
2 cups chicken stock or low-sodium chicken broth
2 dashes Tabasco
salt and white pepper to taste
½ cup heavy whipping cream

Place leeks, garlic, celery seed, and oil in a medium-sized pot and sauté over medium heat until transparent. Add celery leaves, potatoes, and stock. Simmer 10 to 15 minutes until potatoes are soft. Remove and pass through a food mill. Return to stove and add Tabasco, salt and white pepper, and cream. Simmer on low heat until desired thickness is obtained. Serves 2.

CHAPTER 6

Pioneering Women

Odette's

Throughout history, certain individuals have surmounted overwhelming odds to achieve something important to them. This chapter focuses on such women, from the early years of this land to modern-day pioneers. We salute their success!

Widow Finney's

Historic Corner

FOURTH AND CHERRY STREETS
READING, PA 19602
610-378-1774

Joseph and Sarah Finney are considered by local historians to be Reading's first settlers, having begun to farm their homestead in the early 1700s. When Joseph died in 1734, Sarah was in danger of losing their property. Rather than give in to the pressure applied by businessmen who knew the true value of her land, Mrs. Finney fought to keep her home. Thanks to her courage and good business sense, "Widow Finney's" place soon became a haven for weary travelers.

What became of the original structure used by Widow Finney is unknown. In all likelihood, it eventually deteriorated and was torn down in the name of progress. Today's restaurant stands on the Finneys' original parcel of land approximately one block from where they once lived.

The log cabin that houses the main dining room, built in the late 1750s, is unusual in that the walls are made of pine logs rather than hardwood. The unusually large expanse between the logs is filled with stones shaped to fit, then chinked with river clay and straw. Most of that chinking has been whitewashed, but one section has been maintained so guests can see how the original materials were used. The fireplace is located in the center of the room, allowing guests to enjoy it from two different sides. Seated at a table nearby, we enjoyed the room's ambiance. The simple tab curtains at the windows, casually drawn back, gave us a glimpse of the modern world outside while we were whisked back to the eighteenth century by the interior decor. Hand-dipped candles hung from a pegboard, and pewter mugs were displayed on what we surmised were the steps to the original loft. Candles in hurricane globes cast a soft glow, much as they did when Sarah Finney was the hostess.

The second dining room at Widow Finney's is located in an entirely different structure that is very unobtrusively connected to the log cabin. The John Heister House, named after the most prominent of its early owners, was built next to the log cabin around 1810. The floral tablecloths and the more elaborate decor in this room are in keeping with its period of construction.

The menu offers traditional choices alongside modern entrées. We tried the Beef Burgundy Stew and the Black Bean Soup, both of which were good selections for a nippy fall evening. The Lime Cilantro Vinaigrette was a tangy and unusual salad dressing. To our surprise, we were treated with the Widow's Walnuts. Deliciously coated in a meringue of sorts and served warm, they were irresistible. The Lemon Sorbet that arrived next was a pleasing follow-up to the nuts. Our entrées—Pine Nut–Crusted Salmon and Shrimp on Tomato Basil Pasta with Red Wine Marinara— were accompanied by Cauliflower. Both entrées were very filling and tasty.

As we were leaving, the guests at the next table asked our hostess, Louise Mast, if Mrs. Finney was there that evening. It is said that her spirit visits from time to time. It seems that this really is, after all these years, still "Widow Finney's" place.

SWEET AND TANGY NUTS

1 pound pecans
3 egg whites
dash of salt
1 cup sugar
1 cup butter
splash of soy sauce

Preheat oven to 325 degrees. Toast pecans in oven until lightly browned. Beat egg whites in a medium bowl until foamy. Add salt, then gradually add sugar, continuing to beat until stiff peaks form. Fold in nuts. Melt butter in bottom of a sheet pan, add soy sauce, and spread nut mixture over top. Bake for about 20 minutes, stirring nuts every 10 minutes. Cool nuts and break into pieces before serving. Yields 2½ to 3 cups.

APPLE-STUFFED GAME HEN

½ cup onions, diced
½ cup celery, diced
2 medium apples, diced
1 cup butter, divided
16 cups day-old bread cubes
½ pound chestnuts, chopped
2 eggs, beaten
1 tablespoon salt
1 tablespoon pepper
2 Cornish game hens, slit in half lengthwise
2 cups white wine
½ cup water

Preheat oven to 400 degrees. Sauté onions, celery, and apples in ½ cup of the butter until soft. Combine bread cubes and chestnuts. Stir in sautéed ingredients, followed by eggs, salt, and pepper. Set aside. Wash game hen halves and pat them dry. Lift skin and stuff generously with bread mixture. Place stuffed hens in a 9-by-13-inch pan. Pour wine and water over top. Melt remaining butter and drizzle over hens. Bake for about 18 minutes until skin is golden brown and internal temperature is 160 degrees. Serves 4.

146 SOUTH WHITFORD ROAD
EXTON, PA 19341
610-524-1830

When Raymond H. Carr and David J. Knauer developed the old Whitford Farm into a restaurant and country inn, they chose to name it after their mothers, Edith Duling Carr and Lena Kurtz Knauer. Edith Carr is a descendant of a family who, prior to the Civil War, owned twelve river farms in northeast Maryland. Born in Delaware, she moved to Pennsylvania with her husband and lived most of her eighty-five years in Chester County. Lena Knauer was one of eight children born to a miller in Morgantown, Pennsylvania. During her young adulthood, she rode through North Dakota selling cosmetics to the Indians. Not only did she have entrepreneurial tendencies, she had musical talent as well, even playing the piano for silent movies. In her later years, she entertained fellow residents at St. Peter's Village and made several national television appearances playing her musical saw.

The farm goes back long before those fine ladies. Richard Thomas, who traveled to America with William Penn, received a grant of two thousand acres in 1683. Because of Thomas's untimely death, the grant was later claimed by his son. That son and his wife became the first settlers of what is now West Whiteland township.

Through the years, this fertile land was parceled and sold to gentleman farmers. The discovery of limestone and marble in the 1830s changed all that, as mining became an important industry in the area. In addition to limestone quarries and the stone structure now known as the Duling-Kurtz House, this tract also contained a mill, a mill pond and race, a log tenement, and two lime kilns.

In 1885, the property came back into the hands of the original family of owners. J. Preston Thomas, a prominent local resident and a descendant of Richard and Grace Thomas, returned the land to farming. In 1905, the house was bequeathed to J. Preston Thomas's daughter, Martha Gibbons Thomas, who has been described as "one of the best known women in Chester County" for her roles as cattle breeder, politician, and suffragette. In 1922, she was one of the first eight women elected to the Pennsylvania House of Representatives.

All this history provides a backdrop for your dining experience at the Duling-Kurtz House. The home's original beehive oven can be seen in the lounge today. This type of oven was very energy efficient, holding its heat for five to seven hours. Pioneer women conducted themselves accordingly, baking yeast breads requiring the highest temperature first, followed by cakes and quick breads, pies, and finally cookies as the oven temperature gradually fell. The bar area is made from native Chester County walnut. A large pot hangs in the fireplace there; the copper pots and pans hanging from above give the room a colonial feel.

We were seated on the glass-enclosed porch, which offered a lovely view of the gardens. The menu selections were as delightful as the scenery. To start our meal, we opted for the Blueberry-Pineapple Soup and the Mussels, served with yellow and grape tomatoes in Garlic Cream Sauce. Equally enjoyable was our main course, the Smoked Salmon Sandwich, served with Caper Mayonnaise, and the Smoked Chicken Salad Sandwich, served on a croissant. Neither of us typically orders sandwiches, but these were scrumptious, and so unusual. The Parisian Truffle that capped off the meal consisted of a scoop of vanilla ice cream surrounding a center of lemon sorbet, all in a white chocolate coating. It was a fitting end to a lovely meal in a picturesque setting.

LOBSTER AND CRAB CREPES

1 pound jumbo lump crabmeat
8 ounces Maine lobster meat
1¼ cups heavy cream, divided
¼ cup mayonnaise
½ teaspoon Old Bay seasoning
12 crepe shells
vegetable oil

2 cups lobster stock
4 ounces Brie

Combine crabmeat, lobster meat, ¼ cup of the heavy cream, mayonnaise, and Old Bay in a mixing bowl and mix well. Fill crepe shells with mixture and place them on a pastry tray sprayed with vegetable oil. Cover with foil and place in a 350-degree oven for 15 minutes. In a medium saucepan, reduce lobster stock by ½. Add remaining heavy cream and bring to a simmer. Add Brie and ladle over crepes to serve. Serves 6.

HERB-ENCRUSTED RACK OF LAMB

1 rack of lamb, split in the middle, fat removed
salt and pepper to taste
½ cup fresh rosemary leaves, chopped
1 tablespoon oregano
1 tablespoon sage
1 tablespoon basil
1 teaspoon thyme
1 cup mustard

Brush rack with salt and pepper. Chop all the herbs very fine and mix together. Brush mustard on rack, then coat rack with herb mixture. Place rack on a roasting pan in a 425-degree oven for approximately 15 to 20 minutes for rare, 30 minutes for medium. Remove from oven when done and let rest for 3 minutes. Cut between the bones. Serve with your favorite sauce. Serves 4 to 6.

201 SOUTH WINEBIDDLE STREET
PITTSBURGH, PA 15224
412-363-8030

One of Pittsburgh's earliest grand mansions, Victoria Hall was built in 1865 as a private home for the Lynch family during an era when carriages brought couples dressed in silk and velvet to the most important events of the season. Restored to its original beauty, Victoria Hall has been honored as a National Historic Landmark.

As visitors enter the main hall, lit by gilded chandeliers, the grand mahogany staircase immediately captures their eyes. Moving from room to room, guests will notice marble fireplaces, antiques, ornate radiator screens, vintage light fixtures, and beautiful leaded-glass doors. The sun porch with palms and vintage wicker, the turn-of-the-century chapel, the etched-glass entry, and the ballroom-turned-dining-hall all testify to the graciousness of this fine home.

Guests with an eye for authenticity will note that the height of the doorknobs is out of character for a house built during the 1860s, being placed much lower than normal. As Mrs. Lynch was ill during the construction, it has been surmised that this change was to accommodate her wheelchair. Likewise, the low sink in the mud room may indicate Mrs. Lynch's continued interest in gardening, despite her limitations. Unfortunately, she passed away before living in the house, and Mr. Lynch found himself bankrupt shortly afterward.

In 1878, the home became St. Ursuline Academy and Convent. During the early 1900s, St. Ursuline's made changes and additions to the structure, adding a touch of the Federal period to the otherwise Victorian mansion. The modifications included enclosing the solarium and adding a gymnasium and chapel. The mansion was used as a school and convent for over a century, until its last graduating class passed through the doors in 1981.

Joedda and Ben Sampson purchased the property and began restoration in 1994. Mrs. Sampson, a restoration expert responsible for many restorations throughout Pittsburgh, had originally contacted the sisters of St. Ursuline not to purchase the structure but merely to purchase odds and ends that might be handy to her business. However, after other options deteriorated, St. Ursuline contacted the Sampsons, and the idea of Victoria Hall began to blossom.

Victoria Hall's mainstays are business events and private functions such as weddings. However, it is open to the public on Sundays for brunch, when both an à la carte menu and a buffet are available. The quality and presentation of the plentiful feast are equal to its surroundings. The salad table offers eight to ten selections, as does the pastry cart. There are several meat choices, along with potato dishes and vegetable accompaniments. Be sure to save room for dessert, too. We found the Trifle fabulous! As we dined, a strolling violinist played a selection of music and also took requests, which heightened our enjoyment of the meal.

CHILLED CREAMY MANGO SOUP

6 ripe mangoes
1 pint heavy cream
1 tablespoon vanilla extract
juice of 1 orange
juice of 1 lime
1 cup confectioners' sugar

Skin mangoes and remove pulp. Purée mangoes in a food processor; strain through a fine sieve to remove any remaining pulp. In a large mixing bowl, combine mango purée, cream, vanilla, orange juice, and lime juice. Mix until creamy and slightly thickened. Add sugar while whisking slowly. Chill for 1 hour. Serve with whipped cream if desired. Serves 6.

IRISH BREAD PUDDING WITH CRÈME ANGLAISE

Irish Bread Pudding

1½ cups milk
1½ cups heavy cream
pinch of salt
1 teaspoon vanilla extract
5 large eggs
½ cup sugar
4 to 6 2-ounce croissants
½ cup golden raisins soaked in 2 tablespoons water, then drained
1 tablespoon butter, melted
¼ cup peach jam
1 tablespoon water
confectioners' sugar
fresh berries
Crème Anglaise (see next page)

Preheat oven to 300 degrees. Combine milk, cream, and salt in a medium saucepan and heat to simmering. Stir in vanilla. In a large bowl, combine eggs and sugar until well blended. Add the milk mixture to the eggs and sugar, stirring continually; mixture should be smooth and creamy. Cut croissants into ¼-inch slices. Slightly

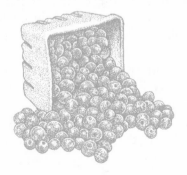

Crème Anglaise

2 cups light cream
2 tablespoons vanilla extract
½ cup sugar, divided
10 egg yolks

overlap slices in a lightly buttered ovenproof dish. Sprinkle raisins on top. Brush melted butter over croissants. Pour the milk, cream, and egg mixture on top. Place the dish in a roasting pan of simmering water and cook in oven for 25 to 30 minutes or until custard is set. Remove from water bath. Melt peach jam with 1 tablespoon water in a small saucepan; strain and brush on top of custard. Dust with confectioners' sugar and serve warm with fresh berries and Crème Anglaise. Serves 6.

Combine cream, vanilla, and half the sugar in a saucepan and heat to boiling. Blend the remainder of the sugar with egg yolks until smooth. Temper this mixture with the heated cream and sugar mixture; blend mixtures together. Cook sauce over low heat, stirring constantly until it lightly coats a wooden spoon. Strain sauce into a clean bowl and cool in an ice-water bath. Keep refrigerated. Yields 2½ cups.

Note: This sauce may be made 1 or 2 days in advance.

MCGILLIN'S OLDE ALE HOUSE

1310 DRURY STREET
PHILADELPHIA, PA 19102
215-735-5562

Chestnut Street's large townhouses were home to many of Philadelphia's wealthy families before the turn of the twentieth century. One block over is Drury Street, where the coachmen and other employees of Philadelphia's society families lived.

The Bell in Hand Tavern was opened in 1860 by William and Catherine McGillin. It was a small Irish pub with an oyster house to one side and the family's living quarters to the other. It was one of the first public places in this little alleyway, but no one called it by its name, saying they were "going over to Pa McGillin's" instead. The name stuck, and the tavern officially became McGillin's Ale House. At that time, its appearance changed from that of an Irish bar to a more traditional English pub. Pa McGillin established another first when, tired of replacing the plank floor, he installed terrazzo instead. It's still there today, looking like brand-new!

After Pa McGillin's death in 1907, Mrs. McGillin and the family continued to run the business. She had a no-nonsense approach, throwing out anyone she considered too rowdy.

If this happened more than once, the individual's name went on a "flag list" that was a kind of anti-social register. In time, it became fashionable to be on that list, which included the names of community leaders, famous entertainers, and other celebrities.

McGillin's was a popular spot for the actors and vaudeville entertainers from the busy Garrick Theater, which was just around the corner. The who's who list of the tavern's patrons included W. C. Fields, John and Ethel Barrymore, and the Marx Brothers. Through the years, celebrities continued to come—Will Rogers, Tennessee Williams, Vincent Price, Ethel Merman, artist Thomas Eakins, "Lord of the Dance" Michael Flatley, Ed Bradley, "Frugal Gourmet" Jeff Smith, and Robin Williams.

The bar had two fireplaces, where the McGillins roasted potatoes, traditionally handed out free to patrons to keep their hands warm. Brothers Joe and Henry Szczepaniak purchased the pub in 1958. At that time, the last surviving McGillin child was still baking potatoes in the fireplace. As a matter of fact, that fireplace is still operational today.

When the brothers retired, Henry's daughter, Mary Ellen, and her husband, Chris, decided to keep up the tradition at what is claimed to be Philadelphia's oldest tavern in continuous operation. The Bell in Hand sign still hangs above the bar, together with all the old tavern licenses. Memorabilia is scattered pleasingly throughout.

The menu encompasses tavern fare and more, offering everything from Nachos to Stir-Fry. There are three whole pages of sandwiches, including two pages of hot choices, such as Philly

Cheesesteak and Tuna Melt. The luncheon and dinner platter selections offer traditional fare like home-style Meat Loaf, Turkey and Dressing, and Seafood Stew, as well as entrées like Chicken Marsala and Shrimp Parmesan. The Coconut Shrimp are excellent, and the sampler, called Ivy's Three Threes—consisting of three Coconut Shrimp, three Deep-Fried Shrimp, and three Grilled Shrimp—is terrific.

BAKED SALMON WITH LEMON CAPER SAUCE

2 6-ounce salmon fillets, skinned
¼ cup dry white wine
salt and pepper to taste
2½ teaspoons lemon juice
2 tablespoons capers, drained
2 tablespoons parsley, chopped
1½ tablespoons butter, softened
lemon slices for garnish

Preheat oven to 450 degrees. Place fillets in a shallow baking pan, top with wine, and season with salt and pepper. Bake for 10 to 12 minutes. Remove from oven. Pour off liquid into a sauté pan. Add lemon juice, capers, and parsley to sauté pan and whisk in butter. Place salmon on plates. Pour sauce over top and garnish with lemon slices. Serves 2.

BEEF SHORT RIBS
WITH FRESH HORSERADISH SAUCE

2 pounds beef short ribs
salt and freshly ground pepper to taste
2 tablespoons olive oil
4 medium onions, sliced thin
2 cloves garlic, minced
1 cup canned Italian plum tomatoes
3 sprigs thyme
2 bay leaves
pinch of marjoram
pinch of savory
2 cups beef stock
3 tablespoons capers, rinsed and drained
4 anchovies, rinsed and chopped
Fresh Horseradish Sauce (see next column)

Preheat oven to 325 degrees. Pat ribs dry and sprinkle with salt and pepper. Heat oil in a large cast-iron skillet over medium-high heat. Cook ribs 4 to 5 minutes per side until brown. Transfer ribs to a platter and add onions to skillet. Reduce heat to low and cook about 10 minutes until soft. Add garlic and stir for 1 minute. Add tomatoes, thyme, bay leaves, marjoram, and savory. Simmer for 15 minutes, stirring occasionally and breaking up tomatoes with spoon. Add beef stock and bring to a boil. Replace ribs and cover. Place in oven and cook about 2 hours until meat is very tender, almost falling from the bone. Remove ribs from skillet. Degrease braising liquid and boil until slightly thickened, stirring occasionally for about 20 minutes. Discard thyme sprigs and bay leaves. Add capers and anchovies to sauce; taste and adjust seasoning. Spoon sauce over ribs and serve with Fresh Horseradish Sauce on the side. Serves 4.

Fresh Horseradish Sauce

½ cup fresh horseradish, peeled and diced
2 tablespoons fresh lime juice
1 tablespoon water
½ cup sour cream
salt and pepper to taste

Combine all ingredients in a small bowl. Refrigerate until ready to serve. Yields approximately 1 cup.

Odette's

SOUTH RIVER ROAD
NEW HOPE, PA 18938
215-862-2432

Built in 1794 and originally known as the River House, this tavern began its life serving boatmen at the head of the dangerous Wells Falls on the Delaware River. The River House was a well-known landmark to local travelers for forty years.

In 1830, the Delaware Canal opened. The New Hope locks, located just above the River House, brought many more customers. Thirty-four years later, an outlet lock was constructed at this location. It allowed barges to cross the Delaware River and connect with the Delaware and Raritan Canal system to the south of Lambertville. The construction left the River House on a man-made island between the two canals. It subsequently became a popular stopping place for the numerous coal barges making their way to New York City. However, as the coal industry began to slow, so did traffic on the Delaware, and the River House fell into disuse.

In the early 1930s, New Hope was revitalized as a tourist area, and the River House opened its doors again as the town's first hotel. In 1961, Odette Myrtil Logan, a Parisian and a former star of stage and screen, purchased the property. Ms. Logan renamed the hotel Chez Odette and

developed a first-class French restaurant. The rich and famous flocked to Odette's to enjoy the charming country atmosphere, the excellent food, and the unequaled entertainment.

The Barbone family, which currently owns Odette's, has preserved the original spirit and ambiance of the establishment and continues to showcase local and big-time talent. Odette's remains a favorite among residents and tourists alike.

It was a lovely, sunny day when we visited Odette's for lunch. We were as charmed by the wooden floors, stone walls, and dark wooden beams as we were by the fabulous view of the Delaware River. We listened to the music of Frank Sinatra playing quietly in the background as we competed over how many stars we recognized in the hundreds of signed photographs lining the walls.

Both the luncheon and dinner menus at Odette's are relatively short, but every item we read sounded more delectable than the last. We thought that the Pine Nut–Crusted Swordfish with Rosemary-Roasted Yukon Gold Potatoes and Sun-Dried Tomato Vinaigrette sounded particularly pleasing, as did the Pancetta-Wrapped Filet Mignon with Parmesan Crackling and Barolo Wine Demi-Glace. Closing the dinner menu, we perused the luncheon items. Debbie chose the Potato-Roasted Garlic Ravioli in Plum Tomato Broth with Wild Mushrooms and Spinach. Karen, who can never resist roasted red peppers, chose the Grilled Portabello Sandwich, served on Rosemary Foccacia with Roasted Red Peppers and Herbed Pesto. The choices were excellent both in flavor and presentation. We completed our experience with Odette's famous homemade sorbets, Debbie enjoying the Cassis and Karen savoring the Key Lime. The sorbets were a delicious end to a delightful luncheon. Long may the two-hundred-year tradition of good food in charming surroundings reign here at Odette's!

WILD MUSHROOM BISQUE

2 tablespoons extra-virgin olive oil
½ carrot, minced
1 stalk celery, minced
½ small white onion, minced
2½ teaspoons fresh garlic, chopped
2½ teaspoons shallots, chopped
2 tablespoons sherry
8 ounces fresh button mushrooms, chopped fine
2 ounces shiitake mushrooms, stemmed and sliced
4 ounces fresh portabello mushrooms, stemmed and chopped
½ stick unsalted butter
¼ cup all-purpose flour
4 cups chicken broth
¼ teaspoon thyme leaf, minced
6 cups heavy cream
¼ cup assorted fresh herbs, minced
salt and pepper to taste

Heat olive oil in a medium-sized pot. Add carrots, celery, and onions. Cook, stirring constantly, until onion is translucent. Add garlic and shallots and cook an additional 2 minutes. Deglaze pot with sherry. Add all mushrooms and cook for 30 minutes, stirring occasionally.

Melt butter in a small saucepan and whip in flour to form a roux. Turn heat to low and cook for 5 minutes. Remove from heat and set aside.

When mushrooms are cooked, add chicken broth and thyme. Bring to a boil. Add roux and whip until it dissolves into soup. When soup begins to thicken, add cream and fresh herbs, stirring constantly. Add salt and pepper. Turn heat to low and simmer for 20 minutes, stirring frequently. Remove from heat and serve. Serves 6.

SEARED MUSCOVY DUCK BREAST SALAD

½ cup gooseberry preserves
3 cup fresh gooseberries, divided
¼ cup white wine vinegar
1 cup blended oil
salt and pepper to taste
4 boneless duck breasts
5 heads frisee, cleaned and chopped
1 cup pecans, split
2 cups Stilton cheese, crumbled

In a blender, combine gooseberry preserves, 1 cup of the gooseberries, and vinegar to make a vinaigrette. Purée. When purée is smooth, continue to run blender while adding oil in a gentle stream. Add salt and pepper. Store in a sealed container in the refrigerator.

In a very hot, dry sauté pan, sear duck breasts skin side down. Season flesh side with salt and pepper, then turn over. Lower heat to medium and turn breasts several times to cook evenly; cook until medium-rare.

In a large bowl, toss frisee in 1 cup of vinaigrette. Divide evenly among 4 plates. Slice duck and arrange around greens. Top salad with pecans, remaining 2 cups of gooseberries, and cheese. Serves 4.

DIMMICK INN

101 EAST HARFORD
MILFORD, PA 18337
570-296-4021

The Dimmick Inn stands in stately fashion on a corner in downtown Milford. Samuel Dimmick, whose life spanned the years from 1793 to 1867, built the structure in 1828. When the inn was leveled by fire in 1854, Samuel's daughter, Frances, vowed to see it rise again from the ashes. "Miss Fan," as Frances was known by the residents of Milford, approved plans for a brick structure to be built on the original site. Completed in the Revival Connecticut Colonial style a year after the fire, the inn consisted of twenty-five guest rooms, a saloon, and a dining room. It also served as the town's post office and stagecoach stop. Since the innkeepers controlled the stage line along the Milford & Oswego Turnpike, which was the main highway west, the fact that the stage stopped at the Dimmick Inn was no surprise.

Frances Dimmick was perhaps the most colorful character associated with the inn. A local newspaper article written in 1898 described her as "not given to frills or frumperies, but she can cast a fly, drive a pair of four, ride a bronco sidesaddle or astride, and draw the sweetest melody from her violin." She wore men's clothing at a time when it was decidedly unfashionable to do so. Never marrying, she managed the affairs of the Dimmick Inn single-handedly for over forty years. Though she put up with no nonsense from her guests, she could also be a charming hostess. Because of this, many distinguished Philadelphians and New Yorkers called the Dimmick Inn their yearly summer home.

Guests have come to the Dimmick Inn from many walks of life. The most notable guest of record was journalist and politician Horace Greeley, who stayed here during the mid-1800s. Over the years, the Dimmick Inn has been used as a hotel, a boardinghouse, a Chinese restaurant, a Jewish delicatessen, a bawdyhouse, and a cabaret. Today, it houses a traditional American family restaurant. The Dimmick Inn is Milford's only hostelry still in existence from the days when stagecoach stops were a plentiful commodity.

The current owners have focused on returning the inn to its earlier appearance, stripping the exterior paint off the blood-red bricks. Inside, guests immediately notice the ceiling, which is made of zinc tiles. In the bar, wooden booths line the eating area. A more formal dining room is just around the corner, off the main entrance. The front porch is also a popular spot to grab a bite to eat during the summer months.

The menu is printed in the center of the place mats, which at first glance appear to be edged with local advertising. After ordering a cup of the Chunky Tomato Soup, which was very good, we gave the ads closer attention. They're all spoofs, and we both got a good laugh as we read. When our Meat Loaf with Mashed Potatoes and our BBQ Pork Sandwich arrived, we were feeling fairly merry as we discussed what sorts of silly ads we would write.

The menu at the Dimmick Inn is varied, like its past. Guests can order a New York Strip or a classic Rack of Lamb, which appears on the list of entrées just above the Down-Home Chicken Fried Steak. They're all in the section entitled "The Barnyard." Other sections are entitled "The Henhouse" (which lists all the chicken entrées) and, of course, "By the Sea" (which features seafood selections). All in all, the Dimmick Inn is a comfortable place with many familiar offerings—the kind of place where you expect to see someone you know.

CHOCOLATE SOUFFLÉ CAKES

2½ cups sugar
2½ cups chocolate chips
3 sticks butter
12 eggs
6 tablespoons cocoa
1 tablespoon baking powder
2½ cups flour
12 scoops vanilla ice cream

Melt sugar, chocolate chips, and butter in a saucepan. Combine eggs, cocoa, baking powder, and flour in a large mixing bowl. Add ingredients from saucepan and combine for 10 minutes with an electric mixer. Butter and flour 12 ramekins; fill each about ⅔ full and refrigerate until needed. Bake at 400 degrees for about 15 minutes until soufflés are well domed. The centers should be visibly moist (dark in color). Serve with ice cream. Serves 12.

SAVORY MEDITERRANEAN DIP

2 8-ounce packages cream cheese, room temperature
8 ounces feta cheese
6½-ounce can marinated artichokes, chopped
⅓ cup frozen spinach, chopped and drained
1 teaspoon garlic, chopped
1 teaspoon red pepper flakes
1 tablespoon olive oil
thin slices of toasted bread or crudités

Combine first 7 ingredients in a food processor. Pulse until evenly blended. Divide mixture evenly among 6 single-serving ramekins. Broil at 450 degrees for about 10 minutes until brown and bubbly. Serve with toasted bread or crudités. Serves 6.

Cliff Park Inn
& GOLF COURSE

155 CLIFF PARK ROAD
MILFORD, PA 18337
717-296-6491

Tradition is long and continuing at the Cliff Park Inn, where the fifth generation of Buchanan family innkeepers is hard at work giving care and attention to the inn and the surrounding golf course. The founder of the clan, Judge George Buchanan, was a shrewd businessman, trading legal services and other payments due him for bits of "worthless," treeless land. Local residents, more interested in timber than the actual land, scoffed at these transactions.

In 1913, this acreage, too rocky to cultivate, was transformed. The sheep were moved from their meadows, and an 1820s farmhouse on the property was refurbished. This was the work of Harry Winters Buchanan and his wife, Annie. It was Mrs. Buchanan, a woman of formidable reputation, who decided that the land should be used for playing a strange new game just becoming popular in the United States—golf. The nine-hole course here became the first golf links in the country to be run by a woman. From that day to this, guests have lounged on the inn's long front porch while watching golfers on the first tee, located just a few steps from the inn's front door. When we asked about the long row of hooks along the entire length of the porch, we were told that in days of fewer security concerns,

golfers would hang their bags there while partaking of light refreshments at the nineteenth hole!

The inn boasts two dining rooms, two sitting rooms, and numerous guest rooms. The comfortable sitting rooms have original fireplaces and beautiful wide-board floors milled on the property. They are filled with ancestral portraits of the Buchanan family, including a portrait of the stern Mrs. Buchanan. The Colonial Dining Room is a delightful combination of the original dining room and original kitchen, complete with working fireplace. The rooms here have antiques, lace-covered tables, organdy curtains, and many fine period pieces of incidental furniture.

We ate at the 19th Hole, a unique wood-paneled room complete with window treatments and carpeting both in the Buchanan plaid. The tables were covered in green linens, and all the chairs were painted red to coordinate with the carpeting. We sat in the corner window and perused both the lunch and dinner menus, which were extensive and appealing. For dinner, we could have chosen such delights as Miali Tuscanna, a boneless pork tenderloin filled with Sausage and Pesto Stuffing, wrapped in bacon, and roasted, or King Salmon, topped with Mushroom Duxelle and baked with Fried Leeks and Tomato Basil Coulis. We longed to savor the Ravioli Sampler—three ravioli served in Tomato Cream Sauce, one stuffed with spinach, one with eggplant, and one with sun-dried tomato.

However, we were there to partake of lunch, so we teed off with the chilled soup. Debbie chose the Plum Soup and Karen the Berry Soup. Both were cool and delicious on that hot, sunny day. We looked out at the scenic golf course while waiting for our salads. Debbie's Spinach and Chicken Salad, with egg, bacon, goat cheese, mushrooms, and Vinaigrette Dressing, was crunchy, delicious, and plentiful. Karen had mescaline greens and iceberg lettuce topped with a Crab Cake, Corn Relish, and a light, creamy Parmesan Dressing that was extremely tasty.

At the end of our meal, when we asked about the recipes we might include in this book, we discovered that Chad Gasiorek, the executive chef at the Cliff Park Inn, had one more treat in store. He decided to provide a five-course meal. Three of the recipes for that feast follow. He suggests that you start off with a Grilled Portabello Mushroom appetizer before the Berry Soup, which should be followed by a salad of fresh baby greens with Dijon Vinaigrette. Next time you have a dinner party for four, you can thank Chad and the Cliff Park Inn, because your menu is already planned!

BERRY SOUP

1 pint raspberries
1 pint blackberries
1 pint blueberries
2 pints strawberries, tops removed
1 cup sour cream
1 cup sugar
heavy cream (to adjust consistency)
Razzmatazz liqueur to taste (optional)

Rinse and combine all ingredients in a blender and blend together. You may need to add more cream or sugar, depending on the consistency and sweetness you desire. Serves 6 to 8.
© 1999 by Chad Gasiorek

POTATO-CRUSTED HALIBUT

4 halibut fillets, 6 ounces each
salt and pepper
1 Idaho potato (raw)
olive oil
lemon wedges for garnish

Take fillets and season with salt and pepper. Shred potato right before sautéing so that it doesn't discolor. Heat oil in pan until it starts to smoke lightly. Lay halibut skin side down and put shredded potato on top (not too thick). Season the top with salt and pepper. This will help it stick to the halibut. Lay the halibut in the pan potato side down. Sauté until potato is brown, then remove and finish in the oven at 400 degrees for 10 minutes. Serve with fresh lemon. Serves 4.

© 1999 by Chad Gasiorek

GRASSHOPPER PIE

1 cup heavy cream
1 jar marshmallow fluff
2 tablespoons crème de menthe
1 chocolate cookie pie shell (Oreo)
½ cup mini chocolate chips

Whip heavy cream to medium peak. Fold marshmallow fluff and crème de menthe into whipped cream until it is evenly incorporated. Pour mixture into pie shell, then sprinkle with chocolate chips. Put in freezer for 1 hour before serving. Keep stored in freezer. Serves 6 to 8.

© 1999 by Chad Gasiorek

Note: By request, these recipes are presented just as they were given to the authors.

CHAPTER 7

Highways and Byways

Cab Frye's Tavern

During the westward expansion of our young country, the going was very difficult until a system of roads was built along Indian trails and rutted thoroughfares. As these routes developed, economic prosperity tended to follow. The restaurants in this chapter are all inns, taverns, hostelries, and hotels that opened along the National Road, the Lincoln Highway, and other major routes as our countrymen traveled and traded.

Since 1790

The Altland House

US 30, CENTER SQUARE
ABBOTTSTOWN, PA 17301
717-259-9535

It's not often that anyone, particularly a restaurant proprietor, is proud of the fact that he serves lumpy mashed potatoes. However, at The Altland House, the Lumpy Mashed Potatoes are considered a house specialty. Made from red potatoes, they're a delicious accompaniment to many of the menu choices.

The menu here leans toward shrimp and crab, though there are selections to suit every appetite. Karen opted for the Margarita Shrimp, which consisted of jumbo shrimp sautéed in tequila and then served with Citrus Beurre Blanc amid field greens and grilled crostini. Debbie had difficulty deciding between the Parrot Bay Coconut Shrimp and the Chicken Napoleon but finally chose the chicken. It was a decision not to be regretted. Her chicken breast was layered with crispy won tons and lightly sautéed spinach, all of which was coated in Herbed Chicken Au Jus. It was as attractive and unusual as it was delicious, and the best part of all was the Lumpy Mashed Potatoes on the side!

After lunch, we remained in the Federal-style dining room to chat with owner Mike Haugh. He pointed out the murals of The Altland House and other town scenes on the walls and reminisced about his young life in Abbottstown. His mother, Betty, was once the town historian, so stories about the village come easily to him.

The town, founded in 1753 by John Abbett, was a full day's travel for the Conestoga wagons heading west out of Lancaster. Because of this, several public eating and drinking houses came into being along the route. The establishment that sits today at the junction of US 30 and PA 194 was purchased in 1880 by Reuben Altland and flourished as an inn and tavern.

Other such establishments died out after the advent of the automobile, but this big hotel continued to do business. Mike's mother, who grew up just a few doors down from the corner, began working as a waitress in the hotel's dining room during her early teens. She commented many times that she would one day own the hotel, but Mike isn't sure how seriously people took her statements. Chicken and Waffles were the specialties back then. Pictures on the walls of chicken pluckers knee-deep in feathers show just how popular those dinners were.

As World War II began, Betty went to work in a nearby factory. It was there that she met Mike's father, a welder. In 1954, Betty's prophecy was fulfilled when she and her husband purchased The Altland House. Shortly afterward, Mike's father concocted his first recipe, Turtle Soup, which is still on the menu. The family continues to run the business today, with Mike at the helm and his son on board.

As our chat came to a close, we gazed across the wide wraparound porch to the cluster of original structures around the town square. Like them, The Altland House has stood the test of time.

SALMON AND ROCKFISH NAPOLEON WITH LEMON GRASS AND CANDIED GINGER BEURRE BLANC

Fish

6-ounce rockfish fillet
8-ounce salmon fillet
salt and pepper to taste
¼ cup clarified butter
¼ cup Chardonnay
Lemon Grass and Candied Ginger Beurre Blanc (see
next column)

Preheat oven to 450 degrees. Slice rockfish into 3 pieces widthwise, then butterfly them open. Slice salmon lengthwise into 4 uniform pieces. Starting and ending with the salmon, stack the fish pieces in alternating layers. Lightly salt and pepper. Using butter and Chardonnay, lightly grease a baking pan. Place fish in pan and place in oven. Bake 10 to 15 minutes. Remove from oven and top with Lemon Grass and Candied Ginger Beurre Blanc. Suggested accompaniments are saffron risotto and steamed asparagus. Serves 2.

Lemon Grass and Candied Ginger Beurre Blanc

1 lemon grass bulb, smashed and chopped
2 tablespoons candied ginger, diced fine
1 teaspoon shallots, chopped
½ cup Chardonnay
½ cup rice wine vinegar
1 cup heavy cream
½ cup sweet cream unsalted butter
salt and pepper to taste
chives, diced fine

Place lemon grass, ginger, shallots, Chardonnay, and vinegar in a heavy-bottomed saucepan and heat on high; if you do not have a heavy-bottomed saucepan, lower heat to medium. Reduce until nearly dry. Add cream and reduce until thick. Remove pan from heat. Cut butter into 1-inch cubes and add cubes 1 at a time to saucepan, whisking until completely incorporated. Finish with salt and pepper and chives. Yields approximately 1 cup.

CRACKED BLACK PEPPER–CRUSTED TENDERLOIN WITH BLUE CHEESE MUSHROOM RAGOUT

Beef

2 8-ounce cuts choice beef tenderloin
¼ cup cracked black pepper
¼ cup grape seed and olive oil with fresh herbs
1 clove garlic, diced
salt and pepper to taste
Blue Cheese Mushroom Ragout (see next column)

Crust outside edge of tenderloins with cracked pepper. Combine oil, garlic, and salt and pepper. Drizzle oil mixture over tenderloins. Grill tenderloins until they reach desired pinkness in center. Top with Blue Cheese Mushroom Ragout. Serve with garlic mashed potatoes and steamed broccoli. Serves 2.

Blue Cheese Mushroom Ragout

¼ cup vegetable oil
1 large portabello mushroom, gills removed and
  sliced thin
4 large shiitake mushrooms, stemmed and sliced thin
10 medium button mushrooms, sliced thin
2 teaspoons garlic, minced
2 teaspoons shallots, chopped
½ cup brandy
½ cup veal or beef stock
½ cup heavy cream
½ cup blue cheese
salt and pepper to taste
4 sprigs fresh thyme, chopped

Heat oil in a medium saucepan, add mushrooms, and sauté for 2 to 3 minutes. Add garlic and shallots and sauté another 2 to 3 minutes. Deglaze pan with brandy and flame until alcohol is burned off. Add stock, cream, and blue cheese. Reduce until thick. Finish with salt and pepper and thyme.

113 EAST MAIN STREET
BOALSBURG, PA 16827
814-466-6241

Upon entering the town, you'll see a sign proclaiming Boalsburg to be the home of Memorial Day. It seems that in 1864, several women decorated soldiers' graves at local cemeteries. The custom then spread throughout the nation, becoming an annual event. This type of patriotism is still obvious on Boalsburg's main street, where we found that many houses were draped with red, white, and blue swags, even though we visited in early August.

Long before the Memorial Day tradition started, the town served as a gateway to the West. Boalsburg was settled by the Scots-Irish in 1806, and its convenience as a stagecoach stop ensured prosperity for its residents. As the town grew, many of its houses were built from native stone. When the tavern was erected in 1819 by Colonel James Johnson, he, too, chose stone construction. The twenty-two-inch stone walls of Duffy's Tavern are as solid today as when they were erected. Their thickness helps keep the indoor temperature of the busy restaurant at a comfortable sixty-eight or seventy degrees, even on hot summer days.

To the left of the entry hall is a large dining room with traditional appointments. The original cash drawer is there, tucked beneath the sill of what was originally an exterior window. On the first Sunday in December, the tavern's annual eight-course feast is prepared in this room. Its enormous fireplace is used for much of the cooking. Just behind this dining room is another, more rustic in character. Cecil Aldin pictures decorate the walls, and a yoke light fixture hangs above. Across the hall is a formal dining room decorated with linens and wallpaper displaying bowls of fruit in the early American style. Located at the back of the restaurant is the Brick Room, which has long plank tables and a narrow, curved staircase leading to loft dining above. At one time, the large, second-floor banquet room was a ballroom with a hinged panel. After the dancing was over, the panel was lowered to separate the space into sleeping quarters for the guests, one side for the ladies and one for the men.

The tavern serves a wide variety of foods, from sandwiches to upscale entrées. The lunch menu, several pages long, continues to be available in the evening. The full-service dinner menu contains such choices as Filet Mignon stuffed with snow crab and Veal sautéed with garlic, mushrooms, and asparagus and topped with Swiss cheese and White Wine Sauce. We tried the Raspberry Brie, followed by the Tavern Salmon, which was stuffed with crabmeat, served on a bed of sautéed spinach, and topped with Béarnaise Sauce. They were both deliciously unusual in flavor. The dessert choices were tempting. After considering the Chocolate Framboise Cake and the Caramel-Topped Apple Pie, we opted to share a Napoleon. This puff-pastry confection, filled with caramel cream and topped with vanilla and chocolate icing, was lighter than air and the perfect ending to a marvelous meal.

Boalsburg is located just off Interstate 80 not too far from State College and Penn State University's main campus. Step back in time after a Saturday of modern-day football and treat yourself to a meal at Duffy's Tavern.

VEAL PURNELL

4 tablespoons clarified butter
2 5-ounce veal cutlets, tenderized
pinch of salt
pinch of pepper
¼ cup flour
2 cloves garlic, minced
1 cup mushrooms
10 asparagus spears, blanched
4 slices Swiss cheese
¼ cup white wine
½ cup chicken or veal stock
2 teaspoons lemon juice
1 to 2 tablespoons butter

Heat clarified butter over a medium flame. Season veal with salt and pepper. Dredge in flour and shake off excess. Lightly sauté veal for 1 minute on 1 side, then add garlic and mushrooms. Flip veal and add asparagus. When mushrooms are just cooked, turn heat to low and stack mushrooms and asparagus on top of veal and lay cheese over the whole stack. Deglaze pan with wine and reduce by ½. Add stock and lemon juice and mix well. Reduce again by ½. Using a spatula, lift veal "stacks" to 2 serving plates. Finish sauce by introducing butter to the remaining liquid a teaspoonful at a time. Pour sauce over veal. Serves 2.

BOURBON- AND MAPLE-FLAVORED SWEET POTATOES

10 medium sweet potatoes
1½ teaspoons salt
2 sticks unsalted butter, divided
¼ cup good bourbon
salt and pepper to taste
1 to 1½ tablespoons maple flavoring

Peel potatoes and dice them into ½- to ¾-inch chunks. Place potatoes in a stockpot, cover with water, and add 1½ teaspoons salt. Bring to a boil and cook potatoes until tender but still firm. Drain well, then lay potatoes in a single layer on a large baking tray. Bake at 350 degrees until completely cooked (baking helps remove the excess moisture). Whip potatoes with 1 stick of the butter and bourbon until all lumps are gone. Season with salt and pepper. Soften the remaining butter and combine it with maple flavoring in a mixer until well blended. Serve sweet potatoes hot with a generous dollop of the Maple Butter. Serves 10.

Cab Frye's TAVERN

914 GRAVEL PIKE (PA 29)
PALM, PA 18070
215-679-9935

The short drive from Allentown into the countryside is well worth the anticipation. Winding our way along PA 29 on our way to Cab Frye's for a late lunch, we thoroughly enjoyed the sunny fall afternoon. As we came within sight of this three-story brick building, we were struck by its profusion of flowers. Window boxes and flowerpots added to the festivity of the exterior decor. The interior was equally appealing. The whimsical accessories scattered throughout the building enhanced antiques such as cast-iron molds and coffee grinders.

We were seated in a light, airy dining room with cafe curtains and floral valences. The fresh flowers that were everywhere complemented the silver chargers. A fireplace with a rough-hewn mantel was centered on the far wall. Doorways with arched woodwork provided lovely transitions from room to room.

After many successful restaurant stops, chef Ed Galgon purchased Cab Frye's Tavern in 1993. He and his wife, Tina, continue a tradition started many years ago. John Steinman and his family built this three-story brick building in 1830 along the gravel pike from Allentown to Philadelphia. It served as their home as well as a stagecoach stop. A century later, Elmer Trollinger purchased the building and the surrounding acreage. He successfully applied for a beer license and began to operate a tavern, growing on his own property most of the food he served. When Cab Frye and his wife, Betty, purchased the tavern in 1953, they began transforming the popular local taproom into a restaurant renowned for its fine food and cocktails. This tradition continued through subsequent owner Robert Eugster and right on to the tavern's current keepers.

Today's menu features continental dishes and seasonal highlights like wild game, seafood, fowl, and wild mushrooms. An extensive wine list complements the entrée selections. Dinner choices such as Scottish Lobster, sautéed with whiskey, curry, pineapple, and peaches, and Wiener Schnitzel, sautéed with Smoked Shrimp, will certainly draw us back for an evening meal.

We began our lunch with a salad of field greens topped with the flavorful house Garlic Vinaigrette, served with freshly baked Bread and Herbed Olive Oil for dipping. Both of us were drawn to the fish selections. Karen chose the Crab Cakes, served with Mango Salsa. She proclaimed them extremely delicious. Debbie did the same with her quiche of the day, a smoked salmon and sun-dried tomato combination. The creativity of the menu items and the superb presentation were a real treat.

As we wandered out to the parking lot, we took note of the delightful alfresco dining area. Lushly green, with a latticework entry, it made us muse about returning on a warm summer evening to renew our acquaintance with Cab Frye's Tavern.

GRILLED FILLET OF BEEF SALAD

⅓ cup blue cheese, crumbled
2 tablespoons hot water
⅓ cup mayonnaise
⅓ cup sour cream
salt and freshly ground pepper to taste
¼ teaspoon Tabasco sauce
2 tablespoons sesame oil
1 tablespoon sesame seeds
1 tablespoon rice vinegar
20-ounce fillet of beef, trimmed
8 cups mixed baby greens
½ pound snow peas, trimmed and blanched
2 carrots, cut and blanched

Place cheese in a bowl. Using a fork, mix in the water, mayonnaise, sour cream, salt and pepper, and Tabasco to make dressing for the salad. In another bowl, combine sesame oil, sesame seeds, and vinegar. Marinate fillet about 20 minutes in this mix, turning once to allow fillet to absorb liquid. Grill fillet over a hot grill until it reaches desired doneness. Divide greens among 4 plates and garnish with snow peas and carrots. Slice beef, arrange on greens, then spoon dressing over top. Serve immediately. Serves 4.

Note: When purchasing the beef for this recipe, ask for the tail end of the fillet, which cooks more quickly, has more flavor, and is less expensive at the butcher shop than other cuts.

PHYLLO TARTLETS WITH LIME CURD AND BERRIES

⅓ cup plus 4 generous teaspoons sugar, divided
1 teaspoon cornstarch
1⅓ cups semisweet white wine
⅓ cup fresh lime juice
1 teaspoon grated lime peel
½ cup egg substitute
4 sheets phyllo dough
2 tablespoons unsalted butter, melted
3 cups berries, washed and hulled
3 teaspoons extra-fine sugar
mint for garnish

To make lime curd, mix ⅓ cup sugar and cornstarch in a heavy saucepan until there are no lumps. Mix in wine, lime juice, and lime peel. Whisk in egg substitute. Whisk over medium heat about 7 minutes until mixture thickens and just begins to boil. Remove from heat and refrigerate.

To make tartlets, lightly butter the outside of 4 custard cups or ramekins. Stack phyllo sheets on a work board. Trim sides and cut 4 6-inch-square stacks from sheets. Lightly butter each sheet in each stack and sprinkle with 4 teaspoons sugar, turning each piece so corners are at different angles. Place each stack of sheets on an upside-down custard cup and press lightly into a bowl shape. Chill for 1 hour.

Preheat oven to 350 degrees. Place custard cups on a cookie sheet and bake about 20 minutes until phyllo turns brown. Let shells cool.

Divide lime curd evenly among shells. Top with berries and sprinkle with extra-fine sugar. Garnish with mint. Serves 4.

Historic

General Warren Inne

WEST OLD LANCASTER HIGHWAY
MALVERN, PA 19355
610-296-3637

Tucked away just off bustling US 202 sits the history-filled General Warren Inne. Originally named the Admiral Vernon Inn, it was built in 1745 to serve as a premier carriage stop for hungry travelers. In 1758, the inn's name was changed to the Admiral Warren, after Admiral Peter Warren, a hero of the French and Indian War.

During the Revolutionary War, the inn was owned by John Penn, grandson of William Penn. John Penn was a well-known Loyalist, and the stage stop became a Tory stronghold where maps were drawn and strategies formed. Generals Howe and Cornwallis used those maps to navigate the valley en route to Philadelphia.

After the war, Penn sold the property to a German Seventh-Day Adventist by the name of Casper Fahnestock. During Fahnestock's tenure, the thriving inn enhanced its reputation for clean lodging and excellent food. Many years later, Fahnestock's great-grandson turned the inn into a temperance hotel, even going so far as to cut down the apple orchards on the property to prevent apple cider from being made and sold. In 1825, in an attempt to diminish ties to its Loyalist past, the inn was renamed to honor General Joseph Warren, the American hero of the Battle of Bunker Hill. Turnpike travel was at its peak during that time, and the inn housed a post office and served as a relay stop for the mail stagecoaches. When the Philadelphia and Columbia Railroad opened in 1831, the decline of the stage began. The last regular coach passed through in 1834.

One hundred and fifty years later, as the local area grew and developed, the current owners took great care to return the inn to its eighteenth-century elegance. In the large dining room where we were served, Oriental rugs covered the plank floor. Old-fashioned prints in antique frames hung on the walls, complementing the Colonial blue-and-white decor. White table linens, fresh flowers, and candles both on the tables and in the brass sconces on the walls gave the dining room a feeling of intimacy. This feeling was enhanced by the hurricane lanterns placed in each of the deep-set windows all along the length of the inn.

The very appealing luncheon menu included choices such as Louisiana Snapper Soup, Smoked Pork Foccacia Sandwich with a sauce of fennel, green olives, and tomato, and Pan-Roasted Beef Tenderloin Medallions, served hunter-style (in a brown gravy). The Pan-Fried Shrimp Dumplings, served in a Ginger Demi-Glace and accompanied by Oriental Vegetable Slaw, caught Karen's eye. The slaw was crunchy and flavorful; the shrimp were innovative and appealing. The day's special, Scrambled Egg and Truffle Crepes, served in a Mornay Sauce, tempted Debbie. Yum, yum, and again yum. Authentic Shortcake followed—not pound cake or angel food cake, but biscuit-style cake with fresh berries and cream. Karen finished it with a smile on her face, proclaiming, "I haven't had Shortcake like this since I left England." Maybe the inn is a Tory stronghold yet.

BANANAS FOSTER

½ cup light brown sugar
2 tablespoons butter
¼ cup banana liqueur
1 banana, peeled and diced large
4½ teaspoons rum
2 large scoops vanilla ice cream

Place sugar and butter in a wide, shallow frying pan over medium heat and melt sugar mixture until it bubbles. Add banana liqueur and mix to combine. Add banana, stirring to coat. Add rum. If you are cooking with gas, tilt pan toward flame to ignite alcohol; otherwise, use a lighter to ignite. Continue to cook until flame goes out. Place ice cream in 2 serving bowls. Pour banana topping equally over each and serve. Serves 2.

PORK TENDERLOIN DIJONNAISE SHIITAKE

2 4- to 5-ounce pork tenderloins
2 tablespoons butter
½ cup flour
3½-ounce package shiitake mushrooms
1½ teaspoons Dijon mustard
1 tablespoon scallions, sliced
1 teaspoon onion or shallots, minced
3 tablespoons white wine, chicken broth, or water
6 tablespoons heavy cream
6 tablespoons brown sauce

Clean pork of excess fat and remove the silver skin. Cut pork into 1-inch medallions; pound medallions flat. Place butter in a sauté pan over medium heat and allow to foam. Dredge pork in flour and sauté until golden brown on both sides. Remove pork from pan. Add remaining ingredients to pan and bring to a simmer. Reduce sauce to desired consistency. To serve, spoon sauce onto 2 plates and place medallions on top. Spoon additional sauce over top. Serves 2.

14 EAST MAIN STREET
LITITZ, PA 17543
717-626-2115

John Augustus Sutter was commonly known as General Sutter because of his involvement in the Mexican War, during which he owned a large parcel of land in the Sacramento Valley. However, he's better remembered for a discovery that changed the future of many people—gold! Unfortunately for him, he was unable to keep his findings a secret. Men in search of a fortune—called "Forty-niners" because of the year they went west—swarmed his property, trampled his crops, and left his livestock and land in ruin. Ironically, their quest of gold left him nearly bankrupt. In ill health, he moved from California to the quiet streets of Lititz, Pennsylvania.

Sutter built his home across the street from the town's hotel. He hoped to provide his three grandchildren the benefits of a fine Moravian education and to cure himself in the town's mineral springs. In his honor, the local inn—founded by the Moravian Church in 1764 as the Zum Anker, or "Sign of the Anchor," and later called the Lititz Springs Hotel—was renamed the General Sutter Inn.

Since its inception, the inn has been regarded as one of the finest in Pennsylvania. In 1803 and again in 1848, it underwent renovations that created the comely three-story brick building of today. The lobby is decidedly Victorian, with settees on either side of the fireplace and a portrait of General Sutter above the mantel. Details such as the plaster molding prettily patterned on the ceiling add to the decor.

The General Sutter Inn houses three separate restaurants. Pearl's Victorian Bar provides spirits of all types, as well as a tavern menu. The Zum Anker Cafe serves hearty breakfast items such as Cornmeal Pancakes and Grilled Pecan Sticky Buns. The many unusual breakfast choices include Eggs Florentine (poached eggs with Canadian bacon and sautéed spinach, served on an English muffin and topped with Mornay Sauce) and Rolled Pancakes, Pennsylvania Dutch–style, stuffed with a variety of fruit fillings. The 1764 Restaurant, named for its founding date and appointed in Federal-style decor, offers a pleasing combination of colonial heritage and a modern menu.

Karen had the Ostrich in Raspberry-Garlic Reduction. Debbie honored General Sutter's Western heritage, choosing the Bison served in a sauce of cumin and pine nuts. Both entrées were served with Flavored Mashed Potatoes, Baby Carrots, and Broccoli Spears. The presentation of the meals, complete with orchid-and-rosemary garnish, was equaled by their flavor.

It had been a long day by the time we arrived at the inn, so we ended our flavorful meal by soothing ourselves with chocolate. The Bailey's Cake was a luscious chocolate layer cake with a layer of Bailey's Irish Cream Mousse. We also tried the Chocolate Gold, a fudge torte with a layer of Chocolate Gâteau, served in a thin chocolate crust accented with gold leaf. Both were certainly worth every calorie!

DRIED SOUR CHERRY QUINOA PILAF

2 cups quinoa
½ cup butter
2 tablespoons shallots, chopped
½ cup dried sour cherries
½ cup cherry wine
4 cups chicken stock
salt and pepper to taste

Sauté quinoa in butter until lightly browned. Add shallots and cherries. When mixture is thoroughly heated, deglaze with cherry wine. Add stock and let simmer until liquid is absorbed and quinoa is tender and moist. Adjust salt and pepper. Serves 12.

BOSC PEAR ARMAGNAC GRANITA

2¾ cups water
1½ cups sugar
½ cup lemon rind, grated
1 cup Armagnac
5 quarts Bosc pears, peeled and seeded

Bring water, sugar, lemon rind, and Armagnac to a boil in a saucepan. Allow to simmer for 5 minutes until a syrup consistency is obtained. Remove from heat. Purée pears in a food processor. Add pears to syrup mixture and thoroughly combine. Line a small roasting pan with clear wrap. Spread mixture in pan, then freeze. When mixture is frozen, cut or break into pieces, return to food processor, and purée until smooth. Repack slush mixture in a plastic container and refreeze until needed. Scoop and serve. Serves 16.

SAFFRON TROUT

½ cup clarified butter
2 10-ounce trout, deboned but with head and skin still on
pinch of salt
pinch of pepper
¼ cup lemon juice
1 cup white wine, divided
¼ cup water
2 pinches of saffron
½ cup fish or chicken stock
¼ cup heavy cream
2 tablespoons butter, dredged in flour

Coat a small baking sheet with the melted butter. Season the inside of the trout with salt and pepper. Place trout on baking sheet by spreading the sides apart, skin sides up. Combine lemon juice, ¼ cup of the wine, and water; ladle over length of trout. Place in a preheated 400-degree oven for approximately 10 minutes. While trout is baking, pour remaining ¾ cup wine into a small skillet. Heat on medium. Add saffron. Allow saffron to steep slightly, then add stock, followed by cream and butter dredged in flour. Swirl 1 to 2 minutes until a glassy, rich sauce is created. Remove from heat. When trout is done baking, skin will begin to bubble slightly; remove from oven. Using tongs, grasp trout by the head and slowly peel backwards to remove head and skin. The fillets are now easily separated into right and left halves. Place hot fillets in an **X** pattern on each of 2 plates and pour warm saffron sauce over the top. Serves 2.

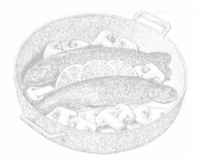

GREEN GABLES
RESTAURANT

7712 SOMERSET PIKE (PA 985)
JENNERSTOWN, PA 15547
814-629-9220

For over seventy years, Green Gables Restaurant has served hungry diners traveling the Lincoln Highway. Opened as a roadside sandwich stand by James Stoughton in 1927, it received national recognition during its second year of operation, when it was awarded second place in the Rockefeller Wayside Stand Competition. Its simple menu of Chicken Salad Sandwiches and Angel Food Cake was so popular it soon undertook a series of expansions to accommodate its growing number of visitors. The first was the Hannah Sellers Dining Room, followed by three glass-enclosed terraces. The addition of the Tuscany Room in 1970 helped make Green Gables the full-service restaurant it is today.

Never at a loss for ways to expand Green Gables' clientele, James Stoughton announced to his family that he intended to add a theater in the backyard. Housed in a gristmill that was relocated through the snow log by log to its present site, the Mountain Playhouse opened in June 1939. It presents a variety of productions from comedies to drama to musical entertainment.

Green Gables' entrance remains very similar to what it was all those years ago. The original white clapboard building is still distinguishable from the additions, which were done in stone. Inside, the slate floors, rough-hewn beam ceilings, and stacked-stone walls are engagingly primitive. Enormous statues reminiscent of ancient Greece, garnered from the estate of steel magnate Charles Schwab, now serve as columns in the Terrace Dining Room.

We were seated window-side, which allowed us a view of the beautifully landscaped grounds. Tall evergreens stood on the banks of the creek as it meandered toward Stoughton Lake. It would have been easy to take in the atmosphere indefinitely, but we managed to focus on the menu long enough to order. It wouldn't be a visit to Green Gables without sampling the Chicken Salad, which was delicious in its simplicity. Accompanied by fresh fruit and Apple Walnut Bread with Cinnamon Butter, it was a good choice for a summertime lunch. Karen tried the Potato-Leek Soup and found it thick, creamy, and flavorful. She followed that with the Salmon Croquettes, served in Dill Sauce. The croquettes were well seasoned and moist.

After lunch, we, like many of the other guests, wandered through Green Gables' nooks and crannies to admire the artwork and the impressive collection of antique glass, china, and pottery. We also explored the Tuscany Room, an expansive dining room. James Stoughton designed the punched-copper lighting himself. Massive oak trees located in each corner of the room were the original survey markers on the family farm. The large fireplace and the window with vines growing across it add to the rustic mood.

Regardless of where you're seated—in the Tuscany Room, the Hannah B. Sellers Dining Room, or the Terrace Dining Room—your experience at Green Gables is sure to be unique.

SALMON CROQUETTES

2 14¾-ounce cans salmon
2 eggs
1 tablespoon heavy cream
½ stalk celery, diced fine
½ teaspoon dill
salt and pepper to taste
3 slices bread, diced fine
1 to 1½ cups dry breadcrumbs

Drain salmon and clean it of bones and skin. Place salmon in bowl. Add eggs, cream, and celery and mix by hand. Add dill, salt and pepper, and bread to bind ingredients. Form mixture into meatball-size portions and roll in breadcrumbs. Deep-fry croquettes. Drain and serve with cream sauce of your choice. Yields 8 croquettes.

BLUE CHEESE DRESSING

4 cups mayonnaise
1 pound blue cheese, crumbled
¼ cup sugar
¼ cup buttermilk
½ tablespoon salad oil
½ tablespoon vinegar
¼ teaspoon white pepper

Combine ingredients in a large mixing bowl. Store in refrigerator in an airtight container. Yields 5 to 6 cups.

HOTEL SAXONBURG, INC.

220 MAIN STREET
SAXONBURG, PA 16056
724-352-4200

What do the Brooklyn Bridge and the village of Saxonburg, Pennsylvania, have in common? On the surface, it seems that a hamlet that is a bastion of turn-of-the-century Americana and an urban bridge renowned for its cutting-edge technology would be worlds apart. What links them is John Roebling.

Originally from Mulhausen, Germany, Roebling founded Saxonburg in 1832 on a 1,583-acre parcel purchased for $2209.50. He intended to create a German community here in America whose economic support would come from agriculture and light manufacturing. Today, Saxonburg is still much as its founder envisioned.

An engineer by education, Roebling labored in his Saxonburg workshop to develop and patent the wire-cable suspension for which the Brooklyn Bridge is famous. His bridge designs using this technology led to his fame and fortune and eventually forced him to move his cable works from Saxonburg to New Jersey for better transportation access.

Thanks to its fresh air and uncluttered countryside, Saxonburg became a weekend retreat for wealthy Pittsburghers escaping the effects of that city's industrial boom. Hotel Saxonburg was one of the town's most popular destinations. In its early years, the hotel was known as the Vogley House. In 1863, it became the Union Hotel. Francis Laube later purchased the structure and renamed it Laube House, a name that remained until the late 1800s.

Today, the hotel's whitewashed exterior hints at what's inside. The dining room to the right of the entry hall has tin-tile ceilings and painted plank walls. The old nails used to construct those walls are still visible. Pictures from Saxonburg's early days line the walls, in and among farm implements from previous eras. Across the way, burgundy wallpaper and a wooden ceiling create an entirely different but equally appealing dining atmosphere.

The day we visited, the town was anxiously awaiting its annual Fireman's Parade later in the afternoon. Chairs and blankets already lined Main Street as we pulled up for lunch. The stone steps and leaded-glass door beckoned us into the hotel, where we enjoyed choosing from a wide variety of luncheon items, including at least six soups. One of the more unusual entrée selections, the Crepe Alex, stuffed with shrimp, proved very good and the perfect size for lunch. For dessert, Karen tried the exotic Fried Ice Cream, while Debbie chose the Strawberry Shortcake, thus bringing an all-American lunch to an appropriate close.

❧ SEAFOOD PASTA ❧

¼ cup garlic butter
8 medium shrimp, peeled and deveined
½ cup scallops
8 fresh mussels (meat only)
¼ cup clams, chopped
2 to 4 tablespoons clam juice
½ cup heavy whipping cream
salt and pepper to taste
1 pound fettuccine, undercooked
2 tablespoons Parmesan cheese, grated
chopped parsley for garnish

Melt garlic butter in an 8-inch sauté pan. Add seafood and clam juice. Sauté slightly until well mixed; be careful not to overcook. Add cream and salt and pepper; cook to reduce by ½. Fold in pasta and toss while adding cheese. When fettuccine is heated through, transfer to serving plates and garnish with parsley. Serves 2.

❧ MUSTARD GRILLED CHICKEN ❧

1 cup Dijon mustard
1 tablespoon pepper
2 tablespoons olive oil
2 tablespoons white wine
2 boneless chicken breasts

Combine mustard, pepper, oil, and wine in a covered container to make marinade. Shake to mix well. Coat chicken breasts with marinade. Cover and marinate overnight. Broil or grill breasts 10 to 15 minutes until they are no longer pink in the center, turning at least once. Serves 2.

136 MARKET STREET
LEWISBURG, PA 17837
570-523-7800

The Lewisburg Hotel sits majestically on the main street of town. Built in 1834, accessible to the Pennsylvania Canal, the Old East-West Turnpike, and two major railroads, the hotel provided accommodations for generations of travelers. It was also home to the first president of the University of Lewisburg (now Bucknell University). The school's first graduation exercises were held here in 1851. In attendance at the commencement were United States senator Simon Cameron and James Buchanan, who went on to become the fifteenth president of the United States. Every governor of Pennsylvania from 1831 to 1901 is said to have been a guest here. Notable people visiting the hotel after the turn of the century included sports figures Jim Thorpe, John McGraw, and Christy Mathewson, poet Walt Whitman, and opera diva Marian Anderson. During the 1930s, 1940s, and 1950s, many of the nation's popular bands performed here.

The hotel was purchased by William Cameron after the Civil War, and the doors were closed for two years of renovations. For the next sixty years, the hotel was known as Cameron House. It was closed again in 1993, when it was purchased by Norman and Nancy Buck. Restored to its original grandeur, it reopened in 1997. The Lewisburg Hotel is the only old hotel in this community to have withstood changes in lifestyle and the wear and tear of time.

During our visit, we were charmed by the Victorian-style floral carpeting and coordinated wallpaper and the magnificent woodwork gleaming in the soft light, which created the effect of a library in two of the main dining rooms. In the third, named in honor of Senator Cameron, guests eat in a Victorian parlor atmosphere. The bar is a comfortable respite full of gleaming oak and capped off by a tin tile ceiling.

In the quiet atmosphere of the Governor's Room, we perused the luncheon menu. Karen chose the Cucumber Dill Sandwich, served on toast, while Debbie enjoyed a sizable bowl of Potato Bacon Soup. Although guests around us sampled a variety of items, the Broccoli Cheddar Quiche and the Ham and Swiss Wrap were overwhelmingly popular.

The delightful town of Lewisburg has many restored buildings for visitors to enjoy. In its regal forest green with cream and burgundy trim, the Lewisburg Hotel again offers solace for another generation of weary travelers.

BRUSCHETTA MIX

12 ripe plum tomatoes, quartered
2 red onions, sliced thin
6 cloves fresh garlic, chopped fine
1 cup fresh basil, cut into thin strips
2 cups virgin olive oil
1 cup balsamic vinegar
fresh-baked Italian bread, grilled
4 slices bucchini (fresh buffalo mozzarella cheese)
Parmesan cheese

In a large salad bowl, combine tomatoes, red onions, garlic, and basil. Mix gently but thoroughly. Emulsify oil and vinegar; add to tomato mixture and toss. Place on grilled bread, top with mozzarella, sprinkle with Parmesan, and serve. Serves 4.

STEAK AND POTATO SALAD

8-ounce New York strip steak
½ cup Italian dressing
2 to 3 cups fresh greens for salad
½ cup green bell pepper, diced
½ cup onions, diced
1 plum tomato, sliced
½ cup potato, diced and fried
½ cup Monterey Jack cheese, grated

Marinate steak in Italian dressing for 30 minutes at room temperature. Grill steak to medium-rare and slice thin. Place fresh greens on a plate. Toss peppers, onions, tomato, and potato and place on top of greens. Add steak on top in a circular pattern. Top with cheese and serve. Serves 1.

Jean Bonnet Tavern
Bed & Breakfast/Fine Dining

US 30 AND PA 31
BEDFORD, PA 15522
814-623-2250

Although it has operated as a tavern since its construction in the 1760s, Jean Bonnet's public house didn't officially receive a license until the third Tuesday in October 1780. The license read that the "Petitioner Lives at the Fork of roads leading to Fort Pitt and the Glades." This was the junction of Old Forbes and Burd Roads, today's US 30 and PA 31.

Records of the property prior to the tavern license show a title transfer of 690 acres from the William Penn family to Hans Ireland, a land speculator. In 1762, the property was transferred to Robert Callender, who was an Indian scout, a deputy for troop supplies, and eventually a scout for General George Washington. The tavern was built during Callender's tenure. Jean Bonnet and his wife, Dorothy, purchased the building in 1779. In mid-1794, with the Whiskey Rebellion gaining momentum, farmers met at Bonnet's to protest the federal excise tax on whiskey. Eventually, George Washington had to call in troops in an attempt to squelch the mounting dissatisfaction.

Today's tavern is in many ways similar to Bonnet's establishment of old. The native stone walls and enormous chestnut beams are still there. Barrels and other memorabilia are gathered around a huge fireplace, which smelled pleasingly smoky during our visit. The quilts hanging throughout the dining rooms provide additional colonial ambiance, as do the twig chairs and wooden furniture. The menu is, no doubt, broader than it was all those years ago. The choices today range from Roasted Duck to Stir-Fry to Vegetable Lasagna.

Comfort food was definitely in order on that incredibly rainy Sunday afternoon. Described as a "Bedford County favorite," the Turkey and Waffles on the brunch menu certainly fit the bill. The entrée was preceded by a salad, served with a French-based Poppy Seed Dressing that included pieces of carrots and beets. It was as tasty as it was unusual. The warm, creamy entrée featured bite-size turkey ladled over a Belgian-style waffle. The waffle was light and fluffy and would have been as delicious with syrup as it was with the creamed turkey. The traditional dessert offerings included Apple Pie, Cherry Pie, Pecan Pie, and Oatmeal Pie.

Just off the Pennsylvania Turnpike, the Jean Bonnet Tavern is ready to cater to weary travelers just as it has served them since the late 1700s. A stop here certainly refreshed us. It also gave us insight into the long-popular all-you-can-eat chicken and waffle dinners that used to be served at so many of the restaurants featured in this book.

OATMEAL PIE

2 eggs
¾ cup white Karo syrup
½ cup butter, melted
½ cup white sugar
½ cup brown sugar
¾ cup oatmeal
1 cup evaporated milk
1 cup shredded coconut
1 teaspoon vanilla
9-inch pie shell, unbaked

Blend eggs, Karo, butter, white sugar, and brown sugar in a medium-sized bowl for 3 minutes. Add oatmeal and evaporated milk and mix for 1 more minute. Add coconut and vanilla and blend well. Pour into pie shell. Bake at 350 degrees for 30 to 40 minutes, until a knife inserted in the center comes out clean. Serves 8.

HOUSE DRESSING

12-ounce bottle French or other Catalina-style dressing
½ tablespoon poppy seeds
⅓ cup fresh beets, cooked and diced
2 pickled eggs, diced

Combine all ingredients in a large mixing bowl. Yields 2 cups.

THE
LOGAN
A Small Luxury Inn

10 WEST FERRY STREET
NEW HOPE, PA 18938
215-862-2300

In 1722, by act of the General Assembly of Pennsylvania, John Wells was licensed to erect and keep a ferry on the banks of the Delaware River on land previously occupied by the Lenni-Lenape Indians. In 1727, he was licensed to keep a tavern. Thus began the Ferry Tavern at the corner of South Main and Ferry Streets. Wells was looked upon as the founder of New Hope. As the community grew, the tavern prospered. Today, it survives as a fine example of the colonial habit of wrapping additions around original buildings.

About a hundred years after the Ferry Tavern was licensed, the name was changed to The Logan Inn. At that same time, a metal Indian was installed above the roof. There are many different accounts of that event. However, the one that seems to be the most popular is that a Lenni-Lenape chief who was acclaimed for his kindness to white settlers developed a close friendship with James Logan. The chief and Logan, who was Williams Penn's secretary, became blood brothers. Indeed, as a sign of respect, the chief took Logan's name. The metal Indian remained above the inn for fifty years and was depicted in many

woodcuts during that period. Now a town landmark, it can be seen on the lawn of the local historical society's museum, which faces the inn.

A tavern is located in the oldest part of the building. Its stone walls, original fireplace, and antique wood paneling give the room a warm, friendly atmosphere. Guests enjoy looking at the beautiful murals that were discovered during renovations and then restored to their former glory.

There are two additional dining rooms at the inn. The Colonial Dining Room, decorated in cream and colonial blue, has wooden furniture, pewter wall sconces, and abundant candlelight. On the day we visited, lunch was being served in the Garden Dining Room. A light, airy room next door to the tavern, it shares one of the original building's beautiful stone walls. The high, arched ceiling and the many floral stained-glass windows serve to make you feel like you're still outdoors. Along one side of the room is a truly fascinating stained-glass wall created by a local artist.

The Logan Inn offers a wide range of choices for lunch. We could have selected from twelve different sandwiches, ranging from Grilled Turkey Sausage with Peppers and Onions to Chicken Salad Maison, which contained morsels of chicken breast with celery and apples. There were ten different salads. Karen almost opted for the Garden Rotini Pasta Salad, which combined tricolored pasta, red peppers, green peas, scallions, and pine nuts in creamy Basil Sauce. Ultimately, we both selected the house specialties—a cold soup de jour followed by the quiche of the day. The creamy Dill Cucumber Soup was perfect on that hot summer day. It was followed by light, fluffy Cheddar and Broccoli Quiche with Roasted Red Peppers. The salad that accompanied the quiche was crisp and tasty.

All in all, it was a delicious sampling from the fifth-oldest inn in America. The Ferry Tavern may be long gone, but the Logan Inn remains to carry on a 275-year tradition of serving appetizing food in comfortable surroundings.

CRAB CAKES

1 tablespoon scallions, chopped
1 tablespoon red bell pepper, diced
1 tablespoon butter
1 pound lump crabmeat
1 tablespoon parsley, chopped
½ cup breadcrumbs
1 teaspoon Dijon mustard
1 teaspoon Old Bay seasoning
1 teaspoon Worcestershire sauce
½ cup mayonnaise
tartar sauce or cocktail sauce

Sauté scallions and red peppers in butter for about 3 minutes. Combine with remaining ingredients. Shape into crab cakes using an ice cream scoop. Bake in a preheated 425-degree

oven for 5 minutes until golden brown. Serve with tartar sauce or cocktail sauce. Yields 6 crab cakes.

CHICKEN LOGAN AU PECHE

2 large chicken breasts, deboned, skinned, and split
salt and white pepper to taste
2 tablespoons butter
1 tablespoon brown sugar
¼ teaspoon fresh ginger root, grated (or ½ teaspoon minced candied root)
1 ripe peach, peeled, pitted, and sliced
1 tablespoon Major Grey's Chutney (optional)
flour for dusting
1 egg, beaten
¾ cup white breadcrumbs
vegetable oil

Pound chicken breasts between sheets of waxed paper as thin as possible without tearing. Season with salt and pepper. Melt butter in a small saucepan. Add brown sugar and ginger root, stirring until sugar is dissolved. Add peach slices and simmer for 1 minute. Cool. Add chutney, if desired. Place peach slices on each flattened breast. Fold envelope-style; fold long bottom side of breast up and over peach, fold sides in next, then fold top flap over all. Chill at least 1 hour. Dust with flour, dip in egg, and roll in breadcrumbs. Chill. Heat oil in a deep fryer to 350 degrees and fry for about 10 minutes. Drain and serve. Serves 4.

The Oak Grill
at The Marshalton Inn

1300 WEST STRASBURG ROAD
MARSHALTON, PA 19382
610-692-4367

An example of early Federal-style architecture, this stone house was constructed in 1793 by Joseph Woodward. It was built along the Strasburg Road, then the main thoroughfare between Pittsburgh and Philadelphia. Nine years later, Woodward sold the property to his son-in-law, Abraham Martin. A thrifty individual, Martin was able to save up at least two thousand dollars over the next two years. He used that money to transform the stone structure into an inn and tavern.

Drovers and teamsters, able to travel only about ten or twelve miles a day, were frequent guests at the inn. Dinner was served for twelve cents, while a drink of spirits cost three cents. Herders were charged eight cents for each head of cattle to be kept for the night; each herder's bed was twelve and a half cents.

Besides Abraham Martin, there have been twenty-four other innkeepers here. The name of the inn has been changed at least eight times; the property has been known as The Marshalton Inn since 1965. The structure was listed on the National Register of Historic Places in 1977.

Guests headed to The Marshalton Inn traverse its original cobblestones. On the porch are an old feedbox and a well-used bench. Shake shingles still top the roof, and the brown door and shutters still have their old slide bolts. The not-quite-level original flooring adds to the charm of this restaurant, which is lit only by candlelight. Each table has its own pewter holder and a simple white candle therein. On the plaster walls are tin sconces, also holding white tapers. Arched molding, painted in colors appropriate to its time period, is coordinated with the corner cabinets and wainscoting. The windows are deep-set; rough linen draperies add to the time-conscious decor.

As we imbibed the peaceful atmosphere of a simpler time, our server brought Rolls, served with Sun-Dried Tomato and Garlic Butter. We were further tempted by the Herbed Goat Cheese Bruschetta, which was tangy and tasty, and the Grilled Pear and Glazed Walnut Salad. The pear was fanned atop of a bed of field greens tossed with blue cheese and sugared walnuts. The blend of flavors and textures was truly unique and very appetizing. Not a morsel was left! After an entrée of Wood-Grilled Salmon, we meandered outside to soak up more of the 1700s.

Next door to The Marshalton Inn is Four Dogs Tavern, a plaster building with a shake roof of approximately the same time period. Its interior is all pine paneling and its atmosphere a more casual alternative to the inn. These are just two of the many early buildings still standing nearby. With so much original architecture here, it's easy to envision what it must have been like way back when.

SOUTHWESTERN CLAMS WITH CILANTRO OIL

2 dozen cherrystone clams on the half shell
salt and pepper to taste
1 tablespoon garlic powder
2 jalapeños, minced
1 large tomato, diced
1 small onion, diced
1 teaspoon red wine vinegar
6 tablespoons cilantro, chopped
1 cup olive oil
2 cloves garlic

Preheat oven to 450 degrees. Place clams on a baking sheet. Sprinkle with salt and pepper and garlic powder. Combine jalapeños, tomatoes, onions, and vinegar. Place on top of clams and bake for 10 to 12 minutes. Place cilantro, oil, and garlic in a food processor and mix until smooth. Remove clams from oven and place on a serving tray. Drizzle with cilantro oil. Serve with French bread and Chardonnay or a Pilsner beer. Serves 6 to 8 as an appetizer.

SOFT-SHELL CRABS WITH CHERRY TOMATO SALSA

Crabs

4 jumbo soft-shell crabs, cleaned
4 cups buttermilk
2 cups flour
vegetable oil
field greens
Cherry Tomato Salsa (see below)

Cover crabs in buttermilk for at least 2 hours. Remove and dust with flour. Place shell side down in about 1 inch of preheated vegetable oil and cook for 3 minutes on each side. Remove and place on paper towels to drain. Place crabs on a bed of field greens and top with Cherry Tomato Salsa. Serves 4.

Cherry Tomato Salsa

1 pint cherry tomatoes, halved
1 red pepper, cut into thin strips
1 red onion, diced
12 scallions, sliced
½ cup red wine vinegar
2 tablespoons olive oil
2 tablespoons sugar
1 tablespoon black pepper
kosher salt to taste

Combine all ingredients in a large mixing bowl. Let stand 2 to 3 hours before serving.

THE STONE HOUSE

RESTAURANT & COUNTRY INN

circa 1822

US 40 EAST
FARMINGTON, PA 15437
724-329-8876

Ah, but for a twist of fate, Fayette Springs Hotel owner Andrew Stewart would have been vice president—maybe even president. Unluckily for him, Millard Fillmore was chosen as vice president instead, then succeeded to the presidency upon the death of Zachary Taylor. Stewart, a colleague of John Quincy Adams, Andrew Jackson, Martin Van Buren, and Abraham Lincoln, was known as "Old Tariff Andy" because of his legislation supporting tariffs along the National Road, which improved transportation in our young country.

Stewart built Fayette Springs Hotel in 1822 as a resort along the National Road. It boasted billiards, a tenpin alley, dancing, and top musical entertainment. After Stewart's death in 1872, the hotel continued to be a thriving summer resort. It benefited from the spa boom of the late 1800s, since the nearby springs were believed to have curative powers.

After the Stewart family sold the hotel in the 1890s, it passed through a number of owners. George Titlow, a hotel baron and grandson of Henry Beeson, one of nearby Uniontown's founders, purchased it in 1909 as a weekend getaway for his family. Although Titlow sold off his other hotels during Prohibition, he kept Fayette Springs Hotel until his death in 1940. The structure subsequently became known as The Stone House, as it is today. In 1954, General George C. Marshall commented about having visited The Stone House as a young man and partaking of the best Chicken and Dumplings he'd ever had.

Award-winning chef Carl Fazio came on board in 1996 with a commitment to providing guests a quality menu. Traditional items like Chicken and Dumplings and pasta dishes appear side by side with innovative choices such as Shrimp Amaretto and Seafood Celena Marie. Chef Fazio has now left The Stone House, but his tradition of quality dishes is superbly maintained by one of his protégés.

The atmosphere enjoyed by diners varies depending on where they are seated. To the left of the main hall, the tone is traditional; wood paneling, family portraits, and other framed artifacts are on the walls. Across the hall, through the arched doorway with Corinthian columns, the floral wallpaper, painted woodwork, and lace curtains create a bright, cheery dining room.

During our visit, we chatted readily with a couple at the table next to us. They recommended the Seafood Chowder, so we tried it. A good choice, it was thick and rich, a wonderful combination of potatoes, mushrooms, and various types of seafood.

Thanks to nearby attractions like Laurel Caverns and the Fort Necessity Battlefield, The Stone House is a perfect place to stop for great food while sightseeing or enjoying a scenic drive down the old National Road. And if you're too tired to drive home, the lovely, antique-filled guest rooms upstairs can provide a welcome respite.

SAFFRON RISOTTO WITH SHIITAKE MUSHROOMS

¼ cup shallots, diced fine
1 cup shiitake mushrooms, sliced
2 tablespoons butter
2 tablespoons olive oil
16-ounce package aborio rice (risotto)
1 cup dry white wine
pinch of saffron
8 cups chicken stock
¼ cup Parmesan cheese, grated
2 tablespoons heavy cream

Sauté shallots and mushrooms in butter and olive oil until golden. Add rice and sauté for 2 minutes. Add wine and bring to a boil. Infuse saffron into chicken stock. Begin adding chicken stock slowly to rice mixture; once rice has absorbed stock, add a little more, continuing for 10 to 15 minutes until all stock is incorporated. Add Parmesan and cream and serve. Serves 6.

FLANK STEAK FAJITAS

2½ pounds flank steak
2 12-ounce bottles dark beer
4 cloves garlic, sliced
2 bay leaves
1 tablespoon red pepper flakes
½ teaspoon cayenne pepper
1 tablespoon Worcestershire sauce
2 tablespoons lime juice
zest of 1 lime, grated
⅓ cup fresh cilantro, chopped
⅓ cup scallions, sliced
4 sprigs fresh thyme
4 sprigs fresh oregano
10 flour tortillas
2½ cups black beans, cooked
½ cup tomato salsa (favorite recipe or commercial low-sodium)
¼ cup guacamole
¼ cup sour cream

Trim steak of all visible fat. Combine next 12 ingredients for marinade; add steaks. Marinate for 48 hours. When ready to grill steaks, drain marinade and pat steaks dry. Grill over hot coals to desired doneness; remove from grill and let rest briefly before slicing thinly on the diagonal. Grill tortillas until crisp but not dry. Place ¼ cup beans on each of 10 plates and top with tortilla folded into a cone. Fill tortillas with steak and garnish with salsa, guacamole, and sour cream. Serves 10.

Temple Hotel Perry's Restaurant

5005 KUTZTOWN ROAD
TEMPLE, PA 19560
610-929-4370

Perry's Temple Hotel Restaurant is a casual eatery that is serious about food. In the twenty-plus years that Perry Cirulli has been involved with the restaurant, it has evolved from a local watering hole that was much like a tavern in appearance and approach. It's now a restaurant known widely for its Italian cuisine, though it's still a favorite local dinner stop. Perry expanded the menu beyond Italian cuisine to keep up with changing consumer tastes, and chef Paula Alexander has added her touch during her more than fourteen years in the kitchen.

Sauces are important here. The recipe created by Perry's father, Asceno Cirulli, is the foundation of the restaurant's Red Sauce. I sampled the Red Sauce in traditional fashion (over Linguine) and found it deliciously thick and robust. Perry and I discussed what else I should sample, the result being a tableful of food. The Garlic-Basil Ravioli was my choice—and I'd gladly choose it again. I gave Perry carte blanche with the rest of the menu, and he ordered a seafood entrée and the steak special. Though not typically a scallop fan, I thoroughly enjoyed the Broiled Sea Scallops. The Petite Filet was done exactly as I like it, and the accompanying Wild Mushroom Sauce was quite nice indeed. The restaurant is well known for its gourmet Cheesesteak (which I'll have to try on

another occasion) and its Roasted Hot Peppers. Perry provided me with an order of the peppers, which I took with me to share with Karen back at the hotel. They were a definite hit with both of us.

The structure that houses Perry's Temple Hotel Restaurant dates to 1795. Originally, the building was a log-and-stone tavern called Solomon's Temple, which had a large, colorful sign depicting King Solomon. The spot became so widely popular that the tavern lent its name to the community, which became known as Temple.

No one knows who built the original tavern, although it is a matter of record that Isaac Levan, a very wealthy gentleman, owned the hotel and the surrounding 116 acres until his death in 1800. The log-and-stone structure was replaced in 1853 during the ownership of Daniel Klechner. Between 1857 and the early 1970s, the hotel was sold eight more times, but its appearance did not radically change. Perry Cirulli's father purchased the property in 1972.

While maintaining the historic integrity of the exterior, Perry has added beautiful hanging baskets and potted plants to the front of the hotel and lovely gardens around the rear entrance from the parking lot. Many of the herbs used in the cooking—some of which are unusual varieties that add a slightly different flavor—are grown right on the property.

Artists gather here annually to paint a variety of exterior scenes incorporating the restaurant and the gardens. Watercolors of the flowers painted over the last several years line the walls of the main dining room, allowing guests on even the snowiest of winter days to enjoy springtime at Perry's Temple Hotel Restaurant.

VEAL SCALOPPINE WITH ASPARAGUS CREAM

½ pound fresh asparagus
½ cup heavy cream
½ teaspoon salt
⅛ teaspoon freshly grated nutmeg
8 2-ounce veal scaloppine
¼ cup flour
2 tablespoons butter
1 tablespoon olive oil
4 sprigs parsley for garnish

Bring 4 cups of water to a boil. Drop in asparagus and cook for 5 minutes. Drain. Reserve the prettiest tips for decoration. Place remaining asparagus, cream, salt, and nutmeg in a food processor. Process until a smooth, even sauce is obtained. Pour into a saucepan and bring to a gentle boil.

Dredge veal in flour; shake off excess. Heat butter and olive oil in a 9-inch skillet. Cook veal about 3 minutes per side until browned. Season with additional salt if desired, then transfer to a platter. Place 2 scaloppine in center of each of 4 plates. Top with reserved asparagus tips and pour sauce over top. Garnish each serving with a sprig of parsley. Serves 4.

WILD HERB VINAIGRETTE

1 clove garlic, chopped
2 pinches of salt
½ cup balsamic vinegar
salt and pepper to taste
⅓ cup mixed herbs (basil, dill, parsley, chives, thyme, etc.), chopped fine
1 cup extra-virgin olive oil

Whisk all ingredients except olive oil in a medium bowl until well blended. To serve, combine well with olive oil and drizzle over salad. Yields approximately 1½ cups.

599 DORSEYVILLE ROAD
FOX CHAPEL, PA 15238
412-963-8717

Having opened its doors well over a hundred years ago, Cross Keys Inn stands along Dorseyville Road in what is now suburban Pittsburgh. In its early years, Cross Keys Hotel, as it was called then, served as a way station between Pittsburgh and Kittanning, a haven for weary travelers during their arduous forty-four-mile journey between the two towns. The inn, designated a historic landmark, has a replica of its original sign swaying in the breeze, just as that old sign must have done way back in 1850.

As travel grew more convenient and roadside inns became less necessary, Cross Keys evolved into a meeting place for area residents and the site of many energetic hoedowns. Eventually, it became a popular taproom before gradually slipping into disrepair.

After careful and authentic restoration (including overcoming the effects of a fire in the early 1990s), Cross Keys Inn again extends its welcome. The plank floors, brick walls, and lantern lights in the entry and the taproom speak to its history. The main dining room is attractively wallpapered, while the wood-paneled library just around the corner provides a cozy alternate dining area. Both rooms allow guests to enjoy a meal in a warm, traditional atmosphere. The attractively appointed upstairs dining rooms are in the old sleeping rooms. On our first visit, we dined in the centermost upstairs room, at a cozy table near the fireplace. The room was decorated with lace curtains, brass mantel accessories, and period wallpaper.

During our most recent visit, the majority of guests seemed to be known by name. As a matter of fact, we frequently heard staff members bedecked in brass Cross Keys shirt studs and cuff links asking, "The usual?"

There were more sandwich selections than we remembered from previous visits, large in size and served with Fries. The other menu selections by chef Regis McGill were creative, appealing, and pleasingly presented. The Meat Loaf, made from a mixture of three different meats, was tasty and not nearly as heavy and filling as Grandma's higher-calorie version. The Dessert Platter, a sampling of five different dessert items, was extremely generous in size and a good choice for two dessert lovers who had difficulty making a decision.

TOURNEDOS OF BEEF

2 8-ounce choice beef tenderloins, cut in half
salt and pepper to taste
¼ cup butter
¼ cup shallots, chopped
¼ cup cherry schnapps or cherry brandy
½ cup black cherries
½ cup veal demi-reduction or brown sauce
4 ounces Brie

Season tournedos with salt and pepper. Melt butter in a medium skillet. Add shallots and cherry liquor. Place tournedos in skillet and sauté. Add cherries and veal demi-reduction. Remove beef and place on broiler pan. Top with Brie. Place under broiler until cheese melts. Top with cherry sauce from skillet and serve. Serves 2.

STUFFED PORTABELLO MUSHROOM

1 portabello mushroom
1 slice provolone cheese
4 fresh basil leaves
1 egg
¼ cup sun-dried tomato flour
¼ cup roasted red pepper strips
1 tablespoon sherry
¼ teaspoon garlic, chopped
¼ cup veal demi-reduction or brown sauce
fresh herbs

Remove stem from mushroom. Lightly steam the cap. Cut cap into half-moons. Layer cap pieces with provolone and basil. Dip in egg and then tomato flour. Lightly sauté both sides. Place in baking dish and top with pepper strips. Bake mushroom, turning until heated through. Remove from dish; drain any oil. Combine sherry, garlic, and veal demi-reduction. Spoon demi-reduction onto plate. Top with mushroom and garnish with fresh herbs of your choice. Serves 1.

CHAPTER 8

What's in Store?

Landis Store Hotel

At some point in their past, all of the structures in this chapter housed a
store of some type. It may have been a grocery, a clothing store, or, not
surprisingly, a general store. For the most part, the architecture is similar,
featuring long, fairly narrow rooms once used to display wares. We no
longer have the penny candy or the pickle barrel, but we can still enjoy the
ambiance of their past.

The Village Inn Restaurant

US 19 AND PA 108
NEW CASTLE, PA 16101
724-654-6851

Harlansburg was once a popular stopping point on the Pittsburgh-Erie Post Road, now US 19. Locals call this road Perry Highway, so named for Matthew Perry, later a commodore, who led troops through here during the War of 1812.

Harlansburg, now part of New Castle, was settled by Jonathan Harlan, who arrived around 1797 to live on his four-hundred-acre land grant. Although many people passed through, the town never grew much larger than about two hundred residents. By 1877, the town and the traffic through it supported three general stores, several churches, two blacksmiths, clothing and shoe stores, three doctors, a drugstore, a gristmill, and a post office. The prospect of oil created a heyday in Harlansburg. The Aladdin Oil Company of New Castle drilled several wells, but no oil was found, and the village returned to its handful of residents.

While several Harlansburg landmarks remain, only two are still open. Unity Baptist Church, built in 1804, is one of the oldest churches in the area. The second landmark, the former Jordan's General Store, is now The Village Inn Restaurant.

Built in the 1870s, the general store was owned by the Jordan family until 1947. It reopened as The Village Inn on June 21 of that year. Pictures on the walls depict the opening day of the smorgasbord, as well as other important events in the inn's history. During the 1992 presidential campaign, Bill and Hillary Clinton and Al and Tipper Gore were dinner guests.

The wooden floors and tables lend a Shaker flavor; period antiques are located throughout the inn. The main dining room is pleasantly decorated with country murals depicting the buildings of Harlansburg in subtle tones.

The homey atmosphere is carried through in the food. Karen found the Beer-Battered Perch delicious, served nugget-style rather than in one large fillet to maximize crispness. Debbie's choice was the Chicken and Biscuits, served just as Grandma used to. The accompanying vegetables—Corn and Peas the night we visited—were served family-style. Both were good, but the Peas, complemented by Pearl Onions, were a real treat. Homemade Raisin Buns served with Cinnamon Spread, both of which are available to take home, rounded out the meal—except, that is, for Karen's Raspberry Vanilla Custard, which she declared to be as delicious as the rest of the feast.

The Village Inn is a casual restaurant perfect for family dining. Its location makes it popular with both visitors to the train museum next door and travelers on nearby Interstate 79.

PARMESAN CHICKEN POT PIE

Pastry

2½ cups flour
½ teaspoon salt
½ cup Parmesan cheese
2 tablespoons parsley
¼ teaspoon pepper
½ cup chilled butter
3 to 4 tablespoons ice water

Sift flour and salt into a wide bowl. Stir in Parmesan, parsley, and pepper. Cut in butter until mixture resembles coarse crumbs. Gradually add ice water until a dough is formed. Knead slightly to ensure mixture is evenly combined. Place onto a lightly floured surface, roll out to a 10-inch circle, place in a pie pan, and set aside.

Filling

3½ cups chicken broth
2 medium white onions, quartered
1 cup white potatoes, peeled and diced
1 cup peeled yams, diced
¾ to 1 teaspoon sage
¼ teaspoon pepper
2 medium carrots, cut in ¼-inch rounds
2 cups broccoli florets
½ cup celery, diced
½ cup flour
5½ tablespoons soft butter
3 cups chicken, cooked and chopped
1 egg, beaten

Bring chicken broth to a boil in a large saucepan. Cook onions, potatoes, yams, sage, and pepper in broth for about 10 minutes until potatoes are tender. Add carrots, broccoli, and celery and continue cooking about 5 minutes. Meanwhile, combine flour and butter to make top crust. Pinch off small pieces of dough and stir into boiling broth to thicken to a stewlike consistency. Stir in chicken. Pour into pastry shell. Add top crust and seal well; brush top with egg. Bake at 425 degrees for 15 minutes, then reduce heat to 325 degrees for 15 more minutes. Serves 4.

CHOCOLATE CARAMEL PECAN CHEESECAKE

2 cups vanilla wafer crumbs
6 tablespoons margarine, melted
14-ounce bag caramels
5-ounce can evaporated milk
1 cup pecans, toasted and chopped
2 8-ounce packages cream cheese, softened
½ cup sugar
1 teaspoon vanilla
2 eggs

½ cup semisweet morsels, melted
whipped cream, if desired
pecan halves, if desired

In a medium bowl, combine crumbs and margarine until well mixed. Press into the bottom and slightly up the sides of a springform pan. In a saucepan, melt caramels with milk over low heat, stirring frequently until smooth. Pour over crust and top with chopped pecans. Combine cream cheese, sugar, and vanilla and mix at medium speed until well blended. Add eggs 1 at a time, mixing well after each addition. Blend in melted chocolate, then pour over pecan layer. Bake at 350 degrees for 40 minutes. Loosen cake from rim of pan and cool before removing rim. Chill. Garnish with whipped cream and pecan halves. Serves 8 to 10.

5018 BAKERSTOWN ROAD
GIBSONIA, PA 15044
724-625-3252

A local landmark since 1914, The Pines Tavern was built as a bakery and ice cream stand for a farmer's wife and daughter. It later became a grocery, a gas station, a speakeasy, a dance hall, and the local watering hole. Wealthy Pittsburgh families such as the Kaufmanns frequented the tavern while staying at their nearby country homes.

The Pines Tavern recently celebrated its twentieth year under the Novak family. Its resurgence has included a change in ambiance from that of a tavern and dance hall to that of a quaint, charming inn. Guests frequently comment to owner Mike Novak that The Pines Tavern reminds them of a special place somewhere else that they've either experienced or read about—for Karen, it was an upscale English pub; for Debbie, it was the genteel antebellum South. Linen tablecloths and fresh flowers grace the tables. The wallpaper and accessories have been carefully chosen with an eye to charm and comfort.

The wine list was chosen in this same spirit, a down-to-earth selection featuring many American wineries. Menu choices include such entrées as Turkey and Wild Rice Tart, Pecan-Crusted Chicken, and a Chicken Salad Club Sandwich served with Blue Cheese Mayonnaise. All the selections are familiar foods and comfortable favorites uniquely prepared and presented.

Regardless of your heritage, you are sure to be transported into yesteryear during the month of December at The Pines Tavern. While the fireplace crackles cheerily, the rooms throughout the restaurant are festooned with traditional decorations and lovely pieces of holiday needlework, done primarily by Mike's sister, Debbie. The tavern hosts an annual Christmas dinner, a five-course meal based on the traditional cuisine of a particular country or region. Previous events have included the Old English Christmas, the German Christmas Dinner, and the Pennsylvania Christmas Heritage Dinner.

Once restaurant-goers experience The Pines Tavern, whether at Christmas or any other time of year, they are anxious to partake of other special dining activities hosted by the culinary staff or sponsored by the restaurant. For that, they can thank the Novak family, which continues to focus on simple pleasures, flavorful food, warm surroundings, and good company.

RASPBERRY PIE

Crust

2½ cups flour
¼ cup brown sugar
1 tablespoon cinnamon
½ teaspoon salt
½ cup vegetable shortening
½ cup chilled butter
6 to 7 tablespoons ice water

Blend flour, sugar, cinnamon, and salt in a food processor. Add shortening and butter; cut in using a pastry blender or by turning food processor on and off until mixture resembles coarse meal. Blend in enough ice water to form moist lumps. Gather dough into a ball. Divide in half and flatten each piece into a disk. Wrap in plastic wrap and chill for 1 hour before rolling out. Roll out top and bottom crusts and fit bottom into an 8-inch deep pie pan.

Raspberry filling

5 cups frozen (not thawed) red raspberries
1 cup granulated sugar
2½ tablespoons dry tapioca
¼ cup lemon juice
Vanilla Sauce (see next column)

Combine raspberries, sugar, tapioca, and lemon juice in a large bowl. Pour filling in crust. Cover with top crust, fold under edges, and make slits in top to vent steam. Place on a cookie sheet and bake at 350 degrees for about 1 hour until top is golden brown and juices bubble. Cool. Serve with Vanilla Sauce. Yields 1 pie.

VANILLA SAUCE

2 eggs
1 cup sugar
3 tablespoons flour
2 cups heavy cream
1½ tablespoons vanilla

Slightly beat eggs in the top of a double boiler. Mix in sugar and flour, then gradually stir in cream. Cook over simmering water, continuing to stir, for 10 to 15 minutes until slightly thickened. Cool to room temperature, then stir in vanilla. Refrigerate. Serve over Raspberry Pie. Yields 3 cups.

1514 EAST CARSON STREET
PITTSBURGH, PA 15203
412-381-5610

From the late 1800s until the last quarter of the twentieth century, Pittsburgh's South Side was comprised of families who made their living in the steel mills. Bars were plentiful along Carson Street, where men stopped off for a brew or two after a hard day's work. In and among the bars, on a convenient corner of East Carson Street, the South Side's main drag, sat Woshner's Haberdashery. As the steel industry declined, so did the South Side. The haberdashery closed, as did many other local businesses.

The South Side experienced a "Yuppie" influx during the 1980s, as young professionals flocked to restore the area, which was convenient to their downtown jobs. Woshner's Haberdashery was the site of one of the earliest renovations. It is now Mario's South Side Saloon, a rollicking eatery and bar that refuses to take itself too seriously.

The facade looks much like it did when the building served as a haberdashery. Mario's has the original tin ceiling, an original staircase, and much of its original woodwork. The conversion from retail space to eating establishment was done in keeping with the era of the old haberdashery, as is evident in the immense wooden back bar and the bench seating with etched-glass dividers. The wooden booths along the brick walls occupy the niches where cupboards once displayed clothing. Overlooking the immense bar are balconies filled with tables and chairs. The several small dining rooms upstairs were once the living quarters of the Woshner family. Among our favorite features are the pocket doors upstairs, the stained-glass windows behind the bar that honor various sports figures, and the moose head to the left of the bar.

The menu at Mario's is extensive. The interesting collection of sandwiches includes the Crunchy Chinese Chicken Sandwich and the Crusty Meat and Potato Caesar Sandwich, both of which captured our fancy and pleased our palates. A Mario's favorite is the Temperature Soup, priced daily according to the outside temperature at nine o'clock in the morning.

So much for history and cuisine, now on to the really important information . . . which is, if you want to imbibe a yard of beer, this is the place to go! This is a skill in which Karen thought only the mad English indulged. Mario's has initiated hundreds of people into the First Down Club, the only requirement for which is that you must quaff ten yards of beer. Or if you're feeling ambitious, try for membership of the Touchdown Club, for which you need consume a hundred yards of beer! For the less thirsty, Mario's serves half-yards and beer by the foot.

PASTA DIABLO

1 red pepper
1 yellow pepper
1 green pepper
1 medium onion
1 cup mushrooms
3 banana peppers
5 pepperocini
¼ cup butter
1 tablespoon salt
1 tablespoon basil, crushed
1 tablespoon oregano, crushed
1 teaspoon red pepper, crushed
3 12-ounce cans tomato juice
2 cups tomato purée
1 pound penne pasta (or favorite pasta)

Slice all vegetables and lightly sauté them in butter. Add salt and spices and continue to cook over medium heat for about 5 minutes. Stir in juice and purée and bring to a simmer. Lower heat and cover. Cook pasta according to package directions. Place pasta on a serving plate and ladle sauce over top. Serves 4.

Note: For an extra treat, serve with either blackened chicken or sautéed shrimp.

PASTA GAMBINO

4 large tomatoes, diced
2 scallions, chopped
1 tablespoon garlic, chopped
5 fresh basil leaves, chopped
2 teaspoons salt
¼ cup olive oil
⅛ cup white wine
12 ounces fettuccine (or favorite pasta)
⅛ cup feta cheese
⅛ cup walnuts, chopped

Sauté tomatoes, scallions, garlic, basil, and salt in olive oil until scallions are translucent. Deglaze pan with white wine. Cook pasta according to package directions. Place pasta on a serving plate and ladle sauce over top. Sprinkle with feta cheese and walnuts. Serves 4 as a side dish.

35 CHAMBERSBURG STREET
GETTYSBURG, PA 17325
717-337-3739

The Blue Parrot Bistro is located on the site of one of the earliest houses built in Gettysburg. For eight years beginning in 1850, a Mrs. Schwartz used the building as an oyster parlor. After its tenure selling oysters, the structure became a private residence, noted in historical records to have housed "a good many surgeons." Based on such accounts, it is thought that the structure may have been used as a field hospital during the Civil War.

After the war, Mr. E. H. Minnigh opened a confectionery here, serving sweet treats from 1868 until his death in 1903. At the onset of the Roaring Twenties, the candy shop was remodeled and reopened as the Blue Parrot Tea Room. Located just off what is now US 30, also known as the Lincoln Highway, the tearoom quickly earned a national reputation. It continued in operation for thirty years, until it was sold in the mid-1950s and converted into the Adam's House Tavern.

The latest change in ownership came in 1988, when this historic building was purchased by Holly Giles, Gary Yount, and chef Alison Giles McIlhenny. Out of respect for Old Town Gettysburg, and with an eye on the building's varied past, they decided to call it the Blue Parrot Bistro.

People have different conceptions of what defines a bistro. Some might say it's an upscale, sophisticated eatery, while others describe it as a casual, homey, relaxed spot to grab a meal. The Blue Parrot's eclectic collection of furnishings and its rotating exhibit of work by local artists help to create an atmosphere that actually fulfills both perceptions. Fresh flowers, white table linens, and Tiffany lamps create a fresh, crisp look. The beam ceilings, original brick fireplaces, and simple whitewashed, half-paneled walls contrast with the furnishings and help create a relaxed ambiance.

Debbie was dining elsewhere when I visited the Blue Parrot Bistro. It was a cold fall evening, and the bistro was extremely busy. I sat in a corner booth and sampled the White Bean and Sausage Soup, together with a selection of fresh Breads and a small ramekin of Olives. The Sweet Blueberry Cornbread was particularly unusual.

The menu is extensive, and I had difficulty deciding among the Pasta Purses (stuffed with mushrooms and tossed in a fresh Tomato Provençal Sauce), the Bistro Meat Loaf (served with Creamy Garlic Polenta), and the Seared Salmon (served with Red Wine and Butter Sauce on a bed of Roasted Garlic Mashed Potatoes). I eventually opted for the salmon and was not disappointed in my choice. Piping hot, it was seared almost crisp on top but was delightfully moist and flavorful underneath. The servings here are large, and I was absolutely full by the time my server presented the dessert tray. The large selection included Boysenberry Cheesecake,

Lemon Torte, Chocolate Divinity, and, most tempting of all, Triple Chocolate Layer Cake. Reluctantly, I left the bistro, and before I could reach the door, other enthusiastic diners had already been seated at my table. It was truly a reflection of good service and exceptional food.

ROASTED RED PEPPER AND GARLIC MASHED POTATOES

8 baking potatoes, peeled and cut into large pieces
1 stick butter
½ cup half-and-half
½ red pepper, roasted, skin removed
½ green pepper, roasted, skin removed
½ yellow pepper, roasted, skin removed
1 head garlic, roasted, skins removed
salt and cayenne pepper to taste

Place potatoes in a large pan and cover completely with water. Bring water to a boil and simmer potatoes until tender. Place butter and half-and-half in a small saucepan and heat until butter is melted. Drain potatoes and mash by hand with a potato masher. Add butter mixture to potatoes very slowly, making sure to add just enough to moisten potatoes. Mash the potatoes again. Finely chop peppers and garlic and stir into mashed potatoes. Season with salt and cayenne pepper. Serves 8.

BAKED ASPARAGUS WITH PROSCIUTTO AND SHALLOT BUTTER

28 stalks asparagus
4 very thin slices prosciutto
4 heaping teaspoons Parmesan cheese, grated
1 cup butter
½ cup white wine
4 large shallots, peeled and sliced
salt and white pepper to taste

Preheat oven to 400 degrees. Blanch asparagus in boiling water for 2 to 3 minutes until just tender. Drain asparagus and shock in an ice-water bath. Wrap each slice of prosciutto around 7 asparagus stalks. Place bundles in a baking pan and top each with a heaping teaspoon of Parmesan. Bake in oven until Parmesan is lightly browned.

To make Shallot Butter, melt butter with wine. When butter is completely melted, add shallots and allow to simmer for 5 minutes. Season with salt and white pepper.

Remove asparagus bundles from oven to individual plates and top each with ¼ of the Shallot Butter. Serves 4.

2901 PENN AVENUE
PITTSBURGH, PA 15222
412-434-0451

The traditional red-brick storefront at the corner of Twenty-ninth Street and Penn Avenue in Pittsburgh's Strip District gives little hint at what lies beyond the front door of this pharmacy turned ice-cream parlor. Much of the original Art Deco interior is there, including the inlaid, diamond-patterned, amber and black terrazzo floor and the cream-colored hammered-tin ceiling. Lining the walls are wooden booths and glass display cases made from either mahogany or cherry, with inlaid cream-colored triangles. The original "inverted wedding cake" light fixtures—so called because of the styling and the frosted glass—are there, too.

If all this isn't enough to make you feel like you're on a movie set, the soda fountain certainly will. Sixteen feet in length, it's made from marble and has ten built-in cast-iron stools. The seats of the stools were styled to resemble bottle caps from the early days of Coca-Cola.

James Klavon and his wife, Mary, opened the pharmacy in the early 1900s. It was a neighborhood place where people frequently dropped in just to say hello. The Klavons continued to operate the business until James's death in 1979, after which the building was boarded up.

The couple's grandchildren grew up listening to stories about the pharmacy, including one in which the Klavons' son, Raymond, had to be rescued from the store. Every spring around St. Patrick's Day, the basement would flood. One year, Raymond went to move things from the basement to higher ground. The water rose faster than expected, and he had to be rescued out of the pharmacy window. A marker shows just how high the water was that day.

It was memories such as these that prompted the grandchildren, including Raymond's son, Ray Jr., to reopen Klavon's as an ice-cream parlor. Like the interior, the menu is from the past. Where else can you still get Phosphates, Malts, and Egg Creams? We had our daughters with us the day we visited, so we insisted on a healthy lunch before we enjoyed the treats. The sandwiches that we tried—the Chicken Salad, the Italian, and the Turkey, Ham, and Provolone—were all very good. The special of the day, Beef and Broccoli Salad, was excellent. Sesame seeds gave it a slightly nutty flavor, and the dressing had a hint of ginger and soy sauce.

Then it was on to what Klavon's does best— ice cream! It was difficult to choose. The selection of floats includes a traditional root beer float called the Monongahela Float, a Coke float listed as the Allegheny Float, and the Ohio Float, made from orange soda and vanilla ice cream. The diet-conscious might prefer the Free Float, made from Diet Coke and sugar-free vanilla ice cream. We ordered two Hot Fudge Sundaes, a Butterscotch

Sundae, and a Crème de Menthe Shake. The sundaes all got a finishing dollop of Flavored Whipped Cream, made on the premises.

People wandered in and out on the day we visited, looking at the old pharmacy books and other memorabilia, including the individually wrapped greeting cards that used to be sold here. Many had grown up coming to the pharmacy and remarked on how similar it is today. One thing certainly hasn't changed. Customers are still encouraged to come in, have some refreshments, and reminisce.

TURTLE SUNDAE

Sundae

4 tablespoons hot fudge sauce, divided
1 large scoop chocolate ice cream
1 large scoop vanilla ice cream
2 tablespoons hot caramel sauce
2 tablespoons pecans, toasted and salted
¼ cup Amaretto Whipped Cream (see below)
1 maraschino cherry with stem on

Drizzle 2 tablespoons of the hot fudge sauce into a sundae glass. Add chocolate ice cream and vanilla ice cream. Drizzle remaining hot fudge sauce and hot caramel sauce over top. Sprinkle pecans on top. Finish with a large dollop of Amaretto Whipped Cream and top with a cherry. Serves 1.

AMARETTO WHIPPED CREAM

2 cups heavy whipping cream
¼ cup to ½ cup amaretto liqueur
1 teaspoon powdered sugar

Combine ingredients in a large bowl and whip until soft peaks form. Store in an airtight container in refrigerator for up to 1 week. Yields 2 cups.

LANDIS STORE HOTEL

4 BALDY HILL ROAD
BOYERTOWN, PA 19512
610-845-2324

Around 1800, Samuel Landis was said to own "all the property in these parts." He allowed a man by the name of John Weller to build a hotel at the crossroads atop Baldy Hill outside what is now Boyertown. After running the establishment for many years, Weller sold it to Landis, who continued its operation. Years later, Samuel Tee rented space in the hotel and operated a store there. Landis eventually took that over, too, adding a post office when he became postmaster in 1853. That addition saved local residents from an arduous three-mile journey to pick up their mail.

At the elder Landis's death, his sons John and Nathan took over the store and hotel. The year 1872 saw John remodel the hotel, a popular spot after the Civil War because of its location. The view was pleasing, and the breezes atop the hill blew gently on warm summer nights. During that time, the eccentric Dr. Augustus Knoske—the only physician for many miles—was a resident of the hotel. He was known for always wearing a coat, even in the warmest weather, as he traveled on foot throughout the countryside, dispensing medicine from his coat pockets.

The building continued in use as a general store and bar until 1970, when Ralph and Helen Hoffman decided to turn it into a restaurant. The general-store business was waning, and regular tavern customers frequently asked for food. The Hoffmans started with Steaks, Boiled Shrimp, Baked Potatoes, and Salad on the menu, then expanded as customers asked, "Is that all you have?" Ralph and Helen viewed the operation more as a service than a business. But the people came, and have continued to come. The Hoffmans' daughter, Janet, and her husband, Gary Henshaw, continue the operation today with the same personal touch and dedication to quality that have made this place a landmark.

Karen was occupied elsewhere the day I visited the Landis Store Hotel. All the ingredients served here are the freshest available, Gary told me as I enjoyed my dinner. Some of them come from the orchards just across the road. The sun-dried tomatoes that garnished my deliciously tender Veal Marengo had been dried by the Henshaws themselves. Entrées come with a choice of two side dishes. I chose a Tossed Salad and the Sweet Potato Soufflé. The sweet potatoes were served in a ramekin piping hot just out of the oven. They were so light and tasty that I think I could get even the staunchest non–sweet potato eaters in my family to enjoy them!

I would have been equally happy with many of the choices on the menu, including the Caribbean Shrimp Soup and the Creamy Onion Soup. The Sweet Potato Shrimp Cakes sounded interesting, as did the Almond-Crusted Crab Cakes and the Pumpkin Risotto. Pumpkin Pie and a beautiful Apple Tart were on the menu, to take full advantage of fall's bounty. I was also drawn to the Chocolate Pecan Raspberry Tart and the

White Chocolate Mousse Torte with Raspberry Center. In the end, I opted for the Banana Macadamia Kahlua Crème Brûlée. The bananas were caramelized with a mixture of sugar, butter, and Kahlua, then spooned on top of the Crème Brûlée, all of which was then garnished with chopped macadamia nuts. When a dish is this tasty, calories don't matter!

PEACH SHORTCAKE

½ cup butter
2 cups flour
2 tablespoons sugar
2 teaspoons baking powder
½ teaspoon salt
1 egg
⅔ cup light cream
4 fresh peaches, peeled and sliced
½ teaspoon nutmeg
1 teaspoon almond extract
4 tablespoons butter, softened
1 cup whipped cream

Preheat oven to 350 degrees. Butter and flour an 8-inch cake pan. Cut butter into flour, sugar, baking powder, and salt until mixture resembles crumbs. In a small mixing bowl, beat egg and light cream. Add to dry mixture and combine thoroughly. Pour into cake pan and bake at 350 degrees for 20 to 25 minutes. Let cool for 10 minutes, then turn out onto cooling rack. Toss peach slices in nutmeg and sprinkle with almond extract. When cake is cool, cut it in half and butter the 2 cut sides with 4 tablespoons butter. Spread peaches and whipped cream on half of the cake and place the other half on top. Serves 8.

VEAL MARENGO

3-pound veal roast
3 tablespoons vegetable oil
salt and pepper to taste
½ cup madeira wine
4 cups veal stock
6 shallots, chopped
4-ounce package shiitake mushrooms
6 tablespoons butter, divided
½ cup sun-dried tomatoes, diced
¾ cup black olives
zest of 2 oranges, chopped and divided
2 12-ounce bags fresh spinach
2 tablespoons fresh parsley, chopped

In a large frying pan, brown veal in oil and season with salt and pepper. Place veal in a roasting pan with madeira, stock, and shallots. Cover with foil and bake for about 3 hours at 375 degrees. Remove veal to a platter. Sauté mushrooms in 3 tablespoons of the butter and add to pan of veal drippings, along with sun-dried tomatoes, olives, and all but 1 teaspoon of the orange zest. Add salt and pepper if desired. Reduce sauce to desired thickness. Sauté spinach in remaining butter until just cooked. Cut veal into 1-inch slices and place on a bed of sautéed spinach. Spoon sauce over top. Sprinkle with fresh parsley and remaining orange zest. Serves 6.

ROOSEVELT TAVERN

YORK, PA

400 WEST PHILADELPHIA STREET

YORK, PA 17404

717-854-7725

For the sum of $275.00, blacksmith Frederick Schaale bought the lot at the southwest corner of Philadelphia and Penn Streets in York. For that purchase, made in 1860, Schaale paid an annual property tax of $2.12. Three years later, he built his residence on the plot of land. In 1868, a relative by the name of Charles Schaale moved into the home and began work as a merchant, tailor, and grocer.

Through the years, the property passed through several owners and uses. In 1911, John Schrantz opened a cigar store here bearing his name. Over the next couple of decades, the cigar shop was variously called Dairyman Brothers, Miller Brothers & Dellinger Cigars, West End Smoke Shop, and, finally, the Roosevelt Cigar Store. The popularity of cigar stores during that time was directly related to the passage of Prohibition. Many cigar stores around the country were fronts for back-room game parlors and speakeasies. Such was the case with the Roosevelt Cigar Store.

Not surprisingly, when Prohibition was repealed in 1933, the Roosevelt Cigar Store's sign came down. In its place, owner Washington Lauer erected a sign that read *Roosevelt Tap Room*. When James Burkholder purchased the business in 1948, he added a dining room and changed the name to Roosevelt Tavern.

Today, Roosevelt Tavern is a thriving restaurant, one of York's most popular. We arrived for a very late lunch and were surprised to find it still fairly crowded at two o'clock in the afternoon. The dining room is decorated with today's creature comforts, but the beamed, stucco ceiling and the dining-room fireplace gave us a glimpse into the establishment's past.

The menu offers a wide variety of soups, appetizers, and entrées for seafood lovers. And be sure to save room for dessert. Debbie has expended many calories during our travels looking for the perfect coconut pie. We discovered it here—Mounds Pie! The coconut filling in between the Oreo Crust and the Fudge Topping was superb—sweet but not too sweet, and lusciously creamy. The portion was large, and we certainly could have shared. However, each of us savored this addition to our list of all-time favorite desserts right down to the very last crumb.

APPLEJACK PORK

Pork

4 6-ounce center-cut boneless pork loins
½ cup flour
8 mushrooms, sliced
2 Granny Smith apples, sliced thin
1 cup Applejack Sauce (see next column)
4 cups wild rice, cooked

Cut pork into 2-ounce portions. Lightly flour meat and sauté in a medium frying pan until cooked through. Add mushrooms, apples, and Applejack Sauce. Cook until mushrooms and apples are hot. To serve, layer wild rice, then apples and mushrooms, then pork. Serves 4.

Applejack Sauce

2 cups apple cider
6 tablespoons dark brown sugar
2½ teaspoons cinnamon
¼ cup applejack brandy
2 tablespoons cornstarch
2 tablespoons water

Combine first 4 ingredients in a medium saucepan and bring to a boil. In a separate bowl, combine cornstarch and water. Stir cornstarch mixture into saucepan and bring to a boil again, stirring until thickened. Yields approximately 1½ cups.

CHAPTER 9

Let Freedom Ring

Dobbin House Tavern

One of the biggest—and most pleasant—surprises as we began our research was discovering that many of the establishments we wanted to include had at one time been stops on the Underground Railroad. This was a network of safe houses where escaping slaves could find shelter, food, and clothing before continuing to freedom. It was fascinating knowing that their time at these places significantly altered the course of their lives.

the Tavern
On the square

108 NORTH MARKET STREET
NEW WILMINGTON, PA 16142
724-946-2020

Someone once said, "Necessity is the mother of invention." That certainly holds true at The Tavern on the Square. After graduating from nearby Westminster College in 1931, Ernst and Cora Durrast saw a need for a quality dining establishment in the New Wilmington community. Obviously, that need was met, because their restaurant flourished against the odds during the Great Depression.

Necessity played an even bigger role in the tavern's future not too long afterward. The cook was sick and unable to come to work, and Cora Durrast was left without enough dough to make the rolls and no recipe to follow. Quickly improvising, she made do with the dough available, turning it into "Sticky Rolls." She didn't think much about her substitution until a customer called the following day to specifically request those Sticky Rolls. They've been a staple here ever since.

Built around 1850, the structure that houses The Tavern on the Square was originally the home of Dr. and Mrs. Seth Poppino. Its massive stone fireplace was uncovered during renovation of the restaurant and again stands proudly in the main dining room. What is now the Little House Gift Shop, located to one side of the house, served for almost thirty years as Dr. Poppino's medical office, where he took care of many area residents. He also took care of many escaped slaves, using the cellar to shelter them on their way to freedom in Canada. The smaller dining room on the first floor is also a special room. Originally a parlor, it saw at least one daughter born, baptized, and married within its walls.

Tradition is obviously important at The Tavern on the Square. After operating the restaurant for sixty-six years, the Durrasts sold it in 1997. New owners Sandy and David Aquaro have maintained the tradition of serving Sticky Rolls and keeping the recipe a strictly guarded secret. Another important tradition is "calling the menu." Although there is a printed menu in the reception area, it has long been the practice for the wait staff to recite the lengthy menu, which sometimes includes as many as thirty items.

The food is traditional as well. It includes offerings such as Ham, Meat Loaf, and Chicken Pie. There are also several seafood selections. An appetizer, two vegetables, a starch, salad, Sticky Rolls, and dessert accompany each entrée. A don't-miss item is the Spinach Salad, served with Egg and Cheese Dressing, which is not meant to be poured like typical salad dressings, but is more like a very creamy egg salad. We'd never seen anything like it but really enjoyed it. If you're lucky, the tavern will also be serving Baked Apples and Cranberries. Warm and tart, they are just delicious. The Sticky Rolls were the highlight of our meal, brought warm just after we were seated. They definitely disappeared too quickly!

Guests at nearby tables saved theirs to take home. We didn't have that kind of self-control and bet you won't either.

HAM LOAF

3 eggs
16-ounce can crushed pineapple, drained, ½ cup juice reserved
2 cups brown sugar, divided
½ pound ground sausage
2 tablespoons mustard
½ loaf bread, processed into breadcrumbs
5 pounds ground ham
½ cup apple juice
1 teaspoon cinnamon
½ teaspoon nutmeg

In a mixing bowl, combine eggs, pineapple, 1½ cups of the brown sugar, sausage, mustard, breadcrumbs, and ham until thoroughly mixed; mixture should have the texture of meat loaf.

Form into 2 logs. Place on a jelly roll pan and bake at 350 degrees for 30 minutes. Remove from oven, add 1 cup of water to pan, and bake another 15 minutes. Combine remaining ½ cup brown sugar with ½ cup reserved pineapple juice, apple juice, cinnamon, and nutmeg. Remove loaves from oven and pour pineapple juice mixture over top. Return to oven for 10 to 15 minutes until completely cooked. Serves 10 to 12.

EGG AND CHEESE DRESSING

½ to 1 cup mayonnaise
1 teaspoon vinegar
½ teaspoon salt
dash of Tabasco sauce
½ cup celery, chopped
½ cup onion, grated
3 hard-boiled eggs, chopped
¾ cup Old English sharp cheddar cheese, grated

Combine mayonnaise, vinegar, salt, and Tabasco. Stir in celery, onions, eggs, and cheese. Serves 6.

Note: The Tavern on the Square serves this dressing over fresh spinach.

The Back Porch

114 SPEERS STREET
LOWER SPEERS, PA 15012
724-483-4500

As the Monongahela River flows its course, allow yourself to be equally carried away. Drift back to the year 1785, when Henry Speers, Jr., bought land just a few steps from the river. His purchase was called the "Speers Intent." A young sycamore tree grew on that land, and in 1806, Speers, using local stone and fashioning handmade bricks from the river sand, built a home next to that tree. As the tree grew, so did the prosperity of the Speers family, who operated several ferries across the Monongahela. Cattle herded from the Western territories for market in Pittsburgh frequently crossed on the family's boats.

The ferry business and the home passed to future generations after the death of Henry Speers, Jr., in 1840. His youngest daughter, Nancy, married the son of Stephen Hill, the founder of Century Inn in Scenery Hill, Pennsylvania. She could little have imagined how her childhood home would be transformed into a restaurant as delicious and appealing as Century Hill, the home where she spent her married life.

More than a hundred years later, Joe Pappalardo had a dream for the old Speers homestead. He wanted to take the abandoned,

dilapidated brick home and turn it into a restaurant. In 1976, he, his supportive wife, and their six young children began the three-year renovation of what was to become The Back Porch. Only the exterior walls remained completely intact. The windows and flooring had to be repaired and replaced. The plaster that covered the original brick walls still remains in the stairs to the cellar and the upstairs offices. It has been rumored that somewhere behind that plaster is a secret tunnel leading from the house to the riverbank; that tunnel was used by escaping slaves. The plaster in the main downstairs dining room was removed, revealing the original bricks fired on the property back in 1806. The sycamore tree still stands, large and strong, beside the house.

The Back Porch continues to be a family affair, according to Patti Pappalardo Keller. She greets guests, takes reservations, and oversees the many subtle details involved in running a successful restaurant. Her mother still stops in from time to time, and her brother Joe Jr. is now the executive chef. Jamie Pappalardo Spadafore makes the restaurant's delicious desserts. Across the street is the Second Street Grille, also owned by the Pappalardos. It's a fun, casual, inexpensive restaurant where sister Michelle keeps everything going and brother Tim oversees the kitchen.

Like the members of the family, The Back Porch is warm. The taupe walls, the eclectic collection of candles and lamps, and the dual fireplaces crackling in the dining room give a homey feeling. Simple hutches both upstairs and downstairs house interesting collections; the birdhouses upstairs vary from cute to creative to unusual.

The menu also has a touch of the unusual. We

engaged in a great deal of discussion and negotiation the day we visited. Debbie chose the Salmon in Tangerine Sauce. The sauce was a perfect balance between sweet and tangy and was absolutely scrumptious! Karen selected the Roasted Vegetable Platter, which included potatoes, zucchini, yellow squash, carrots, and stuffed artichokes, accompanied by a deep-fried feta cheese triangle and a square of polenta topped with a fresh Tomato Salsa. The serving was plentiful and the flavor fabulous. Save room for the White Chocolate Cheesecake with Raspberry Sauce. It's a definite don't-miss item!

CANADIAN CHEDDAR CHEESE SOUP

1 stick butter
1 cup onions, chopped
½ cup flour
7 cups chicken stock
4 cups milk
1 pound cheddar cheese, shredded
salt, pepper, and basil to taste

Melt butter in a large saucepan. Add onions and sauté for 1 minute. Add flour to make a roux. Turn off heat and stir until very thick. Add chicken stock, stirring until well blended. Return to heat and bring to a boil. Reduce heat and add milk. Heat until warm but do not boil. Slowly stir in cheese until completely melted. *Do not boil.* Season with salt, pepper, and basil and serve immediately. Serves 8.

GRILLED TUNA STEAK WITH FETA CHEESE AND LEMON HERB VINAIGRETTE

2 cups olive oil
2 cups vegetable oil
¼ cup plus 2 tablespoons lemon juice
¾ cup red wine vinegar
1½ teaspoons fresh garlic, chopped
¼ cup dried oregano
¼ tablespoon salt
³/₈ teaspoon freshly ground pepper
6 6-ounce fresh tuna steaks, either albacore or
     yellowfin
12 tablespoons feta cheese, crumbled

Place first 8 ingredients in a blender and pulse gently, mixing well to make Lemon Herb Vinaigrette. Set aside 2 cups for marinade and place the rest in the refrigerator to use as a salad dressing later. Marinate tuna in the 2 cups of Lemon Herb Vinaigrette in refrigerator for 2 hours. Remove tuna from marinade and place on warm grill. Grill about 5 minutes per side until tuna flakes easily with a fork. To serve, drizzle tuna with extra Lemon Herb Vinaigrette and sprinkle with feta cheese. Serves 6.

Note: Chef Joe Pappalardo suggests Pine Ridge Chenin Blanc or a French Riesling like Trimbach Emile Cuvee to accompany this dish. Serve tuna with grilled vegetables and a crisp green salad. For a salad variation using this recipe, grill tuna as directed, place on a bed of spring greens, calamata olives, red onions, and feta cheese, and sprinkle with Lemon Herb Vinaigrette. For a fajita variation, grill tuna as directed, flake into bite-sized chunks, and place on flour tortillas with feta cheese and Lemon Herb Vinaigrette. Roll tortillas, place on grill, and turn slowly until all sides are lightly browned. Each tuna steak should be sufficient for 3 tortillas.

89 STEINWEHR AVENUE
GETTYSBURG, PA 17325
717-334-2100

Just as the foundations of a young United States of America were being laid in the year 1776, so were the stones being placed in the foundation of the Dobbin House, Gettysburg's oldest and one of its most historic buildings. Four score and seven years later, the owners of the house probably sat on the porch listening and watching as President Abraham Lincoln delivered his famous speech at the national cemetery just a few hundred yards away.

Alexander Dobbin, born in Ireland in 1742, studied the classics there before bringing his bride, Isabella Gamble, to the New World. Shortly after arriving, Dobbin became the minister at Rock Creek Presbyterian Church, about a mile from Gettysburg. According to one source, he was "a man of keen foresight, highly respected by his peers." He is credited with playing a major role in the founding of Gettysburg.

In 1774, Reverend and Mrs. Dobbin bought three hundred acres in what eventually became Gettysburg and began construction on a farm and a building that was to be used both as their home and as a classical school. The home was so large partly because it was meant to house students and partly because of family necessity. Reverend and Mrs. Dobbin had ten children before her early death. And when the reverend remarried, it was to a widow with nine children of her own. In today's parlance, the classical school was a combination liberal-arts college and seminary. The first of its kind west of the Susquehanna River, the academy enjoyed a superb reputation for educating well-known and successful men of the day.

During the mid-1800s, a crawlspace in the house harbored slaves on their way to freedom. On the back stairs, there is a wall cabinet that slides back to expose a crawlspace big enough for four adults. This is thought to have been the first stop on the Underground Railroad north of the Mason-Dixon line.

Because of its proximity to the Civil War action at Gettysburg, the Dobbin House was shelled several times by both sides. After the battle was over and the armies departed, the home served as a hospital for the wounded soldiers of the North and the South.

Today, the Dobbin House stands much as it did all those years ago. Many colonial ladies and gentlemen dined here in a rich social environment, and today's diners do likewise. The menu reflects the tavern's history, with offerings such as a porridge of the day (Chicken Corn Chowder the day we dined), Fruit Fansey, Sparkling Cyder, and Karen's personal favorite, American Rebellion Tea. The pork recipe included here is one such example, having been handed down from generation to generation since the time the Dobbin family settled.

PENNSYLVANIA DUTCH PORK AND SAUERKRAUT

3 pounds pork, cubed
2 16-ounce cans sauerkraut
2 16-ounce cans chunky applesauce
⅔ cup onion, minced
⅓ cup bacon, cooked crisp and minced
⅓ teaspoon pepper
1½ teaspoons salt
2 teaspoons dry mustard
pinch of ginger
⅓ teaspoon rosemary
1 teaspoon celery seed
⅓ cup brown sugar

Place pork in a roasting pan and brown in a 400-degree oven. Combine all other ingredients in a large saucepan and mix well. Heat sauerkraut mixture slowly to a boil. Add pork and any juice in pan. Simmer on low for 1½ hours, stirring occasionally until pork is tender when squeezed. Serves 6 to 8.

BAKED KING'S ONION SOUP

6 cups beef stock
2 tablespoons sweet butter
6 medium onions, peeled and diced
1 cup stew beef, cut into ½-inch cubes
1 cup dry sherry
6 slices good-quality white bread
12 slices Swiss cheese
12 slices provolone cheese

Bring stock to a slow boil in a large saucepan. Melt butter in a skillet and sauté onions until they begin to yellow. Meanwhile, brown beef in another skillet. Add onions, beef, and sherry to the stock and simmer for 30 minutes.

When ready to serve, fill 6 ovenproof bowls with soup. Place 1 slice bread, 2 slices Swiss cheese, and 2 slices provolone (in that order) on top of each serving. Place under broiler until cheese browns. Serves 6.

WASSAIL

8 cups apple cider
8 cups rosé
1 cup lemon juice
½ teaspoon cinnamon
½ teaspoon nutmeg
¼ teaspoon cloves
¼ teaspoon ginger
2 cups brown sugar

Combine all ingredients in a stockpot or Dutch oven. Heat through and keep warm to serve. Yields 16 cups.

The Lardin House Inn

PA 21

MASONTOWN, PA 15461

724-583-2380

Before the United States of America was even a country, the Lardin House was built. Early maps show a dwelling, built around 1769, on the property. Written accounts describe how the home's attic dormers were used to spot approaching Indians in the early 1800s. The brick Georgian structure was owned by several families through the years, including the Rabbs and the Wilsons. At one time, the property was known as the Miller Plantation. Local history supports the belief that this home was a stop on the Underground Railroad. The graveyard for freed slaves located on the property lends credence to this claim.

During his young adulthood, William Lardin stood atop a hill looking down at this home and thought it would be nice to own it someday. While visiting relatives in the area, he was introduced to a young woman from Masontown who later became his wife. After serving with a unit from Butler, Pennsylvania, during the Civil War, Lardin received a medical discharge and went back to his hometown. He sought work in the oil fields, beginning as a laborer and working his way up through the company. After becoming a primary oil producer, he made as much as two thousand dollars per day, according to reports.

William Lardin was an oil tycoon by the time he purchased the house and property around 1877. He added the large windows and doorways, the slate mantelpieces, and the beautiful exterior gingerbread trim. He also supplied the farm with the finest animals money could buy, including Clydesdales, Longhorns, and other animals considered exotic in those days. Because of his notoriety throughout the area, the property was—and still is—known as Lardin Crossing.

The interior of the home is much as it was during Lardin's time. An antique Windsor pump organ sits just inside the front door. Also occupying the front hall are upholstered chairs and a settee from the period. Small dining rooms in the original parlor and sitting room flank either side of the hall. The inlaid floral design on the fireplace in each of the small dining rooms is duplicated in the cherry mantelpiece in the original dining room. This room has been trimmed in rose woodwork to match the taupe-and-rose floral wallpaper. Antiques are found throughout the home. The Tap Room, located in what was once Lardin's library, contains an antique backbar. During renovation, the home's original oven was discovered. It is now displayed in an alcove behind the Tap Room.

The menu contains a nice blend of traditional offerings such as Shrimp Scampi and Pasta Carbonara and more exotic options like Caribbean Red Snapper and Roasted Breast of Duck Jerome, served in a Melon-Raspberry Sauce. Our rolls, which came to the table straight out of the oven, melted in our mouths. The homemade dressings were a delicious accompaniment to the salad of spring greens. If you're a chocoholic, then be sure to save room for dessert here. The choice will be difficult, however, as more than half the selections on the day we visited featured chocolate as a major ingredient. Enjoy!

❦ SAUTÉED CHICKEN BREAST LARDIN ❧

4 8-ounce split, boneless chicken breasts
¼ cup butter, melted
2 cups button mushrooms, sliced
2 cups portabello mushrooms, sliced
1 tablespoon garlic, chopped
½ cup sun-dried tomatoes, chopped
¼ cup fresh parsley, chopped
1½ cups white wine
¾ cup heavy cream
salt and pepper to taste

In a large sauté pan, sauté chicken in butter until about halfway done. Add mushrooms, garlic, tomatoes, and parsley and sauté for 2 minutes. Deglaze pan with white wine, then cook to reduce by ½. Add cream and simmer to thicken. Season with salt and pepper. Serves 4.

❦   ❦   ❦   ❦   ❦   ❦

❦ ORANGE CHUTNEY GLAZE ❧

3 medium seedless oranges, diced
3 cups orange juice
1 pinch garlic, chopped
1 teaspoon salt
½ cup sugar
1 tablespoon fresh parsley, chopped
¼ cup cornstarch in 1 cup cold water

Combine first 6 ingredients in a large sauté pan and bring to a boil. Add cornstarch mixture and thicken. Cook 2 minutes. Remove from heat and chill. Yields 4 cups.

Note: This glaze goes well with fish and pork.

❦   ❦   ❦   ❦   ❦   ❦

Mendenhall Inn

PA 52
MENDENHALL, PA 19357
610-388-1181

The name Mendenhall dates back to at least 1275, during the reign of Edward I. The family came from the area around Wiltshire, England, and wrote the name as Mildenhall at that time. Family members John and Benjamin emigrated from England in 1685, at which time their last name evolved to Mendenhall.

Heirs of William Penn negotiated the sale of a thousand acres west of the Brandywine River to Benjamin Mendenhall in 1703. Benjamin's second son, Joseph, a captain in the Chester County militia during the Revolutionary War, settled on part of this land. He constructed a large barn and several other buildings around 1796. Benjamin's grandson Isaac also settled on the property, located in what was then referred to as Pennsbury township. Isaac's home, completed in 1838, later became one of the most important links in the Underground Railroad, helping slaves escape to Canada. The family had an excellent reputation as barn builders. Many Chester County barns were constructed by the Mendenhalls. Those built for other local antislavery sympathizers often included hiding places for slaves on the run.

Joseph's large barn has been integrated into the Mendenhall Inn. This main barn is thought to

have housed the mill for cutting the lumber that went into other area barns. Based on an old property plan, it is believed that the present lobby of the inn was one of the original farm buildings. Today, the large brick fireplace is the focal point of the room, which features many pieces of simple, farm-style furniture. Farm implements decorate the walls, and lantern sconces hang nearby. Off the lobby area are two dining rooms that are frequently used for special events.

Connecting this farm building with the old barn that houses the Tavern and the Mill Room is a walkway, which steers guests past two inviting terraces, a perfect setting for sipping a glass of Lemonade. The Tavern has an Old World feel about it, thanks in part to the several hunting prizes displayed atop the backbar. Hunting prints line the walls, and a rustic chandelier hangs overhead. The original bar is well worn, and the large fireplace is still in use during the winter months. On the stairs leading up to the Mill Room, signs from the old Mendenhall Lumber Mill are displayed alongside blacksmith signs from the same era. The original barn framing can be seen in the Mill Room, where the atmosphere has been attractively softened for modern-day diners. Stenciled shutters are at the windows, and stenciled wagon-wheel chandeliers are overhead.

Both the lunch and dinner menus at the Mendenhall Inn provide patrons with a wide variety of selections. The Mendenhall Luncheon is a popular choice. It's a fixed-price meal that allows guests to choose from among the Onion Soup, the Snapper Soup, and the House Salad, then from among the crepe of the day, the quiche of the day, Oysters Rockefeller, Clams Casino, and a Chicken Breast. Seafood is most definitely the house specialty. Eight of the appetizer selections feature seafood. There are eight seafood entrées as well, alongside options such as Tenderloin en Croûte, which is a tenderloin of beef covered with smoked cheddar and Mushroom Purée, baked in a puff pastry, and served with Bordelaise Sauce. The inn's version of Beef Wellington, it is served up deliciously different and is very tasty indeed. The poultry portion of the menu features not only Duck but also Pheasant and Quail, certainly a reflection of the Mendenhall Inn's early history.

BANANA FLAMBÉ

2 tablespoons granulated sugar
3 tablespoons butter
2 bananas, cut in half widthwise and lengthwise
3 tablespoons Meyer's dark rum
3 tablespoons banana liqueur
½ teaspoon cinnamon sugar
2 large scoops vanilla ice cream

Add sugar and butter to a hot Suzette pan, or flat-bottomed skillet, and caramelize. Add bananas and coat with caramel. Remove pan from flame. Add rum and banana liqueur. Return to flame and ignite. While pan is still ignited, sprinkle cinnamon sugar over top. Place ice cream into serving dishes. When flame subsides, place 4 banana pieces over ice cream and pour sauce on top. Serve immediately. Serves 2.

CHERRIES JUBILEE

2 tablespoons granulated sugar
½ lemon
3 tablespoons kirschwasser
3 tablespoons Peter Heering liqueur
10 dark sweet cherries, pitted
6 tablespoons cherry juice
2 large scoops vanilla ice cream

Heat a small pan and sprinkle sugar over bottom. When sugar is totally caramelized, place lemon on a fork and use it for stirring to speed up reinversion of hardened sugar. Once inversion is completed, remove pan from heat and add kirschwasser and Peter Heering. Flambé. Add cherries and juice; move cherries to side of pan to prevent them from being overcooked. Bring sauce to a froth. Place ice cream in serving dishes. Spoon 5 cherries over each scoop of ice cream and continue to thicken sauce until it coats a spoon. Spoon sauce over cherries and ice cream and serve. Serves 2.

Note: There are 3 variations on this recipe. You can sprinkle cinnamon sugar over cherries while liquor is still ignited; you can replace Peter Heering with crème de cacao or Vandermint; or you can replace kirschwasser with brandy.

The Thomas Lightfoote Inn

2887 SOUTH REACH ROAD
WILLIAMSPORT, PA 17701
570-327-9330

Thomas up den Groff and his brothers, Derrick and Abraham, came west to the Susquehanna Valley from Germantown, Pennsylvania. They were induced to settle here by their good friend Thomas Lightfoote, the original surveyor of the valley.

The up den Groff brothers were direct descendants of a signer of the Bill of Rights. They, like Lightfoote, were Quakers who believed in the equality of all men. When the family's plantation house was renovated before the Civil War, provisions were made for escaping slaves. A tunnel was dug from the nearby Susquehanna River into the basement of the home. In this manner, slaves traveling along the river could enter and leave the house unseen. Thomas up den Groff's grandson was a conductor on the Underground Railroad and risked his life many times during slave escapes. One young slave known as Levi was so appreciative of the family's kindness that he came back to the plantation after the war and lived with the up den Groffs as a free man. At his death, he was buried in the family cemetery as a token of the family's esteem for him.

The trapdoor used by escaping slaves to come from the tunnel into the main part of the house is located in the dining room at the front of the structure. We found it, after some careful searching. After all these years, it's still very hard to spot. This room is decorated in burgundy and has a lovely floral rug. The seating is intimate, with tables for two or four. A large working fireplace dominates the end wall. Copper utensils hang as they did in 1792, when the house was built. A large arrangement containing pine cones and a pheasant adorns the chimney above the mantelpiece. The decor is completed by a spinning wheel and antique toys quietly placed in the corner of the room.

We ate in the back dining room, which has mustard walls, wood paneling, hanging tapestries, a slate floor, and large windows that allow a wide view of the grounds. We started off with a salad and Seafood Bisque, which was delicious and chock-full of all the right ingredients. The Smoked Salmon Sandwich and the Stuffed Sole that followed provided extremely ample lunch portions. The dessert choices were four cakes, all of which sounded equally delicious. How were we to choose among Champagne Cake, Chocolate Mousse Cake, Chocolate Chambord Cake, and White Cake with Lemon and Raspberry Filling, frosted in Orange Cream? We chose to be guided by our server, and jolly good advice it was, too! As the saying goes, all good things must come to an end, and thus we departed, promising to return on our next visit to Lycoming County.

CHICKEN OREGANATO

4-pound roasting chicken, quartered
2 pounds potatoes, quartered
5 cloves garlic, chopped
juice of 1 lemon
½ cup olive oil
1½ cups chicken stock
1 teaspoon salt
½ teaspoon pepper
1 teaspoon paprika
2 teaspoons oregano

Preheat oven to 350 degrees. Place chicken in a deep roasting pan and surround with potatoes and garlic. In a separate bowl, combine lemon juice, olive oil, and chicken stock. Pour over chicken and vegetables. Sprinkle salt, pepper, paprika, and oregano over contents and bake for 1½ hours. To serve, divide chicken among 4 plates and surround with equal quantities of vegetables. Serves 4.

VEAL PAPRIKA

1 cup onions, chopped
3 pounds veal, cubed
¼ cup olive oil
¼ cup Burgundy
2 cloves garlic, quartered
1 cup tomatoes, crushed
2 cups water
¼ teaspoon cumin
2 teaspoons paprika
1 teaspoon salt
dash of cayenne pepper
6 1-cup servings of rice, pasta, or mashed potatoes

In a large pan, braise onions and veal in oil. Add burgundy to deglaze pan. Add next 7 ingredients. Bring to a boil, then reduce heat and simmer for about 45 minutes until veal is tender. Serve over rice, pasta, or mashed potatoes. Serves 6.

CHAPTER 10

A Ghost *of a* Chance

First Fork Lodge

With so much rich history at these restaurants, it's not surprising that rumors about individuals who were a part of that history linger. The stories might be about a previous owner, a guest, a passerby, or a neighbor. Regardless, each seems to be linked to strange occurrences or visitations from the spirit world. Although locals enjoyed regaling us with stories, we have no personal experiences to tell, other than those of good food and terrific atmosphere.

Since 1885

Riverside Inn

1 FOUNTAIN AVENUE
CAMBRIDGE SPRINGS, PA 16043
800-964-5173

The birth of Riverside Inn came in 1884, but its conception took place twenty-five years earlier, with the discovery of oil in nearby Titusville. That discovery caused "black gold fever" in the surrounding area. Dr. John H. Gray, a landowner along French Creek, was one of those infected. In early 1860, he was strolling along the bank of the creek with a metal probe when he discovered not oil but a spring. Over the next fifteen years, Gray paid little attention to his discovery—until, that is, rumors began to circulate that laborers who frequently drank from the spring never got sick. After accompanying a patient to Hot Springs, Arkansas, in 1884, Gray noticed the similarity between the water at the two sites in separate states. Upon returning home, he probed again and discovered four more jets of the same "special" spring water, which he used to treat dyspepsia and kidney and liver complaints. According to an old Riverside Inn pamphlet, he found that the "waters, unassisted, affected many cures." He erected a springhouse and began selling the mineral water at a "nominal price."

Riverside Inn, built near the springs by W. D. Rider in 1884, was one of the first health spas of its kind. Licensed physicians supervised treatments while guests indulged in Russian, Turkish, sea-salt, and mineral baths. In 1895, the hotel was sold to the William Baird family, who also purchased Gray's springhouse. At that time, numerous hotels were popping up around Cambridge Springs, the closest town. Thanks to its location a hundred miles from Pittsburgh, Buffalo, and Cleveland and its status as the halfway point on the route between Chicago and New York, Cambridge Springs flourished.

Like all fads, the mineral-water craze eventually died out. But during the fifty years of the Bairds' ownership, Riverside Inn developed into a complete resort. It was the last of Cambridge Springs' grand hotels.

Since purchasing the property in 1985, Michael and Marie Halliday have worked to re-create Riverside Inn's Victorian aura. Stepping into the lobby, we immediately noticed the original tile floor and the bellhops' bench. Today, it's cushioned, but back then, the bellhops sat straight and tall on the wooden bench waiting for someone to ring. Reminders of past glory adorn the lobby, from the key cubbyholes to the vintage cash registers. Along the adjoining hallway are historic pictures of the inn and other memorabilia. The most intriguing items are the stoneware jugs, which were placed outside bedroom doors by guests. It was the duty of the bellhops to collect them, walk the quarter-mile or so to the springs, fill them, and return them to the guests. And that was at six o'clock in the morning! Interestingly enough, Mrs. Halliday explained that some guests feel there are also relics that go unseen—namely, the spirits of two men and a woman, all in Victorian attire, who watch over the resurgence of Riverside Inn.

The multiple dining rooms are frequently in use for private parties, while the Victorian Room functions as a popular dinner theater. The Concord Room serves as the main dining area. On the lunch menu, you'll find familiar favorites such as a Club Sandwich, a Chef's Salad, and a Tuna Melt, as well as daily specials. The dinner menu includes Beef, Chicken, Veal, and Seafood choices. We found the food very good and reasonably priced. Combine all that with fabulous service and you have a terrific dining experience! But make other dining plans for the winter, because Riverside Inn is closed from late December until mid-April.

ARTICHOKE FROMAGE

6 canned artichokes, chopped
1 cup cream
2 teaspoons basil
1 teaspoon garlic, minced
¼ teaspoon salt
2 tablespoons Parmesan or Romano cheese
toast points

Combine all ingredients except toast points in a saucepan and simmer until thickened. Place in a baking dish under broiler until golden brown. Serve with toast points. Serves 2.

OLD-FASHIONED COUNTRY TOMATO SOUP

1 tablespoon butter
½ cup onions, diced
½ cup carrots, diced
½ cup celery, diced
2 cups fresh tomatoes, diced
1 tablespoon basil
1 tablespoon garlic, chopped
2 cups tomato juice
1 cup chicken stock
1 cup cream
¼ cup cornstarch
¼ cup water
salt and pepper to taste

In a 3- to 4-quart pot, melt butter and sauté onions, carrots, celery, and tomatoes until lightly browned. Stir in basil and garlic. Add tomato juice and chicken stock. Cook for 15 minutes. Add cream. Thicken with equal parts cornstarch and water. Add salt and pepper. Serves 6 to 8.

Historic Cashtown Inn circa 1797

1325 OLD US 30
CASHTOWN, PA 17301
717-334-9722

Actor Sam Elliott, who starred in the epic film *Gettysburg*, was a guest here during the making of the movie. Many of the scenes were actually filmed at this location. Dirt was hauled in to cover the parking lot and the road out front to create a landscape that echoed the authenticity of the inn.

Built in 1797 as the first stagecoach stop west of Gettysburg, the Old Hotel, as the inn was originally known, was a haven for weary travelers. Its name was changed as a result of how the owner did business. During that era, goods and services were frequently paid for by barter. However, the gentleman who ran this inn accepted only cash. Since the surrounding town had no name, travelers up and down the pike began referring to the area as "Cashtown." The name stuck, and, eventually, the Old Hotel's name was changed to Cashtown Inn.

Prior to the Battle of Gettysburg, the hotel served as the headquarters of Confederate general A. P. Hill. Civil War art and memorabilia decorate the dining room, the sitting room, and the adjacent tavern room. Glass-topped tables with jacquard cotton tablecloths provide comfortable seating for about twenty-five guests. Under the glass are maps of the Gettysburg campaign for diners to peruse while waiting to be served. The brick walls, the original fireplace, and the wide-plank bar at one end of the room add to the coziness of this casual dining area. At the back of the inn is a more formal dining room with linen tablecloths and napkins. Civil War music plays quietly in the background while guests enjoy classic country cuisine. On the front wall is an impressive mural of the inn, sketched and painted from memory by Gettysburg postmaster John Meckley, a relative of former owner Bud Buckley.

During our travels, we met a family from Boston who highly recommended Cashtown Inn's Herbal Mushroom and Cheese Casserole and its Soup Trio. We didn't have the Soup Trio, but we did try the chilled Pear Soup and the creamy Tomato Basil Soup. Both were wonderful and would be delicious accompaniments to a salad, topped with a choice of the inn's homemade dressings. The house dressing is Creamy White Chablis. For dieters, a fat-free French-Style Honey Pineapple is available. We also thought the Maple Dijon sounded interesting. No trace of Karen's Crab Imperial, served on foccacia bread, was left at the end of the meal; her empty plate spoke for itself.

While we were eating, we noticed a photograph of Jason Hoover, one of the innkeepers. Behind him in the picture was an aberration that looked vaguely like a spinal x-ray. The note on the back of the picture, from a 1999 guest, suggested that maybe it was something supernatural. She wasn't the first to capture such an image; similar pictures hang on the walls as well. It has been suggested that the spirit of a Civil War soldier may be at work. Regardless of whom the presence represents, the guest who sent the picture of Jason mentioned unusual experiences during her visit. Ours was very straightforward, but if you go, maybe the ghost will visit you, too.

BAKED BRIE WITH FRUIT

8-ounce wheel Brie cheese
¼ cup nuts (slivered almonds, pecans, or walnuts)
6 to 8 slices fresh fruit (strawberries, peaches, cantaloupe, or other melon)
1 sheet puff pastry
1 egg
1 cup milk
½ cup honey

Preheat oven to 350 degrees. Slice Brie horizontally and place nuts and fruit in the middle to make a Brie sandwich. Roll puff pastry to ⅛-inch thickness and wrap around cheese. Combine egg and milk to make an egg wash; seal pastry by brushing with egg wash. Bake about 10 minutes until pastry is golden brown. Remove from oven, drizzle with honey, and serve immediately. Serves 6 to 8 as an appetizer.

ARTICHOKE DIP CYNTHIA

10-ounce can artichoke hearts
2 3-ounce packages cream cheese
¼ cup mayonnaise
2 tablespoons chives
4 tablespoons salsa
½ cup cheddar cheese, grated
foccacia toast points

Preheat oven to 350 degrees. Drain and quarter the artichoke hearts. Combine next 5 ingredients thoroughly, then stir in artichokes. Place in a baking dish and bake 15 to 20 minutes until warm and bubbly. Serve with foccacia toast points for dipping. Serves 6 to 8.

Note: This recipe is named after chef Keeney's wife.

38 NORTH UNION STREET
MIDDLETOWN, PA 17057
717-944-5373

Definitely a grand old lady, this home was designed in the post–Civil War era, and its brownstone exterior and intricate, fanciful details reflect the optimism of its time. Extravagantly built in 1888 by Charles Raymond, the house went to Middletown National Bank twelve years later to pay off Mr. Raymond's creditors.

In 1898, Redsecker Young purchased the dwelling for the then-exorbitant sum of sixty-six hundred dollars! Four years later, the home passed into the hands of the locally prominent Simon Cameron Young, who eventually bequeathed it to his two daughters, Emman and Eliza. The house gradually deteriorated, but its beauty and craftsmanship were still evident when Herman and Sara Baum purchased it in 1949 and began their twenty-year occupancy. Alfred Pellagrini rescued the home in 1970, purchasing it just one day before it was scheduled to be demolished.

As was customary with Victorian architecture, the roof is peaked and gabled and has dormers and many gingerbread adornments. Most of the exterior windows are crowned with stained-glass transoms. An intricate stained-glass window signed by a Philadelphia artist decorates the semicircular landing on the staircase leading from the entry area. Other details include ball-and-spindle grilles, carved wainscoting, and inlaid ceramic floors. In the dining room to the left of the hall, the inlaid wooden floor is original, as is the richly colored wallpaper. The fireplaces have intricate woodwork, cubbyholes, and beveled mirrors. One of the home's unique features is what appear to be floor-to-ceiling windows in the dining room. Actually, they are doors that slide into the ceiling, allowing passage to the porch.

Enormous pocket doors separate the individual rooms from the rest of the house. Those that divide the original dining room from the parlor area are particularly beautiful because of the stained-glass inserts decorating the top halves of the doors. Pellagrini once heard footsteps behind the doors and called police about an intruder. But when they searched the mansion, they found no one. Research into the matter suggested that the footsteps may have belonged to the ghost of Emman Young, who is said to pace the floor mourning the young man she loved but was not allowed to marry.

In our window seat, tucked away in a cozy turret room off the parlor, we wondered if Emman might have sat in the same location, wistfully watching for her young man to walk by. We enjoyed the view of the nearby downtown as we lunched on Garlic Soup, salad, and the pasta special of the day, a Cinnamon-Basil Linguine made on the premises. Wanting to linger, we managed to find room for dessert. The Chocolate Louise was yummy, and the Tiramisu, which our waitress, Carolyn, had made, was declared by Karen the best she'd ever eaten.

STRACCIATELLA SOUP

4 cups fresh chicken broth
4 eggs
4 heaping tablespoons grated Parmesan or Romano
  cheese
pinch of nutmeg
pinch of salt
pinch of pepper
2 tablespoons fresh spinach, chopped

Heat broth to a boil. In a bowl, beat eggs, cheese, nutmeg, salt, and pepper. Add to stock. Remove from heat. Add spinach, stirring gently. Place in serving bowls and sprinkle additional grated cheese over top. Serves 4 to 6.

STEAK DIANE

2 tablespoons butter
1 teaspoon Tabasco sauce
2 tablespoons Worcestershire sauce
2 tablespoons fresh chives, minced
2 teaspoons lemon juice

salt and pepper to taste
2 3-inch-thick filets mignons, butterflied
6 tablespoons brandy
2 tablespoons cream sherry

Melt butter in a small sauté pan over medium-high heat, being careful not to burn. Add Tabasco, Worcestershire, chives, lemon juice, and salt and pepper. Place steaks in pan and sear on 1 side. Turn steaks. Blend brandy and sherry in a flambé cup and heat until mixture ignites; *be careful*. Pour flaming liquid over steaks, spooning sauce around meat until flame extinguishes. Continue cooking until meat reaches desired doneness. Serves 2.

FISH IN LEMON PEPPER
BRANDY SAUCE

¼ cup olive oil
½ cup butter or margarine
½ cup dry white wine
1 teaspoon salt
black pepper, ground coarse
2 tablespoons plus ¾ teaspoon lemon juice
4 8-ounce fish fillets of your choice
¼ cup brandy

Combine first 6 ingredients in a sauté pan. Add fish and cook each side on medium heat for about 3 minutes, depending on thickness. Flambé with brandy to finish. Squeeze additional lemon juice over fish just prior to serving, if desired. Serves 4.

First Fork Lodge

PA 872
AUSTIN, PA 16720
814-647-8644

If you're in the mood for a good story in addition to a delicious meal, both served up in a unique atmosphere, then First Fork Lodge is the place for you. During March, April, September, and October and around Christmas and New Year's as well, the Krafft family stages a dinner theater that tells the story of the Costellos, the original owners of First Fork Lodge. The four-course dinner consists of the soup du jour, possibly a Spinach Salad, entrées of Seafood Casserole and sliced Roast Beef, served with vegetables, and Bread Pudding for dessert. The story is full of intrigue and marital discord.

The house was built in 1883 by the owners of what was reported to be the largest tanning factory for shoe leather in the world at that time. Mr. Costello also owned the company store and the houses in which his workers lived. His brother owned the rest of the town. Since the Costellos ran the town, it's not surprising to learn that they built a jail cell in the basement of the family home. Anybody who broke the law was thrown into their personal brig until the next time an official lawman came to this rural area. Due to family problems that eventually led to the divorce of Mr. and Mrs. Costello, the family sold the home during the early 1900s.

In 1925, the family living in the house lost their daughter to measles. Her spirit has been reported wandering through First Fork Lodge. Many guests have mentioned seeing or hearing the twelve-year-old. Objects left in one room are found in another, and items are knocked over when no one is around. Once, when Linda Krafft was on the sofa taking a nap, a fire was laid in the wood-burning stove. Jack, her husband, thought Linda had done it; Linda thanked Jack for such a nice fire.

Focused on the myriad attention-drawing collectibles throughout the house, many guests never experience the ghost. Each room is filled with antiques and sundry items from Linda's many collections. Mantelpieces from Linda's childhood home, unexpectedly discovered at a local antique shop, can be found in the living room and the upstairs hallway. Every room houses a collection of hunting prizes such as deer heads, a fox, and other local game. Each bedroom at First Fork has a decor befitting its theme. You might find yourself deep in the forest in a tree-house bed surrounded by lush silk greenery out of which various stuffed animals peer.

The day we visited, Steve Brooks, a First Fork employee, entertained us with abundant stories as we toured the home. First Fork houses hunters and fisherman, as well as those just wanting to get away from it all. We recommend that you try the dinner theater, so as to get the full history of the lodge. Regardless, reservations are a must. The menu is predetermined but is sure to be delicious.

BREAD PUDDING WITH CARAMEL SAUCE

Bread Pudding

2 cups milk
¼ cup margarine
½ cup sugar
½ teaspoon nutmeg
1 teaspoon cinnamon
¼ teaspoon salt
2 eggs, beaten
6 cups homemade bread, cubed
½ cup raisins

Preheat oven to 350 degrees. Heat milk and margarine in a 2-quart saucepan over medium heat until margarine is melted. Set aside. Mix sugar, nutmeg, cinnamon, salt, and eggs in a large bowl. Stir in bread cubes and raisins. Pour milk over bread mixture, then transfer entire mixture to an ungreased 1½-quart casserole. Place casserole into a 13-by-9-inch pan. Pour boiling water into the pan until water is 1 inch deep. Bake 40 to 45 minutes. Serves 6 to 8.

Caramel Sauce

½ cup butter or margarine
1¼ cups brown sugar
2 tablespoons corn syrup
½ cup whipping cream

Melt butter in a medium saucepan over medium heat. Add sugar and continue cooking until it dissolves. Stir in corn syrup and cream. Continue cooking and stirring as mixture thickens; do not boil. When thickened, pour over top of Bread Pudding just before serving. Yields enough sauce for 1 batch of Bread Pudding.

PEACH-STUFFED FRENCH TOAST

2 28-ounce cans diced peaches
2 8-ounce packages cream cheese, softened
¼ cup walnuts, crushed
¼ teaspoon nutmeg
1½ teaspoons cinnamon, divided
2 teaspoons vanilla, divided
1 loaf Italian bread, cut into 1½-inch slices
¼ cup brown sugar
1½ tablespoons cornstarch
1½ tablespoons water
2 cups milk
6 eggs
1 tablespoon sugar
whipped cream

Drain 1 can of peaches, reserving juice. In a large mixing bowl, combine ½ can of drained peaches with cream cheese, mashing the peaches into the cheese. Add walnuts, nutmeg, ½ teaspoon of the cinnamon, and 1 teaspoon of the vanilla. Mix well with a fork and set aside.

Starting at the top of the bread slices, cut a pocket down into the bread about ¾ inch from each side. *Do not slice all the way to the bottom.* Stuff the pocket with 2 to 3 tablespoons of cream cheese mixture. Place the remaining 1½ cans of peaches, with juice from both cans, into a large saucepan. Warm slowly, adding brown sugar. In a small bowl, stir cornstarch into water until dissolved. Stir cornstarch mixture into peaches in saucepan. Heat until bubbly, stirring frequently. Continue to heat until mixture is thickened to a syrupy consistency. If necessary, add additional cornstarch mixture 1 teaspoon at a time until thick. Reduce heat to warm. In a medium-sized bowl, mix milk, eggs, sugar, remaining 1 teaspoon cinnamon, and remaining 1 teaspoon vanilla. Roll stuffed bread in mixture, then place it in a heated skillet or on a griddle. Cook until it turns golden brown. Serve topped with peach sauce and whipped cream. Serves 6 to 8.

Harmony Inn

230 MERCER STREET
HARMONY, PA 16037
724-452-5124

"Agreement in feeling, approach, action, or disposition" is the dictionary definition of *harmony*. Such agreeable feelings were the ideal of the German settlers, known as Harmonites, who founded the community of Harmony in 1804. Their five thousand acres of land north of Pittsburgh became one of America's most successful examples of communal living. Today, Harmony is preserved much as it was during its heyday. Most of the buildings in the three-block-by-four-block community are from the era of the town's founding; plaques indicate their original owners or purpose. Harmony residents are proud of the heritage of their community, and rightly so.

In 1856, Harmony was to become a northern railroad terminus. In anticipation of this, Pittsburgh and New Castle railroad magnate Austin Pearce built a mansion in Harmony for his summer home. The scale and magnificence of the Italianate home reflected the optimism of both Pearce and much of the country. Although the original Harmonites had died or moved to new settlements at New Harmony, Indiana, or Economy, Pennsylvania, their descendants felt that the home's extravagance bordered on being sinful.

When Pearce's grand expectations were not realized, he sold the home to the Ziegler family, who had purchased the town from the Harmonites. The home was converted into a hotel and saloon, becoming one of the earliest licensed establishments in Butler County. From that time until now, a restaurant has been in continuous operation here.

The atmosphere today is that of an upscale hunting lodge, complete with a rack of antlers above the fireplace in one of the dining rooms. Vintage pictures and memorabilia line the walls. The large arched windows and mammoth arched doors were part of the original structure. Horsehair is visible protruding from the old mortar. The original tile floor is still intact in the bar area.

A violent murder once took place on the premises. Although accounts vary as to whether it was a shooting or a stabbing, locals feel that the murder could be the source of the friendly presence at the inn. The day we were there, the clientele urged owner Carl Beers to tell us the story. He said that he and others have experienced unexplained air movement and electrical impulses, that some have felt a warm presence, that objects have been misplaced and found in unusual places, and that unexplained images have been sighted. Psychics have been invited in to document what they say is a presence that watches over the inn and its customers.

Regardless of whether you experience the presence (and we didn't), you're sure to experience great food in ample quantity.

Sandwiches dominate the lunch menu, while the dinner menu boasts a full range of entrées, from Pasta to Chicken to Beef to Sandwiches. While Debbie thoroughly enjoyed her Smoked Turkey Reuben, Karen tried the Smoked Beef Dip Sandwich, made from brisket smoked at the inn, then slow-roasted overnight. Mr. Beers offered us the recipe, but we felt it was something that guests ought to go and try at the inn itself.

COMANCHERO FRIES

1 large potato, skin on
¼ cup Monterey Jack cheese, shredded
½ cup green chili sauce or regular salsa, heated
½ cup refried beans, heated
½ cup (or to taste) jalapeño peppers, chopped
¼ cup bacon bits
¼ cup cheddar cheese, shredded
2 tablespoons ranch dressing

Hand-cut potato into fries and place in fryer. Combine Monterey Jack, green chili sauce, and refried beans, mixing well. When fries are golden brown, remove from oil and drain. Top with Monterey Jack mixture, then sprinkle jalapeños, bacon, and cheddar over top and drizzle with dressing. If desired, commercially prepared waffle fries can be substituted for fresh potato. Serves 1 to 2.

SMOKED TURKEY REUBEN

1 tablespoon butter, melted
2 slices marbled rye bread
2 tablespoons Thousand Island dressing
1 slice Swiss cheese
5 ounces smoked turkey breast, sliced
⅓ cup coleslaw

Butter 1 side of each slice of bread. Place on a grill or in a skillet, buttered side down. When bread is browned, spread dressing on unbrowned side of 1 slice. Place cheese on top of turkey and put under broiler until cheese melts. Place turkey and cheese on the other slice of bread and top with coleslaw and then the other slice of bread. Yields 1 sandwich.

U.S. HOTEL

401 SOUTH JUNIATA STREET
HOLLIDAYSBURG, PA 16648
814-695-9924

Pioneer Adam Holliday survived Indian attacks and the turmoil of the American Revolution before starting his homestead on the banks of the Juniata River. By 1796, he prospered so that he began laying out a town in the valley. When Holliday's son, John, opened a tavern in 1814, there were still just a few homes and farms in the area. Four years later, when the Huntingdon, Cambria, and Indiana Turnpike was completed, the tavern and town became a popular stopping place for travelers.

The Pennsylvania Canal, finished in 1832, opened Hollidaysburg to trade with Philadelphia and other points east. Two years later, the Allegheny Portage Railroad joined the canal with the growing American West. Hollidaysburg became a vital link in the development of industrial areas such as Johnstown and Pittsburgh. To accommodate the growing number of travelers, John Dougherty built the U.S. Hotel in 1835 to provide food, lodging, spirits, and entertainment for man and beast (or so the gaudy signs of the times proclaimed). By 1837, the Juniata Street basin was a hub for shipping and trading warehouses.

The town's status as a transportation center lasted only about twenty years, until the Pennsylvania Railroad's main line caused Altoona to emerge as the new center of activity. The U.S. Hotel survived that downturn, only to be destroyed by fire in 1871. Several years later, a German immigrant rebuilt the hotel and established a brewery on the premises. In 1905, a barroom was added to the brick structure. It continues to function as such today. The original tile floor is still in place. If you know where to look, you can find the name Sarah Smith written on one of the small tiles. Actor John Wayne once bellied up to the bar in this room, where many relics of the hotel's past are still housed. The hand-carved mahogany backbar is impressive in its size and workmanship. On the walls are old pictures of the town and the hotel, as well as beveled, silvered mirrors and leaded stained-glass windows. The brass foot rail is still there, too, under which still flows a running-water spittoon.

Alongside the tavern are the dining rooms, appointed in burgundy and hunter green. The smaller of the front rooms was once the lobby and later served as a poolroom; an old abacus used for keeping score still hangs on the wall. Across the hall is the largest of the dining rooms, which was once the waiting area. Ladies waited in the front and men in the back, from where they had direct access to the bar.

The dining room where we ate has always been used as such. We enjoyed the Filet Mignon Sandwich, the Juniata Street Turkey and Cheddar Croissant, and the Onion Rings. As we considered dessert, we heard a story about an unusual visitor. One evening after dining, a guest came to owner Karen Yoder and told her that she definitely felt a presence in the room. What seemed to be a friendly female presence visited again late one evening as Karen and her son painted the room. Occasionally, she has been felt in the cellar or seen upstairs.

As usual, we experienced nothing but good food in a very pleasing atmosphere. We'll certainly come back to try other tempting entrées, such as the Rigatoni with Wild Mushrooms and Sausage, the Blackened Blue Chicken, and the Veal Santa Monica.

MIXED GRILL

2 4-ounce beef tenderloins
2 5-ounce chicken breasts
2 teaspoons garlic, chopped
2 tablespoons butter
6 shrimp, peeled and deveined
1 cup honey
2 tablespoons whole-grain mustard
½ cup demi-glace or brown sauce
fresh herbs for garnish

Place tenderloins and chicken on a grill and cook to desired doneness. While they are grilling, place garlic, butter, and shrimp in a sauté pan and cook until done. Combine honey and mustard in a small bowl.

To serve, place demi-glace in a small circle on 2 plates and top each circle with a tenderloin. Place chicken breasts beside tenderloins and top with Honey Mustard Sauce. Place 3 garlic shrimp between each tenderloin and breast. Garnish with fresh herbs and serve. Serves 2.

DRUNKEN MUSHROOMS

4 tablespoons butter, divided
3 cups fresh mushrooms
½ cup brandy
1½ cups heavy cream
salt and pepper to taste
2 teaspoons parsley, chopped
8 slices French bread, sliced on the bias

Melt 2 tablespoons of the butter in a sauté pan. Add mushrooms and sauté for 30 seconds. Add brandy and flame over burner. Add cream, remaining butter, salt and pepper, and parsley and simmer over a low flame until mixture begins to thicken. Toast bread under the broiler. Arrange bread on a plate in the shape of a cross. Once sauce has thickened, pour over toast points. Serves 2.

CHICKEN FROMAGE

2 8-ounce boneless, skinless chicken breasts
4 slices tomato
4 slices mozzarella
4 slices provolone
parsley for garnish

Split breasts in 2 and grill until done. Remove chicken from grill and top with tomato and cheeses. Broil chicken until cheeses are melted. Garnish with parsley and serve. Serves 2.

SIGN OF THE SORREL HORSE

4424 OLD EASTON ROAD
DOYLESTOWN, PA 18901
215-230-9999

Sign of the Sorrel Horse was fashioned in the 1920s from a gristmill built in the 1700s. The surrounding area was originally called Dyertown, after John Dyer, who arrived in Philadelphia in 1714, then settled here on twenty-five hundred acres in 1718.

Dyer's grandson, John Dyer, Jr., kept a diary that provides an account of traveling many miles in August 1777 to Warwick Township to see the Continental Army, "consisting of about 18,000 men." The Marquis de Lafayette is said to have dined with the Dyers during that time. John Jr. later described the English leaving Philadelphia on June 18, 1778, but he omitted Washington's arrival near Dyertown two days later. It has been claimed that the Dyers' mill provided Washington's men with flour in June 1778 as the army camped on a hill known as Doyltown. John Jr. wrote nothing of this, however, in his usually thorough diary. In fact, the diary is blank from his June 18 entry until March 1779—the biggest lapse of time throughout the entire diary. It is not known what kept him from recording his thoughts during that six-month period, when surely there was much to be noted.

Lafayette is said to have enjoyed his visit with the Dyers so much that his ghost returns each year on the anniversary of the meal. Mr. and Mrs. John Corcoran, the owners of the establishment many years ago, went out of their way to provide hospitality to Lafayette's restless spirit. The Corcorans set aside a table—complete with a burning candle, a loaf of bread, and a bottle of wine—for their guest from the other world. After the restaurant passed into the hands of Ruth and Charles Kiker, an employee was alone in the inn one evening. Needless to say, he was startled when he heard a low voice call out, "John! John!" The employee swallowed hard and responded, "My name is not John." The unidentified voice answered, "Oh!" and said no more that evening.

On the night I dined, the only unusual sounds were those of the parakeets and white doves in the birdcages that decorated my little alcove. This intimate setting was just off the Escoffier Room, a lovely dining room with chandeliers reminiscent of Sweden's Santa Lucia Day. The walls of the Escoffier Room are a bittersweet color that coordinates beautifully with the navy wing chairs and Oriental rugs. The atmosphere is completed by one of the building's three fireplaces, accessorized with candles and copper wares.

Game is a specialty here. Elk, Caribou, Antelope, Venison, and Wild Boar are prepared seasonally. Eventually, I settled on the New Orleans Barbecue Shrimp, four large prawns in a sweet and tangy glaze. In the mood for seafood, I followed this up with Swordfish and Salmon, served in Whole-Grain Mustard Sauce with a wedge of Blue Cheese Polenta. It was a deliciously light entrée for a hot August evening. Before rejoining Karen, I decided to finish out the meal with the fresh Sorbet. The mango flavor was the perfect ending to a delightful meal.

COLORADO ELK LOIN IN SWEDISH LINGONBERRY AND CASSIS SAUCE

Bouquet garni

3 sprigs whole thyme, chopped fine
1 celery heart, chopped fine
1 leek casing, chopped fine
2 bay leaves
4-inch-square cheesecloth
9-inch kitchen string

Place thyme, celery heart, leek, and bay leaves in center of cheesecloth. Draw corners together and tie with string.

Elk and veal stock

2 pounds elk bones
2 pounds veal bones
2 carrots, chopped
2 onions, chopped
2 stalks celery, chopped

Preheat oven to 425 degrees. Place elk and veal bones on a roasting tray and roast until they reach a deep caramel color; turn bones periodically. Place bones into a soup pot with 12 cups of cold water and bring to a slow simmer. Continue cooking for 4 hours. Add carrots, onions, celery, and bouquet garni. Cook an additional 30 minutes. Strain mixture through cheesecloth.

Elk loin

1 cup cassis
½ cup lingonberries

30 ounces elk loin
salt and pepper to taste
olive oil

Add cassis to elk and veal stock and reduce mixture to about 2 cups. Add lingonberries and simmer for 2 minutes. Sauce should coat the back of a spoon.

Season elk loin with salt and pepper. Coat an ovenproof pan with olive oil. Heat pan in oven. When oil just begins to smoke, add elk loin and sear at high heat until browned. Finish cooking elk in a 350-degree oven until it reaches desired doneness. Slice into 6 equal portions and serve. Serves 6.

CHOCOLATE VOLCANO

5 1-ounce squares semisweet chocolate
1½ 1-ounce squares unsweetened chocolate
14 tablespoons sweet butter
4 eggs
4 egg yolks
1 1/3 cups confectioners' sugar
1 scant cup pastry flour
Pam spray or butter

Melt semisweet chocolate and unsweetened chocolate with butter. Add eggs, yolks, and sugar; mix well. Sift in flour. Spray or grease 4 soufflé dishes. Pour batter into dishes and bake for 10 minutes in a 500-degree oven. Serves 4.

KING GEORGE INN

CEDAR CREST AND HAMILTON BOULEVARDS
ALLENTOWN, PA 18103
610-435-1723

Now a National Historic Site, this "publik coach house serving tired and hungry wayfarers" was established in 1756 in the hamlet then called Dorneyville. Built during the French and Indian War, the tavern served as a way station between Philadelphia and the Allegheny Mountains. During that difficult time, a group of Indians is said to have kidnapped and killed several babies from the area, disposing of their bodies by throwing them into various Dorneyville wells. More than 150 years later, an employee of this inn accidentally locked herself in the cellar, located near the inn's well. As she waited for someone to realize she was there, she was terrified to hear a baby's scream. Fortunately, such demons of the past have given way to gaiety today. The well now serves as the inn's wine cellar. The basement, a paneled room, now functions as a tavern, where jazz was being played the night we visited.

Following the French and Indian War, the inn saw its day as a town hall, meeting house, news center, church, and courthouse. It was also the site of a staging field for regular and irregular citizen-soldiers during the American Revolution. Perhaps Dorney's Tavern, as it was called back then, even hosted a few meetings of the Sons of Liberty, those revolutionary planners.

From regular dinner seating to special events, this stone structure carries on its legacy of congeniality and delicious food. Recently, it hosted a *Titanic* reenactment dinner, which proved to be a huge success. In doing the research for that event, restaurateur Clifford McDermott discovered that there was a Dahlia McDermott on the *Titanic*'s passenger list. A relative? It's doubtful, but who knows?

Two appealing dining rooms on the main floor and a central bar provide service to guests of the King George Inn. The Hearth Room, which has thick, exposed-stone walls and wooden mantelpieces, is a favorite with dinner guests because of its coziness. Seated across the hall in the other dining room, we were intrigued by our room's decor. Its stone walls were accented by forest-green beams spanning the ceiling. The quotations on either side of the beams made for interesting reading. "When the wife drinks to the husband all is well," read one, credited to John Ray. Our personal favorite, from Sententin in 50 B.C., said, "In quarreling the truth is always lost."

The menu had plenty to peruse as well, including myriad appetizer choices. The Cream of Fennel and Potato Soup was thick like chowder and very tasty. The service was very prompt; before we knew it, our salads were served. These were quickly followed by Panned Sea Bass with Shrimp, Ancho Chilis, and Spinach, served in a Cumin Tomato Broth. One of six entrées from the list of specials that evening, it was just spicy enough to suit the palate. We left no room for dessert, but as we departed, we promised to return for the Prime Rib with Yorkshire Pudding, a Christmas tradition for the last twenty-seven years!

CAESAR SALAD

1 large head romaine lettuce
1 ounce anchovies
1 teaspoon garlic, chopped fine
½ teaspoon Worcestershire sauce
½ teaspoon dry mustard
½ teaspoon freshly ground black pepper
1 egg, beaten
¼ cup lemon juice
¼ cup good-quality olive oil
½ cup freshly grated Parmesan cheese
¾ cup Croutons (see below)

Separate lettuce leaves. Wash well, then tear green portion into bite-sized pieces, discarding stalks. Place anchovies in a large wooden salad bowl and crush with the back of a spoon. Add garlic, Worcestershire, mustard, pepper, egg, lemon juice, and olive oil. Whip ingredients until well blended and slightly frothy. Add lettuce and toss. Top with cheese and Croutons and serve on cold glass plates. Serves 2.

Croutons

1 to 2 slices French bread, slightly stale
1 clove garlic
1 tablespoon olive oil

Cut bread into ½-inch cubes. Peel garlic and halve lengthwise. Sauté garlic in olive oil, stirring, until it begins to brown. Remove garlic and stir in bread cubes. Sauté, stirring, until croutons are browned on all sides. Yields enough croutons for 2 Caesar Salads.

KING GEORGE CHEESECAKE

1½ cups graham crackers, crushed
2¾ cups sugar, divided
6 tablespoons butter, melted
9 egg whites, whipped
6 8-ounce packages cream cheese, room temperature
1½ teaspoons vanilla extract, divided
2 cups sour cream

Preheat oven to 400 degrees. Combine graham crackers, ¼ cup of the sugar, and butter; mix well. Press firmly into a 10-inch springform pan. Bake crust for 5 to 8 minutes until edges are brown. Set aside to cool.

In a large bowl, beat egg whites and 2 cups of the sugar until stiff. In a separate bowl, beat cream cheese and 1 teaspoon of the vanilla extract until smooth. Fold egg white mixture into cream cheese mixture, then pour into pan on top of cooled crust. Bake for about 45 minutes until a knife poked into center of cake comes out clean. Allow to cool for 1 hour.

Using the back of a large spoon, press down edges and center of cheesecake until they are at least ½ inch below top of pan. In a medium bowl, fold together sour cream, remaining sugar, and remaining vanilla until thoroughly combined. Pour mixture over cooled cake and bake for 10 more minutes. Allow to cool for at least 4 hours.

Loosen cheesecake by running a knife around edge of pan. Remove cheesecake from pan, place on serving plate, and decorate as desired. Serves 12.

CHAPTER 11

All in a Day's Work

The Gamble Mill Tavern

We all have a job to do. This chapter highlights the places where people worked and the jobs essential to their communities. Restaurants have been fashioned from all sorts of workplaces, such as post offices, fire stations, and even schoolhouses, where children persevered. The staffs at these establishments now work hard at providing great food and quality service while proudly displaying the type of work done by their predecessors.

664 CENTERVILLE PIKE
SLIPPERY ROCK, PA 16057
724-794-1899

Built in 1899 with foundation stone from the construction on Moore's Bridge, Wolf Creek School originally stood on the western edge of the cemetery at Wolf Creek United Presbyterian Church. Through most of its history, the school housed students in grades one through eight. However, by the time of its closing, only first-graders were in attendance. The teacher at that time was Mrs. Mary Shaner Wimer, who had taught in the school district for thirty-three years. She was Butler County's last teacher in a one-room schoolhouse.

Beginning in November 1989, the badly dilapidated building was dismantled and moved in sections to its present location adjacent to the Applebutter Inn on Centerville Pike in Slippery Rock, just down the road from Slippery Rock University. The structure has been restored to its original condition with the exception of new flooring and the addition of a modern fireplace, a kitchen, and restroom facilities. The inviting exterior's crisp gray and white paint and stone chimney entice passersby to sample a traditional home-cooked meal.

Once inside, guests can revel in Wolf Creek's many school artifacts. These carefully refurbished items are on display in the cafe's two appealing rooms. The day's menu items are written on old blackboards. Presidential pictures and maps adorn the walls. We were charmed by the original school desks, the potbelly stove, and the American flag standing in the corner next to an old copy of the Pledge of Allegiance. Tin cups holding sugar and sweetener are on the tables. A must-see item is the delightful water-stained painting done by an unknown schoolchild on brown wrapping paper. It has since been entitled "The Horse."

The deck and pagoda add pleasant warm-weather seating to this delightful cafe. The service is friendly and helpful. The menu is varied, and serving sizes are plentiful. As we chatted with owner Mike Thompson, we tried the delicious Apple Nut Cake featured here.

❦ APPLE NUT CAKE ❦

2 eggs
4½ cups apples, chopped
2 cups sugar
1 teaspoon vanilla
½ cup nuts, chopped
½ cup plus 1 teaspoon vegetable oil
2½ cups flour
¾ teaspoon salt
2 teaspoons cinnamon
2 teaspoons baking soda

In a large bowl, break the eggs over the apples. Stir lightly with a fork. Mix in sugar, vanilla, nuts, and oil. Stir well. Gradually add dry ingredients. Pour into a 13-by-9-inch baking pan. Bake at 325 degrees for 1 hour. Serve warm with favorite vanilla sauce or ice cream. Yields 1 cake.

❦   ❦   ❦   ❦   ❦   ❦

❦ ITALIAN PORTABELLO APPETIZER ❦

2 large portabello mushrooms
2 tablespoons butter
½ teaspoon fresh garlic, minced
½ cup tomatoes, diced
¼ teaspoon basil leaves, chopped
2 tablespoons Parmesan cheese, grated
2 slices provolone cheese
Greek dressing

Rinse mushrooms and pat dry. Remove stems and save. Melt butter in a medium saucepan and add garlic. Brush garlic butter onto mushroom caps and grill each side for 1 minute. Chop stems and sauté in remaining garlic butter. Add tomatoes, basil, and Parmesan. Place caps in a baking dish and spoon tomato mixture onto caps. Place provolone on top of mixture. Bake at 350 degrees for 5 minutes. Drizzle with Greek dressing and serve. Serves 2.

❦   ❦   ❦   ❦   ❦   ❦

THE CLASSROOM RESTAURANT

133 CAMP LANE
MCMURRAY, PA 15317
724-942-4878

Thompsonville School, built in 1904 as the first schoolhouse in the rural farming community of McMurray, educated children from first grade through sixth grade. Today, there are local residents who can remember ringing the school bell (which still hangs atop the schoolhouse) and eating lunch on the banks of the creek running near the front of the building.

After educating local children for thirty-five years, the school was closed in 1939. The building was subsequently used for craft and antique shops and for office space. Two French gentlemen opened a restaurant here in the 1970s. Rather than adding a kitchen, they prepared menu items table-side.

The current owners, Chuck and Shawn Davis, have preserved this piece of nostalgia and created an outstanding dining experience. The past mingles with the present as guests, seated in either the loft or the main dining room, enjoy structural features such as original flooring and well-worn wainscoting. Many old books sit perched upon a bookshelf. The cursive alphabet borders the room high on the rust-colored walls, where primitive prints hang alongside art created by the Davis children.

Guests can survey the menu on the blackboard at the front of the classroom or scan the miniature chalkboards brought right to the tables. The menu choices are innovative, surprising, and flavorful. You'll find sauces like Horseradish Sour Cream and Papaya Coulis. The Oven-Roasted Duck is served with seasonal Marmalades. On the menu the night we dined were Grilled Beef Medallions, served with smoky bacon and Tomato Pepper Sauce.

We enjoyed a complimentary appetizer of White Bean and Parsley Pâté with crispy toast wedges. Its rapid disappearance spoke for itself. The Baked Spinach Crepes, served with Balsamic Onions in Mozzarella and Pepper Sauce, were as delicious as they were unusual. The Penne Pasta in Garlic Oil, tossed with pistachios and cherry-berry tomatoes, was a popular choice at our table and with other dinner guests as well. The entire meal was wonderful, down to the last bite of the Apple Spice Cake and Vanilla Ice Cream topped with Cinnamon Sauce. Do make reservations—it's busy, and you don't want to risk missing this experience.

❦ BALSAMIC VINAIGRETTE ❧

2 cloves garlic, chopped
1 tablespoon parsley, chopped
½ teaspoon fresh rosemary, chopped
½ teaspoon fresh thyme, chopped
1 tablespoon cracked black pepper
1 teaspoon salt
2 cups balsamic vinegar
6 cups virgin olive oil

Combine all ingredients except olive oil in a large bowl. While whisking, slowly drizzle in oil until well blended. Yields 8 cups.

❦ DEVILED CRAB CAKES ❧

Crab cakes

1 pound Maryland blue crabmeat, cleaned
½ cup mayonnaise
¼ cup Dijon mustard

1 tablespoon Tabasco sauce
salt and pepper to taste
1 cup fresh breadcrumbs
oil for frying
lemon wedges for garnish
Tabasco Tartar Sauce (see below)

Combine crabmeat, mayonnaise, mustard, and Tabasco in a mixing bowl. Add salt and pepper. Stir in breadcrumbs. Mix well and form into 4 cakes about 4 inches wide and 1 inch thick. In a skillet, brown cakes on both sides in hot oil. Serve with lemon wedges and top with Tabasco Tartar Sauce. Serves 2.

Tabasco Tartar Sauce

½ cup mayonnaise
3 tablespoons balsamic vinegar
1 tablespoon Tabasco sauce

Combine all ingredients and mix well. Yields ¾ cup.

INTERSTATE 80, EXIT 40

WHITE HAVEN, PA 18661

570-443-4480

The cold, dry air of the Pocono Mountains is heralded as being therapeutic for many ailments. It was this climate that encouraged a group of late-nineteenth-century philanthropists to choose White Haven as the location for a sanatorium for individuals suffering from consumption—or, in today's term, tuberculosis. The site was also desirable because it was accessible by rail from both New York and Philadelphia, yet was isolated enough to keep the tuberculosis contained.

The disease was widespread at the turn of the century. In 1901, when the White Haven Sanatorium was founded, Dr. Lawrence Flick supervised patients in only a few buildings. As the disease reached epidemic proportions, the facility grew; it even included a nursing school. The expanded sanatorium required additional power, which was provided by a coal-to-steam plant. The plant was funded by a donation of $125,000 from industrialist Pierre DuPont, a gift of gratitude for the care given his personal secretary, who was afflicted with the disease. Eventually, the introduction of the antibiotic streptomycin and the development of modern immunization techniques brought tuberculosis under control. Because of its dwindling patient population, the sanatorium eventually was forced to close, which started a gradual decline of the property.

Pictures on the wall of Powerhouse Eatery show what an eyesore the old power plant became. The structure began getting a facelift in 1989. Much of the existing building and plant hardware were preserved.

The power plant's original smokestack, visible from Interstate 80, beckons travelers to an unexpected treat. Relics from the plant adorn the parking lot. Inside, a gray steel door separates the waiting area from the dining rooms. We were seated in the back dining area underneath two enormous Type H Stirling Boilers. No, we're not experts in power plant equipment. Rather, we were educated by the menu's back cover, which tells about the relics found throughout the restaurant. Among those items are original metal beams and pipes and various gauges. In the front dining room, a Babcock-Wilcox Boiler is on display. Metal doors are still embedded in the brick walls.

While the decor is reminiscent of the workaday world of yesteryear, there is nothing mundane about the food served here. Brand-new on the appetizer menu the night we visited was Shrimp and Roasted Corn Risotto. It was so tasty that we would have been happy to have an entrée-sized portion. Debbie ordered the tender and tasty Pork Tournedos in Bourbon Demi-Glace, served with Sausage Bread Stuffing, pecans, and dried cranberries. Karen enjoyed the Pork à la Powerhouse. Not yet out of steam, we managed to find room for Tiramisu and a light, refreshing All-Berry Mousse. Fueled up, we were ready to hit the road again!

BUFFALINA SALAD

1 cup fresh mozzarella, shredded
¼ cup green onions, chopped
1 tablespoon roasted garlic, minced
1 tablespoon fresh basil, chopped
2 plum tomatoes, sliced
½ cup extra-virgin olive oil
1 heart of romaine, chopped
1 tablespoon balsamic vinegar

In a mixing bowl, combine mozzarella, onions, garlic, basil, tomatoes, and olive oil. Pour mixture over romaine. Drizzle vinegar over greens. Serves 2.

PORK À LA POWERHOUSE

2 cloves garlic, minced
3 shallots, chopped
¼ cup butter
¼ cup all-purpose flour
¾ quart chicken stock
2 cups heavy cream
2 bunches dill, minced
1 pound jumbo lump crabmeat
salt and pepper to taste
4 8-ounce boneless pork loins
oil

Sauté garlic and shallots in butter until translucent. Add flour to make a roux. Cook 5 minutes until pale. Add chicken stock and cream. Cook sauce until it coats the back of a spoon, then strain. Add dill, crabmeat, and salt and pepper. Cook pork in oil until desired doneness. Split each pork loin, fill with crabmeat mixture, and coat with sauce. Serves 4.

THE CRESTMONT INN

CRESTMONT DRIVE
EAGLES MERE, PA 17731
570-525-3519

The highest point in Eagles Mere is twenty-one hundred feet above sea level. Some call this mountain Hemlock Hill, while others call it Cyclone Hill because of the 1892 storm that stripped the peak of its native timber. Several years later, William Watson was sitting in his hotel room and gazing up at the bare mountain when he felt a call to build a family resort. In June 1900, The Crestmont Inn opened. During its heyday, vacationing families returned to The Crestmont year after year to escape the heat and the pressures of turn-of-the-century city life. They looked forward to the wonderful food, the excellent service, the enjoyable activities, and the leisurely acquaintances they built up over time.

The last of the grand hotels to open in Eagles Mere, The Crestmont Inn was also the last to close, in 1969. In 1971, the Eagles Mere Conservancy purchased the hotel and its 320-plus acres. When the property was purchased by Robert and Kathleen Oliver several years later, the hotel was so dilapidated that it had to be torn down. Kathleen, who had fond memories of spending her summers at The Crestmont Inn, longed to re-create her experiences. Although the main building was gone, the Olivers saved and restored other buildings on the property through a labor of love.

Today's Crestmont Inn consists primarily of two buildings, a pool, tennis courts, and the surrounding grounds. Rooms for overnight visitors are located in the staff house, which once had forty rooms used by maids, bellhops, and other employees. It has now been converted to fourteen bedrooms, all with private baths. The Crestmont Inn's dining room is located in what was the original wash house, which once contained numerous commercial irons, washing machines, and no fewer than twenty-four ironing boards to do the myriad table linens and other laundry.

The linens are still in evidence, pressed and fresh on the tables. The fresh flowers and the crystal create a beautiful dining atmosphere. The dinner menu has something for everyone. There are several Seafood choices and at least a Veal, a Beef, and a Chicken entrée. Grilled Country Ham frequently appears on the menu as well.

We had breakfast at the inn and thoroughly reveled in the experience. As we entered the dining room, the tables were already set with Orange Juice and Melon Cups. The choices for the morning included eggs any style, Blueberry Pancakes, and Eggs Benedict. Each plate was garnished with fresh blueberries and strawberries and a fresh apricot, halved, in which was a dollop of homemade Strawberry Butter. The pancakes were light, fluffy, and chock full of berries; the Strawberry Butter added a delightful touch. The Hollandaise Sauce on the Eggs Benedict was perfect, creamy, and light. As if this wasn't yummy enough, we then tried the Bananas Caribbean, a citrus version of Bananas Foster. It was creative and gastronomically superb. If breakfast is this good, then lunch and dinner are not to be missed!

Eagles Mere, where lovely vacation homes beg visitors to have a walk about town, has an aura of bygone days. Thanks to its repertoire of excellent food and the kind of sincere, genteel service where the staff readily calls guests by name, The Crestmont Inn has captured the spirit of its predecessor.

STUFFED FILLET OF FLOUNDER

8-ounce package cream cheese, softened
1 cup lobster, cut into small pieces
1 cup shrimp, cut into small pieces
1 cup crabmeat, flaked
1 tablespoon lemon juice
1 tablespoon lobster base
½ cup mayonnaise
1 teaspoon Tabasco sauce
½ cup breadcrumbs
12 4-ounce portions flounder
Imperial Sauce (see next column)
6 slices lemon
parsley and fresh herbs for garnish

Place first 9 ingredients in a mixing bowl and mix with hands, adding extra breadcrumbs if necessary to bind. Form into 6 oblong shapes the size of a very large egg. Preheat oven to 400 degrees. Place 6 flounder fillets skin side down on ovenproof seashells. Place stuffing mixture on flounder. Put remaining 6 fillets on top of stuffing, also skin side down. Gently fold fish pieces around stuffing. Place a generous amount of Imperial Sauce over entire fish mixture, covering to seal edges. Bake uncovered for 20 minutes until sauce forms a golden glaze. Serve immediately with a lemon slice and parsley or a sprig of fresh herbs. Serves 6.

Imperial Sauce

1 tablespoon butter
1 tablespoon flour
¾ cup milk
2 cups mayonnaise
1 tablespoon Worcestershire sauce
¼ teaspoon salt
¼ teaspoon Tabasco sauce
1 tablespoon lemon juice
dash of pepper
1 egg, beaten

Melt butter in a 2-quart saucepan over medium heat. Slowly stir in flour; whisk for about 5 minutes. Gradually add milk and cook until thick. Cool completely, then add mayonnaise, Worcestershire, salt, Tabasco, lemon juice, and pepper; combine thoroughly. Fold in beaten egg. Yields approximately 3 cups.

Note: This sauce may be stored in a tightly covered container in the refrigerator for up to 1 week.

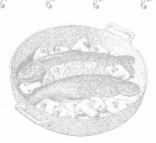

THE GAMBLE MILL TAVERN

160 DUNLAP STREET
BELLEFONTE, PA 16823
814-355-7764

In its advertising, The Gamble Mill Tavern says it offers "fine dining in a casual atmosphere surrounded by the warmth of old wood, brick, and stone in a historic grist mill." The minute we walked in, we had to agree. Relics from the mill decorate the lobby, and one of the old mill wheels sits just outside the front door. Water still flows through the raceway and under the building, and enormous wooden beams are visible throughout. Large, original windows keep the interior bright.

The mill was built by William Lamb, who is credited with organizing the first permanent settlement in the Nittany Valley. Lamb constructed his home along the west bank of Spring Creek in 1785. A year later, he built the mill just south of his home. The mill was a drawing card for new settlers, helping the area prosper. It became known as Lamb's Crossing, and a sign outside the restaurant still proclaims it as such.

In 1794, John Dunlop, an ironmaster from the Cumberland Valley, bought all of Lamb's properties, including the Big Spring, called Beautiful Fountain at the time. The town's name, Bellefonte, is derived from that spring. James Harris and the Dunlop family are credited with laying out the town.

The mill passed through various owners over the years. John Gamble purchased it in 1901. After his retirement in 1923, the building slowly deteriorated until it was eventually condemned and marked for demolition. With the support of a dedicated local group, Ted Conklin purchased the mill in 1975. The following year, it became the first local building to be placed on the National Register of Historic Places.

The food here is as memorable as the building's past. We had difficulty choosing an appetizer from the innovative list, finally settling on a Mushroom Turnover and a dish called Rajas con Queso, which consisted of roasted red peppers, jalapeños, tomatoes, onions, and cream cheese served warm with tortilla chips. Both were as tasty as we'd hoped. The creamy Raspberry Dressing on the salad that came with Karen's Mushroom Turnover was unbelievably good. The entrée choices weren't any easier than the appetizers had been. Sandwiches like Chicken Giuseppe (a chicken breast marinated in Balsamic Vinaigrette and then topped with prosciutto, provolone, pepperocini, olives, roasted red peppers, and Basil Mayonnaise) and Mango Barbecued Chicken were tempting. Eventually, Debbie selected the Butternut Ravioli (spinach ravioli filled with butternut squash, served in a sauce of roasted garlic, mushrooms, and sun-dried tomatoes). The flavors were exquisite. Karen found her Polynesian Chicken (a warm salad of diced chicken, melon, avocado, and bell peppers in Orange Ginger Sauce) equally flavorful. By the time the dessert tray arrived, our decision-making skills had deserted us entirely, so we asked our server to choose for us. The rich Cappuccino Torte proved the perfect ending to a perfect meal. Oh, to have to face such choices every day!

GRILLED ASPARAGUS WITH RASPBERRY VINAIGRETTE

Salad

1 pound asparagus spears, trimmed to 5 inches
1 cup Raspberry Vinaigrette (see below)
12 to 16 cups mesclun lettuce
¾ pound Montrachet cheese

Brush asparagus with Raspberry Vinaigrette. Grill over medium-hot coals for 3 to 5 minutes. Toss mesclun with remaining vinaigrette and divide among 8 plates. Fan asparagus over greens. Slice cheese into 8 rounds and place at base of asparagus fan. Serves 8.

Raspberry Vinaigrette

2 egg yolks
⅓ cup dry white wine
⅓ cup raspberry juice
½ cup raspberry vinegar
2 teaspoons granulated sugar
1½ teaspoons garlic, peeled and chopped
¼ teaspoon raspberry extract
2½ cups oil
2½ tablespoons fresh tarragon, chopped

Combine first 7 ingredients. Drizzle in oil. Mix in tarragon by hand. Yields approximately 4 cups.

VEAL MOREL

¼ cup brandy
⅓ cup dry white wine
⅓ cup dry red wine
3 tablespoons shallots, peeled
2½ cups veal stock
¼ cup demi-glace stock
¼ cup heavy cream
¼ cup unsalted butter, cubed
salt and pepper to taste
1 ounce dried morel mushrooms
8 1½-inch-thick veal loin chops

Bring brandy, wines, and shallots to a simmer in a noncorrosive pot. Add stocks. Reduce by ½, strain, and return to pot. Add cream and heat; do not boil. Whisk in butter and add salt and pepper. Soak mushrooms in hot water until soft; drain. Season veal with salt and pepper and grill 10 minutes per inch of thickness for medium-rare. Stir morels into sauce. Ladle sauce over meat and serve with garlic mashed potatoes. Serves 8.

~ THE MINERS' REST ~
A Dining Landmark Since 1893

807 FOURTH AVENUE
PATTON, PA 16668
814-674-5532

The staff and the customers are on a first-name basis here, just as they have been since 1890, when this hotel and restaurant opened. It was built to serve the men working in nearby mines, who were paid here, ate here, and some say sought female entertainment here. Pictures on the walls from the early days show dozens of miners lounging on the expansive porch, perhaps after a filling evening meal. Most of the food served at The Miners' Rest today is homemade. The delicious Meat Loaf and the Chili are local favorites. Equally popular are desserts like the ample Apple Dumpling, served warm with vanilla ice cream, and the old-fashioned Coconut Cream Pie.

The restaurant's decor is charming in its simplicity. Not only does The Miners' Rest have a tin-tile ceiling, but it is one of the few places we've seen with tin tiles on the walls as well. Attractively arranged and proudly displayed is an assortment of mine equipment, from lanterns to helmets to tin lunch buckets. Picks and coal scuttles are here, too, alongside photographs of the men who may have used them. An antique radio plays in the corner of the room. Pictures of local attractions such as Horseshoe Curve further emphasize the restaurant's pride in the county's heritage.

Seldom Seen Mine is just down the road, about four miles north of Patton. This mine and many others took advantage of the area's rich natural resources. Those resources and the county's geographic location allowed the area to play a significant role in Pennsylvania's rise as an industrial leader.

Seldom Seen Mine was originally called Chest Creek Mine Number 1, which began operation in the early days of mechanization. Seldom Seen Mine employed a relatively small number of miners—approximately fifteen to twenty. In small mines such as this, coal was typically extracted using old-fashioned techniques like hand-loading. These mines were at one time owned by wealthy local families, who employed immigrants on a production basis, sometimes paying them as little as twenty-five cents a ton for coal mined and loaded! Even though the miners were paid only for this work, they were also personally responsible for the safety of their work areas inside the mine. This included timbering and shoring up the roof, tasks that sometimes were not done as thoroughly as possible, due to the time they took away from the actual production of coal.

Today, descendants of the immigrants who made their living in these mines give tourists an idea of what life was like for coal miners at Seldom Seen Mine. The Miners' Rest allows a glimpse into a small part of this history as well.

TUNA SALAD

4-pound, 2-ounce can chunk light tuna, packed in
  water
2 cups celery, diced
1 cup onion, diced
1¾ teaspoons pepper
1¾ teaspoons celery salt
1¾ teaspoons celery seed
1 teaspoon garlic powder
1 tablespoon dill weed
1 tablespoon parsley flakes
1 to 1½ cups mayonnaise

Drain tuna thoroughly. Combine all
ingredients except tuna and mayonnaise. Add
tuna and mix again, breaking up any large pieces.
Add enough mayonnaise to hold together, making
sure mixture is not too dry and not too moist.
Cover and refrigerate. Serves 12.

CHILI

2½ pounds ground chuck
1 medium onion, chopped
1 tablespoon fresh garlic, chopped
2 cups water
2 cups green pepper, chopped
3 cups dark red kidney beans
6 cups canned tomatoes
2 tablespoons salt
1 tablespoon chili powder
pepper to taste

Brown ground chuck, onion, and garlic. Add
water, green peppers, kidney beans, and
tomatoes. Bring to a boil, stirring constantly, then
reduce to a simmer and cook for about ½ hour.
Add seasonings and simmer for about 2 more
hours, stirring every 15 minutes. After cooling,
skim off fat. Serves 12.

MEATBALLS

1¼ cups Italian breadcrumbs
5 large eggs
1 cup milk
¼ cup mozzarella, shredded
¼ cup provolone, shredded
4 tablespoons dried parsley flakes
1 tablespoon dried garlic granules
½ teaspoon pepper
2½ pounds ground chuck

Combine all ingredients except ground chuck
in a large bowl and mix thoroughly. Add ground
chuck and mix thoroughly again. Using a 2¾-
ounce ice cream scoop, make meatballs. Place
meatballs on a large baking tray. Add a small
amount of water on tray and bake at 450 degrees
for 20 to 25 minutes. Let cool and refrigerate until
ready to use. Yields approximately 15 meatballs.

33–35 NORTH MARKET STREET
LANCASTER, PA 17603
717-299-4602

Although this building was completed and in use around 1893, the tavern license granted to George S. Deering, on display as you enter, gives a date of March 1916. During the early twentieth century, the Grape Tavern, a local social organization, used this spot as its headquarters. No one is quite sure what the group did, other than to meet and imbibe. After it disbanded, the Commercial Printing Company occupied the building, serving Lancaster's printing needs until the late 1970s.

When the printing company relinquished its space in 1978, the building returned to its original use, thanks to The Lancaster Dispensing Co., a Victorian pub featuring spirits, good food, and entertainment. It's located on an adorable pedestrian street just off of Lancaster's main drag.

As you enter, you can't help noticing the enormous bar that runs the length of the restaurant's back wall. The stained-glass windows on either side of the bar and the leaded-glass cupboard doors speak to the building's era of origin. The ceiling fans quietly spinning overhead provide an additional Victorian touch, as do the leaded-glass transoms and wooden flooring. As we chatted with Judy Ross, one of the owners, she pointed out that the building's wainscoting was fashioned from shutters of the period. Augmenting the decor are the shiny brass railings around the bar, hanging plants, and red cloths graced by fresh flowers at each table.

Fresh ingredients for many of the menu items are purchased right next door at the Lancaster Central Market House, a historic building in its own right. Variety is plentiful, as the menu features multiple appetizers and salads. The Lancaster Dispensing Co.'s Chicken Salad can be prepared six different ways: with Honey Mustard; with Sun-Dried Tomatoes; with Herbed Mayonnaise; Cajun-Style; Jamaican Jerk–Style; and Thai-Style with Peanut Sauce. Burgers and open-faced sandwiches are on the menu, alongside a lengthy list of overstuffed sandwiches, served with Chips, Potato Salad, Macaroni Salad, or Coleslaw. The seven vegetarian selections on the menu suggest how our eating habits have changed over the years. However, one thing at The Lancaster Dispensing Co. that hasn't changed is the original wallpaper. Several years ago, the owners discussed an update, but after looking at many, many samples, they couldn't find anything better than what was already there, so they decided to leave well enough alone. We're glad they did.

BLOODY MARY MIX

46-ounce can tomato juice
46-ounce can V-8
4 tablespoons horseradish
2 tablespoons Worcestershire sauce
2 tablespoons Rose's lime juice
2 tablespoons celery salt
several dashes of Tabasco
several dashes of bitters

Combine ingredients and mix well. Pour over vodka and ice. Serve with a twist of lemon and lime and a fresh celery stalk. Serves 10 to 12.

ARTICHOKE AND SPINACH DIP

½ cup onions, diced fine
2 tablespoons vegetable oil, divided
2 14-ounce cans artichoke hearts, drained and chopped coarse
1½ teaspoons salt
¾ teaspoon pepper
¼ cup white wine
1½ teaspoons roasted garlic
10-ounce bag fresh spinach
3 8-ounce packages cream cheese

Sauté onions in 1 tablespoon of the vegetable oil until they start to soften. Add artichoke hearts, salt, pepper, and wine. Continue to sauté about 10 minutes until soft. Add garlic and cook 5 minutes more. In a separate pan, cook spinach in remaining oil. Drain and chop spinach and add it to the artichoke mixture. Add cream cheese and mix thoroughly. Refrigerate. To serve, heat desired quantity of dip by placing under broiler until lightly browned. Serve with baked bread or crackers. Yields 6 cups.

10 REED STREET
PHILADELPHIA, PA 19147
215-462-4646

Upon entering the Engine 46 Steakhouse, there is no mistaking it for anything other than the 1894 firehouse that it is. The tables are covered in Dalmatian-print cloths, and pictures of the lovable animals are everywhere. Red chairs and woodwork accent the black and white, creating a fun, upbeat atmosphere. The raised bar area, which encompasses the entire left side of the downstairs dining room, has old-fashioned ladders hanging above it. Decorating the shelves that house the liquor stock are patches from a wide variety of fire companies.

Our favorite table is on the first floor, tucked away just off the front door. The arched entry to this table has the station number in tile. The brass firemen's pole, situated where it's been for over a hundred years, now has a table for six surrounding it. The grill and headlights from one of the fire company's old engines hang on the wall nearby. Farther into the restaurant, a pegboard holds the coats and helmets of some of the fireman who were called to action from this station.

The creatively decorated stairway leading to the second floor has been painted in gray, then sponge-painted in black. Black-and-white photographs of Philadelphia fireman in action over the years have been decoupaged on the walls, creating historical firefighting wallpaper of sorts.

In the upstairs dining room, additional photos on the walls chronicle the efforts of area firefighters. Cast-iron insignias representing these men are displayed along one wall, as are license plates from a variety of local fire companies. Antique call boxes are on view throughout the room, as is a large collection of vintage fire extinguishers and hose nozzles.

Stopping in at Engine 46 for a Saturday-afternoon snack, we were immediately attracted to the Coconut Onion Rings listed on the specials board. Served with Sweet and Sour Sauce, the onion rings were not too sweet and had just a hint of coconut. More importantly, they were not too greasy. We enjoyed every bite. Next came dessert. Karen ordered the Caramel Apple Granny, a torte with buttery caramel- and toffee-laden custard combined with fresh Granny Smith apples. Debbie ordered a hot fudge brownie sundae, foolishly expecting it to be served in a typical parfait glass. Diners beware! When something is named the Towering Inferno, as this sundae was, take note. It was huge enough to be served on a dinner plate and had ice cream and whipped cream mounded several inches high! In fact, it was so large that everyone in the dining room gasped when our waitress placed it on the table.

The rest of the menu is All-American. Buffalo Wings, Potato Skins, and Four-Alarm Cheese Fries are among the appetizer selections. There are seven sandwich selections, and the entrée menu ranges from Steaks and Ribs to Shrimp and even Lobster Tails.

As we began our afternoon snack, a birthday party of energetic young boys was just winding down. From the young to the young at heart, Engine 46 Steakhouse provides a good time.

❦ ❦ ❦ ❦ ❦ ❦

❦ SECRET SPICY RANCH DRESSING ❦

4 cups ranch dressing
3 teaspoons fresh lemon juice
1/3 cup horseradish
2½ teaspoons cayenne pepper

Combine ingredients in a medium bowl. Yields about 4½ cups.

Note: This dressing is great on wrap sandwiches and as a dip for fresh vegetables or other appetizers.

❦ ❦ ❦ ❦ ❦ ❦

❦ PRIME RIB SOUP ❦

2 to 3 cups fresh vegetables of your choice, diced
28-ounce can tomato purée
½ cup beef base
2 thick slices prime rib, diced
3 large potatoes, diced
pinch of seasoned salt
salt and pepper to taste
8 cups water

Place all ingredients in a large soup pot. Bring to a boil and stir. Reduce heat to medium and cook for 4 hours. Serves 8 to 12.

❦ ❦ ❦ ❦ ❦ ❦

Post Office
DELI & CATERING

120 WEXFORD BAYNE ROAD
WEXFORD, PA 15090
724-934-3354

The president was Theodore Roosevelt, baseball's National League batting title was won for the fourth time by Honus Wagner, and the Ford Model T was being developed. It was 1906. That year also saw the beginning of an electric streetcar—known as the Harmony Short Line—that furnished transportation from Pittsburgh through Wexford and on to points north.

The Harmony Short Line's wooden, one-room station, operated by Alphonsus Brooker, was located at the corner of Brennan and Wexford Bayne Roads. The Harmony Short Line continued in operation until 1931. Late that year, Mark Brooker and a team of draft horses pulled the station to its current location at the corner of Church and Wexford Bayne Roads. From then until 1963, the station served as Wexford's post office.

Located just around the corner, the General Store and Cole's Hotel and Bar look just as they did at the turn of the century. The name Wexford Post Office Deli was chosen in tribute to the history of the building and the area.

Wexford Post Office Deli is the type of place that makes you smile when you just drive by. It's a cheerful, cozy, one-stop delicatessen offering a wide variety of foods. The selection includes cheeses, luncheon meats, soups, sandwiches, main dishes, breads, cookies, cheesecakes, tortes, and pies. For example, the repertoire includes four different varieties of Potato Salad! The deli allows local residents a delicious alternative to fast-food eateries and expensive restaurants. It's also a popular catering choice for both families and businesses.

Our favorite time to visit Wexford Post Office Deli is in warm weather. We like to dine alfresco at the gingham-checked picnic tables surrounded by a white picket fence. Then again, the deli is appealing during a tour of the area's fall foliage, as we also like to enjoy a sandwich and a bowl of soup when there's a nip in the air.

🌿 LEMON BARS 🌿

Crust

2 cups flour
½ cup powdered sugar
1 cup butter

Preheat oven to 350 degrees. Combine ingredients in a bowl or food processor, forming a course meal. Press into a sheet pan. Bake for 15 minutes.

Filling

2 cups sugar
6 large eggs
¾ cup flour
1¼ teaspoons baking powder
1⅓ cups lemon juice
powdered sugar for garnish

Combine all ingredients except powdered sugar in a large mixing bowl. Pour mixture over crust. Bake at 350 degrees for 45 minutes until firm in center. Cool. Sprinkle with powdered sugar and cut into bars. Yields about 2 dozen bars.

🌿　🌿　🌿　🌿　🌿

🌿 AMERICAN POTATO SALAD 🌿

5 pounds Idaho potatoes
½ bunch celery, chopped
½ large green pepper, chopped fine
½ large red pepper, chopped fine
1½ teaspoons celery seed
salt and white pepper to taste
1½ to 1¾ cups mayonnaise
1½ tablespoons Dijon mustard

Cook potatoes in a pot of water until a fork goes through easily. Cool potatoes in refrigerator, then peel and cube. Add remaining ingredients and mix well. Use more mayonnaise if necessary. Serves 16 to 20.

🌿　🌿　🌿　🌿　🌿

CHAPTER 12

All Aboard!

Railroad House

Get on board for a terrific dining experience. The restaurants in this chapter have one thing in common—trains. Most have been fashioned from old stations, but there are a couple of railroad cars, too. The abundant memorabilia transports guests back to a golden age. You don't want to miss these choo-choos!

DiSalvo's Station

325 MCKINLEY AVENUE
LATROBE, PA 15650
724-539-0500

One of only eleven restaurants in the nation to be nominated for the Culinary Institute of America's prestigious Augie Award in 1996, DiSalvo's is definitely unique. Guests enter the restaurant by traversing a tunnel formerly used for the arrival and departure of rail passengers. At the end of the tunnel, the old train yard has been transformed into an vast atrium with cobblestone floors, lush greenery, and an elaborate marble fountain. A full-size railroad dining car is dwarfed by the room's proportions.

Each nook and cranny of the former train station, now a nationally registered historic landmark, has its own personality and collection of memorabilia. The main dining room was originally the concourse. A lush green Victorian floral carpet covers the floor. At the peak of the high, mahogany ceiling is a stained-glass window bearing the Pennsylvania Railroad insignia; that insignia is duplicated in the leaded-glass windows of the nearby taproom. The taproom was formerly used for ticketing and luggage, while the Latrobe Room served as the railway express office.

A special feature of DiSalvo's is its Prima Classe, or what it terms "a restaurant within the restaurant." Guests are seated in the atrium's dining car, which has been fully restored to opulence, boasting hand-carved Italian wood, linen tablecloths, silver, crystal, and beautiful sconces. The menu here, offered on Friday and Saturday, is delivered verbally. Only fresh products available from market that day are served. Attentive service is provided by executive chef Gaetano DiSalvo and host Joseph DiSalvo.

While the menu is predominantly Italian, other favorites are also available. In addition, guests are invited to make special requests. If the kitchen has the ingredients, the staff will make the dish. That option was tempting, but we found the Fettuccine with Mushrooms, Bacon, and Sweet Peas even more so. The pasta was prepared perfectly al dente, and the accompanying Garlic Bread was just the right balance between crisp and moist.

During our meal, an Amtrak train rumbled overhead, bringing to life the restaurant's past. This past can be traced back to 1851 and credited to Oliver Barnes. It was in that year that Barnes, a civil engineer for the Pennsylvania Railroad, bought a 140-acre farm with the intention of developing a new town. He donated 3 acres of his purchase to the railroad for a right of way, then began laying out the streets of Latrobe on either side.

By the turn of the century, Barnes's town was becoming a hub for industrial transportation. A train station was needed to help manage the load. This structure was completed in 1903. For almost seventy years, it served Latrobe's bustling populace, only to be closed, abandoned, and scheduled for demolition. Now, as DiSalvo's, it serves the town once more.

ZABAGLIONE CON LO SPUMANTE

4 egg yolks
¼ cup sugar
½ cup sparkling wine, divided
1 pound mixed fresh or frozen berries (raspberries, blueberries, strawberries)
4 sprigs mint

In the top half of a double boiler, whisk egg yolks and sugar to a creamy consistency. Heat water in bottom of double boiler. Place top half over the water, making sure it doesn't touch the water. Beat mixture with a whisk about 5 minutes until it starts to thicken; be careful not to beat too long, or you will cook the eggs. Remove from heat and stir in ¼ cup of the wine, whisking until well incorporated. Return mixture to double boiler and whisk 3 to 5 minutes until thickened. Remove from heat and set aside. Divide berries among 4 wineglasses or dessert bowls and spoon 1 tablespoon of remaining wine over each. Top with the custard and decorate with a mint sprig. Dessert can be eaten warm or chilled. Serves 4.

Note: Guests call ahead to make sure chef Gaetano DiSalvo has this ready for them!

HOMEMADE BISCOTTI

6 eggs
1¼ cups sugar
1 orange rind, grated
1 teaspoon vanilla extract
1¼ cups vegetable oil
2 cups flour
2 tablespoons baking powder
2 pounds toasted hazelnuts or cashews, chopped coarse
cooking spray

Break eggs into a small mixing bowl. Add sugar, orange rind, and vanilla. Beat on medium speed for 10 to 12 minutes. *Slowly* add vegetable oil. In a separate bowl, combine flour and baking powder. *Slowly* add flour mixture to egg mixture. Beat on low for 2 minutes. Fold mixture by hand until smooth; there should be *no* lumps. Gently fold in nuts with a rubber spatula. Spray 6 loaf pans with cooking spray. Divide the dough evenly into pans, using approximately 1 inch of batter in each. Bake at 350 degrees for about 15 minutes. Let stand in pans for 5 minutes. Remove from pans and place on cooling rack for 5 minutes. Using a sharp knife, slice each loaf into 1-inch slices; you should have 10 to 12 slices per loaf. Arrange slices on a cookie sheet and place in oven for 5 to 6 minutes until lightly toasted. Yields 5 to 6 dozen cookies.

LACKAWANNA STATION
700 LACKAWANNA AVENUE
SCRANTON, PA 18503
570-342-8300

The history of Scranton is strongly tied to the emergence of the iron, coal, and railroad industries, as George and Seldon Scranton utilized the iron-ore deposits discovered throughout the Lackawanna Valley. The 1840s saw the construction of the city's first iron mills, which inspired the addition of several railroad lines to support them. This service allowed Scranton to capitalize on the fact that it possessed one of the world's largest stores of anthracite coal.

As Scranton flourished, entrepreneurs flocked to the city. In 1899, the president of the Delaware, Lackawanna, and Western designated that railroad headquarters and a new passenger station be built in Scranton. When completed in 1908, Scranton's Lackawanna Station was heralded as one of the most beautiful stations in the country. A five-story structure in the French Renaissance style, it summed up Scranton as a city in one architectural fete. As the iron, coal, and railroad industries declined, Lackawanna Station was closed, and the hustle and bustle were silenced.

Under the supervision of the Pennsylvania Historical Museum Commission, an extensive renovation of Lackawanna Station was completed in 1983. The original brass was polished and the limestone, marble, and tile were all restored to their original tones. Terrazzo floors and faience panels depicting scenes from the old rail route testify to the workmanship from days gone by. Once again, visitors can enjoy the story-and-a-half waiting room with its barrel-vaulted ceiling of leaded glass. The building is now Scranton's Radisson Hotel, and the Grand Lobby is now Carmen's, a Four Diamond restaurant.

Seated in the plum-upholstered Victorian parlor chairs, we immediately began to crane our necks to take in the opulence. The original station clock was there, still keeping time, while the fountain gurgled quietly and classical music played softly in the background. Everything on the breakfast menu was appealing. With a little encouragement from John Birtel, the manager of Carmen's, we sampled several of the dishes. The Delaware and Hudson Omelet was full of chunky extras such as ham, sausage, red onions, peppers, and mushrooms. The Wyoming Valley French Toast was wonderfully crunchy and absolutely perfect without syrup. Likewise, the Cinnamon and Apple Crepes were delicious without any additional topping.

The lunch menu offered choices every bit as appealing, like Shrimp Lucian, which consists of shrimp stuffed with crab and served in Tomato-Lime Beurre Blanc. For dinner, how about Teriyaki-Marinated Ahi Tuna, served with Mango Purée and coconut milk? Or Tomato Basil Risotto, served with crab, shrimp, asparagus, and mascarpone cheese?

For those looking for a sandwich menu, the old station also offers Trax Bar & Grille, where meals are served under the very canopy where trains once entered to load and unload. Whether you choose the nostalgia of Trax or the more formal Carmen's, a trip to Lackawanna Station is sure to sate both your interest in history and your appetite.

VEAL CHOPS WITH BLUE CHEESE SAUCE

Veal chops

½ teaspoon cayenne pepper
½ teaspoon dried thyme
½ teaspoon garlic powder
¼ teaspoon white pepper
¼ teaspoon black pepper
¼ teaspoon salt
4 10-ounce veal chops, trimmed
oil

Combine cayenne, thyme, garlic powder, white pepper, black pepper, and salt in a small bowl. Brush both sides of chops with oil. Sprinkle spice mixture over both sides. Grill over medium-high heat to desired doneness, about 4 minutes per side for medium-rare. Arrange 1 veal chop on each of 4 plates. Spoon Blue Cheese Sauce over top and serve. Serves 4.

Blue Cheese Sauce

¾ cup dry white wine
¼ cup shallots, minced

1 cup whipping cream
¾ cup blue cheese, crumbled
salt and pepper to taste

Boil wine and shallots in a medium saucepan about 6 minutes until reduced by ½. Strain mixture and return wine to pan. Add whipping cream and boil about 10 minutes until sauce is reduced to ¾ cup. Whisk in blue cheese. Boil about 3 minutes until thickened to a sauce consistency. Season with salt and pepper. Cover and refrigerate. Rewarm over low heat before serving. Yields approximately 1 cup.

Note: This sauce can be prepared 4 hours ahead.

WYOMING VALLEY FRENCH TOAST

4 ounces cream cheese
4 slices Texas toast or thick slices French bread
¼ cup strawberry jam
2 eggs
1 tablespoon sugar
½ cup almonds, toasted and sliced

Spread half of cream cheese on 2 pieces of Texas toast. On the other 2 pieces, spread remaining cream cheese, then top with strawberry jam. Put slices together to make 2 sandwiches. Whisk eggs and sugar together in a shallow dish. Dip each sandwich into egg batter, then into toasted almonds. Place on a griddle or in a skillet over medium heat. Cook 2 to 3 minutes on each side until browned. Serves 2.

BOWERS HOTEL

BOWERS ROAD AND OLD BOWERS ROAD
BOWERS, PA 19511
610-682-2900

Located midway between Reading and Allentown, this hotel came into being when Jonas Bower donated land in back of his farmhouse to the Reading Railroad Company for the line running from New York City to Harrisburg via Reading. The land was originally part of a 147-acre plantation purchased by Jonas's father, Michael Bauer, who arrived from Germany in 1766.

As the rail company was constructing a station for this East Penn Branch of its railroad, Jonas Bower built a simple, square log cabin to provide lodging, food, and beverages to the rail passengers. Shortly afterward, the stone-and-brick structure known today as the Bowers Hotel began to emerge.

In the tavern area, the original hand-carved backbar has been preserved, as has an original gas lamp, which is still lit every business day. Adorning a wall of the barroom is a picture of Calista "Sis" Mathias, who for fifty-four years ran the tavern for a drinking crowd of factory workers from the Fleetwood and Topton areas. Black-and-white photos from those days are displayed for current visitors to enjoy.

The remainder of the restaurant consists of three lovely dining rooms. The original high ceilings and Federal-style woodwork are still there, thanks to the renovation efforts of current owners Jeffrey Milkins and Steven Parker. Milkins's eighteenth-, nineteenth-, and twentieth-century oil paintings are lovely accents to the decor. The Green Room, the smallest of the three dining rooms, is decorated in a quiet hunter green. Mr. Milkins is particularly fond of the Red Room, a cheery room with red-and-white Victorian-inspired wallpaper. The Blue Room has lovely blue-and-white woodwork, with Federal-style striped wallpaper above. Brass chandeliers provide elegant lighting, while white lace curtains at the windows allow additional soft light. The six-panel shutter-style room dividers are original and quite unique. During the renovation, the owners considered removing them. However, after seeing similar room shutters during a visit to The Hermitage—Andrew Jackson's former home in Nashville, Tennessee—they decided to keep the dividers, which are now a favorite topic of conversation.

It was in the soothing Blue Room that we chatted about the hotel and its renovation over a delicious lunch. Mr. Milkins recommended the Baked Spinach Balls, served with Honey-Mustard Sauce. It was a delicious combination. Debbie also tried the soup du jour, a Spicy Thai Beef, which was tastefully garnished with chopped peanuts. It was a good choice on a blustery fall day. The lunch-sized Stir-Fry portions were incredibly large. We also tried the Chicken Caesar Sandwich, which consisted of two thin chicken breasts in a

Caesar Dressing, topped with lettuce and tomato, all served on toasted Garlic Bread. It was most unusual and very flavorful.

Special events are popular at the Bowers Hotel. Once a year, the restaurant participates in the Chili Festival, held at the park just down the street. Vendors come from across Pennsylvania, as well as from other states. Festival-goers can sample a wide variety of chili peppers, take a wagon ride to the nearby pepper farm, and, most importantly, sample the three chili recipes of chef Tamara of the Bowers Hotel—tomato-based Chili, White Chili, and Seafood Chili. You can even have chili for dessert, but you have to get there early. Each year, the supply of Chocolate-Chili Ice Cream disappears before the guests do!

TRIO OF ROASTED POTATOES

2 large sweet potatoes, peeled and diced
4 large Yukon Gold potatoes, peeled and diced
8 small, new red potatoes, quartered
¼ cup olive oil
1 tablespoon fresh garlic, chopped
2 tablespoons fresh thyme, chopped, or 1 tablespoon dried thyme
1 teaspoon salt
½ teaspoon pepper
cooking spray

Preheat oven to 400 degrees. Mix diced and quartered potatoes with olive oil and spices; make sure potatoes are well coated. Spread out potatoes on a baking sheet sprayed with cooking oil. Make sure pan is big enough for potatoes; in order for potatoes to roast properly, they shouldn't be crowded. Bake in oven for about 15 minutes until soft. Serves 6.

PORKCHOPS WITH APPLE STUFFING

1 medium onion, diced
4 stalks celery, diced
4 tablespoons olive oil, divided
2 tablespoons butter
8 Granny Smith apples, peeled and diced
½ teaspoon sage
½ teaspoon nutmeg
1 teaspoon cinnamon
½ teaspoon salt
½ teaspoon white pepper
¼ cup brown sugar
2 cups bread, diced
8 ½-inch-thick center-cut porkchops
½ cup flour

Preheat oven to 350 degrees. Sauté onions and celery in 2 tablespoons of the olive oil and the butter until onions are transparent. Add apples and sauté for 5 minutes. Add spices and brown sugar. Cover and reduce heat to low. Cook 10 to 15 minutes until apples are soft. Add bread cubes and stir. Dip porkchops in flour. Brown chops on both sides in the remaining 2 tablespoons of olive oil, using more if needed. Lay 4 porkchops in a baking dish and top with apple stuffing. Place remaining 4 chops on top of stuffing and bake for 25 to 35 minutes. Serves 4.

On the banks of the Monongahela River just across from downtown Pittsburgh sits the old Pittsburgh & Lake Erie Railroad terminal, now known as the Grand Concourse. It was built in 1901, during the golden age of railroads, when the wealthy traveled in opulent style. The terminal had been vacant for nearly a decade when it was rescued by Chuck Muer, a visionary who has made a career out of salvaging such buildings.

One of the biggest challenges came in undoing a World War II renovation. As part of a blackout during that time, the vaulted, stained-glass ceiling was painted. It took gallons and gallons of oven cleaner to restore this marvelous part of the architecture to its original state. First-time visitors frequently crane their necks trying to appreciate the magnitude and beauty of the workmanship.

As a matter of fact, the entire concourse, now the main dining room, is breathtaking in its lavish excess. Extraordinary floral arrangements, lovely table appointments, and luxurious seating create a truly posh experience. Adjacent to the concourse is the Oyster Bar, once the baggage-claim room and now a great place to grab a drink or wait for a coveted table during the very popular Sunday brunch. Our favorite thing to do is partake of the Cinnamon-Sugar Donuts, made while you watch by an old-fashioned donut machine. Next door is the Gandy Dancer, originally the ticket office. It's a casual alternative to the more upscale main dining room. The name *gandy dancer* is derived from the Gandy Company, which made railroad equipment. Through the years, anyone who worked with this equipment became known as a gandy dancer. If it's a great view you covet, the River Room should be your choice. Once the loading dock, it's now glassed in and boasts a terrific view of the river, Pittsburgh's skyline, and the Smithfield Street Bridge, more than a century old.

Nary a detail has been overlooked at the Grand Concourse. Menus are posted where old train bulletins once were. The seating from days of old has been replicated, in keeping with the ambiance. Attention to detail is obvious on the menu as well. For lunch, appetizer choices such as Crepes Aubergine, Escargots in Puff Pastry, and Baked Brie Almondine can be augmented with a soup or side salad. There are also plenty of sandwich, fish, pasta, main salad, and entrée choices. Many of the lunch items are featured on the dinner menu as well, with other delicious choices added. Seafood, a house specialty, can be prepared according to your preference. The Mussels à la Muer are wonderful, and the Lobster Ravioli, served in Basil Cream Sauce, are divine. Always, always, always save room for dessert. Debbie would be hard pressed to pick a favorite. Karen, on the other hand, gives her vote unwaveringly to the Bananas Foster.

SMOKED BLUEFISH PÂTÉ

1 pound smoked bluefish
8-ounce package cream cheese, room temperature
4 tablespoons margarine, room temperature
¼ cup heavy cream
1 tablespoon horseradish
⅛ teaspoon Tabasco sauce
chopped parsley for garnish

Prepare bluefish by skinning it and removing bones. Place cleaned bluefish in the bowl of an electric mixer. Mix until fish is reduced to small flakes. Add cream cheese, margarine, cream, horseradish, and Tabasco. Continue mixing until smooth. Transfer pâté to a storage container with a lid and refrigerate until ready to use. To serve, place pâté in a serving bowl and smooth its top surface with a hot knife. Garnish with chopped parsley. Serve with assorted crackers. Yields 3 cups.

TUNA AU POIVRE

4 tablespoons butter, divided
2 tablespoons shallots, diced fine
½ cup brandy
1 teaspoon Worcestershire sauce
1 tablespoon plus 1 teaspoon Dijon mustard
1 cup heavy cream
½ teaspoon salt
⅛ teaspoon white pepper
1½ pounds yellowfin tuna, cut into 8 medallions, each ¾ inch thick
4 tablespoons olive oil
3 tablespoons ground black pepper
1 teaspoon salt

Melt 2 tablespoons of the butter in a small stainless-steel saucepan and sauté shallots on medium heat for 1 minute. Add brandy. Briefly let brandy warm, then carefully ignite it with a long kitchen match. After alcohol has flamed away, add Worcestershire and Dijon and simmer for 1½ minutes. Add cream and let sauce cook until it is reduced by ⅓. Using a whisk, whip in remaining butter. Add salt and white pepper. Keep sauce warm until ready to serve. Brush tuna medallions with olive oil, cover top and bottom surface with black pepper, and season with salt. Serves 4.

Railroad House

WEST FRONT AND SOUTH PERRY STREETS
MARIETTA, PA 17547
717-426-4141

The town of Marietta was created from the vision of David Cook and James Anderson. In 1803 and 1804, the two men began developing towns side by side on the banks of the Susquehanna River. Eight years later, they decided to join forces. They named the combined community Marietta, after their wives, Mary and Henrietta. The town soon became vital to the lumber industry and for transportation along one of Pennsylvania's main rivers. In addition, the Pennsylvania Main Line Canal, which ran from Philadelphia to Pittsburgh, passed right through town.

Accommodations were soon needed for those traveling the river and canal. Construction on an inn and tavern located on the edge of the canal began in 1820 and was completed in 1823. The hotel became a mecca for hardworking, rough-living river men. Its walls "reverberated with inebriate good cheer, and an occasional brawl," according to one account.

The Portage Railroad, later known as the Pennsylvania Standard, eventually replaced the canal. The waiting room and ticket office for rail passengers were located in the old inn and tavern

until Marietta Station was constructed across the street in 1860. More than thirty years later, the Railroad House, as the inn had become known, came under the ownership of Colonel Thomas Scott, who had been assistant secretary of war under Abraham Lincoln.

The Railroad House continued to prosper until the 1930s, when the accumulated neglect of the Depression and the effects of a flood in 1936 caused extensive deterioration. It sat vacant until it was sold at auction by the federal government in the late 1950s. Restoration began during the next decade and continued into the 1970s. Today, under the ownership of Richard and Donna Chambers, the Victorian home serves as a bed-and-breakfast, tavern, and restaurant.

Three dining rooms fill much of the first level, which has original plank flooring throughout. Guests seated to the right of the hallway enjoy a Victorian atmosphere. Across the hall, the surroundings are slightly more casual. Tucked away in the inn's original kitchen is another cozy dining room, where the focal point is the enormous fireplace.

No longer as rowdy as it once was, the Railroad House has a more refined menu as well. The restaurant has been featured in *Bon Appétit* magazine, among other publications. Richard prepares classic American cuisine with continental overtones. Dinner entrées range from Chicken Moutarde to Seafood Mélange to Straw and Hay, a delicious dish made from shrimp, scallops, and lobster, served over Spinach and Egg Fettuccine and topped with Mornay Sauce.

We chose to experience breakfast, and what an experience it was! The Fruit Cups and Muffins that started us off were just teasers for the fabulous entrée to come. Accompanied by Sausage Links and Home-Fried Potatoes, the Pandora French Toast was exquisite, topped with lightly cooked apples in creamy Cinnamon Sauce. It is rare that either of us feels that we've tasted something really unusual at the breakfast table, but we can assure you that we enjoyed every bite of this creative dish.

PUMPKIN PECAN CHEESECAKE

Cheesecake

1½ cups graham cracker crumbs
1 cup sugar, divided
6 tablespoons butter, melted
3 8-ounce packages cream cheese, room temperature
¾ cup brown sugar, packed firm
5 large eggs
16-ounce can pumpkin
½ cup whipping cream
½ teaspoon ground cinnamon
½ teaspoon ground nutmeg
¼ teaspoon ground cloves
topping (see next column)

Blend graham cracker crumbs, ¼ cup of the sugar, and butter in a medium bowl. Press mixture in bottom and up sides of a 9-by-2½-inch springform pan. Chill. Preheat oven to 325 degrees. Using an electric mixer, beat cream cheese in a large bowl until smooth. Mix in remaining ¾ cup of sugar and brown sugar. Add eggs 1 at a time and beat until fluffy. Blend in pumpkin, cream, cinnamon, nutmeg, and cloves.

Pour into crust. Bake about 1½ hours until center no longer moves when pan is shaken. After cheesecake sets, sprinkle topping over top and bake an additional 15 minutes. Transfer to wire rack to cool. Cover and refrigerate overnight. Can be prepared 2 days ahead. Yields 1 cheesecake.

Topping

¾ cup brown sugar, packed firm
6 tablespoons chilled butter
1½ cups pecans, chopped

Place brown sugar in a small bowl. Cut in butter until mixture resembles coarse meal. Stir in pecans.

SHRIMP CHAMPAGNE BISQUE

1 cup celery, diced fine
1 cup carrots, diced fine
½ cup chicken consommé or chicken stock
1 tablespoon Old Bay seasoning
¼ cup champagne
1 to 2 cups uncooked shrimp, ground
8 cups heavy cream

In a stock pot, cook celery, carrots, consommé, and Old Bay until vegetables are tender. Add champagne and stir. Add ground shrimp and stir with a whisk until smooth. Add heavy cream and cook until done. Serves 8 to 10.

TARENTUM STATION

101 STATION DRIVE
TARENTUM, PA 15084
724-226-3301

Trains don't stop here anymore, but Tarentum Station is still a busy place full of hustle and bustle. Owner John Azzara shouts a cheery hello from behind the bar, stops at tables to greet guests, and answers the train-shaped phone as it chugs, puffs, and toots within earshot of everyone. We ate here twice during the writing of the book, both at lunchtime. On each occasion, the restaurant was full and people were waiting. Tarentum Station certainly is a popular spot with the locals.

Once upon a time, the Pennsylvania Canal ran through town on its way from Philadelphia to Pittsburgh. During the late 1800s, the railroad replaced the canal. The old train station, located a couple of blocks down the street from where Tarentum Station now stands, burned to the ground in the early 1900s. Tarentum Station was built as a replacement in 1913, becoming the town's third building for this purpose. The structure was ready for use in 1914 for passengers traveling on the Pennsylvania Railroad via the Apollo train.

The tracks still run just outside the stained-glass front door. The period benches available for the overflow crowd are frequently full. The cream and colonial blue interior and the ceiling fans whirring overhead are in keeping with the history of this relic. Train-related bric-a-brac is in almost every nook and cranny and above some of the doors. Switching lanterns hang in each window. Timetables, train pictures, and period photographs adorn the walls. Tin lunch buckets, lanterns, and other assorted items sit on the stairway ledge leading up to the additional dining rooms.

The menu is Italian-American and the portion sizes ample. The Meatball Soup is hot and delicious, especially on a cold, rainy day. The Garlic Bread is wonderful, amply buttered, with Romano cheese sprinkled over the slices. The sandwiches are huge and delicious. They appear on the menu in a section labeled "Club Car Sandwiches," while the salads are categorized as "Dining Car Salads." Each of the burger choices is named for a railroad company, such as the Conrail and the Atchison, Topeka, and the Santa Fe. The dinner menu boasts the same type of creativity. The "Through the Farmland" section highlights chicken, veal, and pork selections. "Building up Steam" houses the appetizer choices, while "A Whistle Stop in Italy" rounds out the menu with Tarentum Station's pasta selections.

Remember to go early and hungry for maximum enjoyment of your trip to Tarentum Station.

ITALIAN PORKCHOPS

2 7-ounce porkchops
1 banana pepper, cut into small rings, seeds removed
½ leek or scallion, white part only, sliced fine
6 mushrooms, sliced
1 clove garlic, minced
2 plum tomatoes, diced
3 tablespoons cooking oil
½ cup beef or veal stock
½ cup white wine
fresh parsley for garnish

Score porkchops on a hot grill for about 2 minutes per side. Sauté banana pepper, leek, mushrooms, garlic, and tomatoes in oil until tender. Pour off oil. Add stock and wine. Place porkchops in a baking dish and pour mixture from skillet over top. Bake in a 325-degree oven for 15 to 20 minutes. To serve, place a porkchop on each of 2 plates, pour stock and vegetables over top, then sprinkle with parsley. Serves 2.

BEANS AND GREENS

2 bunches escarole
4 cloves garlic, minced
1 cup olive oil
15-ounce can canellini beans
1 stick butter
½ cup chicken stock
salt and pepper to taste
pinch of red pepper flakes
½ cup freshly grated Romano cheese

Clean escarole and cut into small pieces. Boil in salted water until tender. Drain well. Sauté garlic in oil until browned. Add escarole and bring to a simmer. Add beans and butter and bring back to a simmer. Add chicken stock and continue to simmer a few more minutes. Season with salt and pepper and red pepper flakes. Stir in Romano. Heat through and serve. Serves 4.

CHAPTER 13

Guess Who Came to Dinner?

Summit Inn

The average citizen enjoys hearing of the comings and goings of prominent individuals. From our founding fathers to modern entertainers, well-known guests have visited the restaurants in this chapter. We can't promise that anyone other than John Q. Public will be dining during your visit, but you're sure to enjoy the menu selections, just as the celebrities did.

CITY TAVERN

138 SOUTH SECOND STREET
PHILADELPHIA, PA 19106
215-413-1443

When its door first opened in 1773, this place was described as "a large and commodious tavern." It was commissioned and built by subscription. A group of fifty-three investors who wanted to create the atmosphere of a London tavern came together to raise the money. Situated near the city's center, the City Tavern soon became a place for important people to meet. The first proprietor, Daniel Smith, is known to have leased the tavern for the princely sum of three hundred pounds a year.

In late 1774, it was used as an informal gathering place for the members of the First Continental Congress. Such well-known men as George Washington, Thomas Jefferson, and Richard Henry Lee could be found here discussing politics and taking their meals in the private dining rooms. Indeed, John Adams once called it "the most genteel tavern in America."

Throughout the next eighty years, the City Tavern maintained its importance by serving the public in many ways. American and British forces both used the tavern for housing prisoners of war during 1776 and 1777. Many famous court-martials were held here during that time. In 1789, the tavern became the Merchants' Coffee House and Place of Exchange, the first place that merchants visited upon their arrival in Philadelphia. Patrons could share newspapers, discuss the latest shipping news, and conduct business. By 1799, the City Tavern was the most important financial institution in the city.

Today, the City Tavern continues to reflect the ambiance of the eighteenth century. The wait staff dresses in historically correct, handmade period clothing, adding charm to the elegant colonial surroundings. Culinary historians have lent their expertise to determine the ingredients and beverages used in days gone by.

On the day we visited, we were met by Karina Kachurak, the director of public relations for Walter Staib, the current proprietor. She recalled tales about the painstaking research carried out to ensure that countless items in the tavern are in keeping with the time period. Everything—from the lead-free pewter serving ware on all the tables to the brass candlesticks to the specially made dishes—has been researched and verified.

Karina encouraged us to sample many of the delightful dishes on the lunch menu. We began with a glass of Shrub, a fruit-and-vinegar concentrate usually topped off with water (or something a little stronger). Then came a fine selection of breads—Sally Lunn, Anadama, and Sweet Potato Biscuits made with pecans and molasses, reputed to be Thomas Jefferson's favorite! Both the Mallard Duck Sausage and the West Indies Pepper Pot Soup were delicious and full of flavor, though the Cold Cucumber Soup was our personal favorite. Karen enjoyed the

Colonial Turkey Pot Pie, which contained tender chunks of turkey, mushrooms, early peas, and red potatoes in a Sherried Cream Sauce, topped by light, flaky pastry. Debbie opted for the Roast Platter, which consisted of smoked chicken, roasted meats, and baked ham. She found her dish just as appetizing. We have to be honest and relate that we sampled every single dessert on the menu, and they were all fabulous. We encourage you to step back in time and visit the City Tavern, "a triumph of tradition."

WEST INDIES PEPPER POT SOUP

¾ pound salt-cured pork, chopped
¾ pound salt-cured beef, chopped
2 tablespoons vegetable oil
1 medium white onion, chopped
4 cloves garlic, chopped
¼ Scotch Bonnet pepper, seeded and chopped
1 cup scallions, chopped
1 pound taro root, peeled and cut into 2-by-¼-inch
    strips
16 cups chicken stock
2 bay leaves
1 teaspoon fresh thyme, chopped
1 tablespoon freshly ground allspice
1 tablespoon freshly ground black pepper
1 pound callaloo or collard greens, rinsed and
    chopped
salt and pepper to taste

In a large stockpot, sauté pork and beef in oil over high heat for 10 minutes until brown. Add onions, garlic, and Scotch Bonnet pepper and sauté for 3 to 5 minutes until onions are translucent. Add scallions and sauté for 3 minutes. Add taro root and sauté for 3 to 5 minutes until translucent. Add chicken stock, bay leaves, thyme, allspice, and black pepper. Bring to a boil over high heat, then reduce heat to medium and cook for about 30 minutes until meat and taro root are tender. Stir in callaloo. Reduce heat and simmer for about 5 minutes until wilted. Season with salt and pepper. Serves 10.

Note: To salt-cure pork and beef, rub an entire well-marbled shoulder of meat with coarse salt and refrigerate for at least 3 days. Wash salt off meat before cooking.

RICE PUDDING

2 cups water
¾ cup long-grain white rice, uncooked
2½ cups whole milk
½ cup granulated sugar
3 large eggs
1½ tablespoons unsalted butter, softened
1½ teaspoons vanilla extract
2 teaspoons ground cinnamon, divided

Preheat oven to 325 degrees. In a 2-quart saucepan, bring water to a boil and add rice. Simmer covered for 15 to 20 minutes, then let stand covered for 5 minutes; drain if necessary. In a separate saucepan, bring milk to a boil. Stir in rice and cook for 10 minutes until grains become soft. In a large bowl, whisk together sugar, eggs, butter, vanilla, and 1 teaspoon of the cinnamon. Gradually stir rice mixture into egg mixture. Place in a 2-quart ovenproof glass or ceramic dish, then place dish in a larger, high-sided roasting pan. Carefully pour boiling water into roasting pan to a depth of 1½ inches around dish. Bake covered for 20 to 30 minutes until a knife inserted near the center comes out clean. Sprinkle remaining cinnamon on top as a garnish. Serves 6.

THE JEFFERSON HOUSE RESTAURANT

2519 DEKALB PIKE
NORRISTOWN, PA 19401
610-275-3407

The elegant structure that we now know as The Jefferson House Restaurant was built as a private residence in 1848. When the estate was partially destroyed by fire in 1920, an architect rebuilt the home in a style strongly influenced by a Thomas Jefferson design. Today, the property encompasses not only the mansion and its seven dining rooms but also ten acres of landscaped grounds, a wooded duck pond, a 150-year-old springhouse, a fountain, and two Italian gazebos.

Angelo Romano and his wife, Betty, have a thirty-year history here. The Romanos, their daughter, Linda Romano Groff, and their son-in-law, Thomas Groff, own and operate The Jefferson House. Angelo's career includes significant events dating back to when he was seventeen years old. At that time, he was apprenticed to master chef Henry Sidoli at the Warwick Hotel in Philadelphia. One day, none other than baseball legend Joe DiMaggio walked in and ordered a hamburger. The chef told young Romano to instead prepare a seven-course meal. Duly impressed, DiMaggio asked to meet the creator of his feast. The athlete predicted that the young man would one day own his own restaurant. Romano responded by saying, "Mr.

DiMaggio, if that comes true, I will owe you another dinner." Thirty-five years later, DiMaggio booked a table at The Jefferson House Restaurant. Unbeknownst to him, his prediction had come true, and Romano now owned the restaurant. Once again, Angelo Romano created the most elaborate meal he could concoct. Afterward, he revealed his identity and reminded DiMaggio of the earlier occurrence. As Romano began the story, the ballplayer quickly chimed in and finished the tale of the dinner thirty-five years prior. DiMaggio didn't pay for his meal after this second encounter. After all, Romano had made a promise that he intended to keep.

During our Sunday visit to The Jefferson House, Mr. Romano greeted guests and saw to their needs with a well-deserved pride. The mansion-turned-restaurant is exquisite in its decor. We were thrilled to be seated in the elegant dining room overlooking the patio and the springhouse, where we enjoyed a lovely view of the grounds. We opted for the prix fixe menu, which is very reasonably priced and available during certain hours every day. Although Karen started with a salad, she had to taste Debbie's Crab Bisque, which we declared the best soup either of us had eaten in quite a while. It was creamy and absolutely full of crab. Nut-Encrusted Pork Loin topped with Berry Sauce and an entrée of Cajun Catfish followed. Both were served with a selection of Steamed Fresh Vegetables. Since we had skipped breakfast, we both had room for a lovely dessert. Karen chose a Profiterole, served with Ice Cream and Chocolate Sauce. The Tart that satisfied Debbie's sweet tooth was full of mixed berries housed in a soft crust. It was a choice that was popular with the guests around us, many of whom were regular visitors. What a bright spot in anyone's week—a lovely Sunday lunch at The Jefferson House!

CHANTERELLES CROSTINI

12-ounce package bacon, chopped
3 pounds chanterelle mushrooms
1½ sticks butter
¼ cup shallots, minced
750-milliliter bottle white wine
1 cup veal or duck demi-glace
1 loaf bread, sliced ⅜ inch thick
3 tablespoons parsley, chopped

Sauté bacon in a large skillet until colored. Add mushrooms and sauté for 5 minutes. Add butter and shallots. Add wine and reduce. Add demi-glace and sauté until mushrooms are coated. To make crostini, place bread slices on a large baking sheet and toast in a 350-degree oven until very crisp. To serve, spoon mushrooms over crostini, then sprinkle with parsley. Serves 12.

SALMON WITH SESAME CRUST AND HONEY MUSTARD VIN BLANC SAUCE

2 cups water
2 cups white wine
2 cups fish stock
1 onion, peeled and cut in half
2 stalks celery
1 carrot, top removed
6 cups heavy cream
1 tablespoon Thai curry paste
10 red peppercorns
1 cup whole mustard
¼ cup honey
salt and pepper to taste
10 6-ounce salmon fillets
1 egg, beaten
½ cup sesame seeds

Put water, wine, stock, onion, celery, and carrot in a thick-bottomed stainless-steel pot. Cook until reduced to 1 cup. Strain and return to pot. Add cream, curry paste, and peppercorns and reduce by ⅓. Add mustard, honey, and salt and pepper. Brush salmon with egg, then coat top of each fillet with sesame seeds. Bake for 10 minutes at 350 degrees. Toast seeds under broiler for color just before serving. To serve, use approximately ½ cup Honey Mustard Vin Blanc Sauce per fillet. Serves 10.

CENTURY INN
EST. 1794

US 40
SCENERY HILL, PA 15360
724-945-6600

What is now US 40 was once a Nemacolin Indian trail and later the oft-traveled National Road, which opened the West to settlers and immigrants. Stephen Hill built Century Inn atop a panoramic knoll along this road in 1794 as a respite between the Pennsylvania towns of Washington and Brownsville. In those days, a team of oxen could travel only ten to twelve miles before needing rest, so hostels of this type were necessities along the National Road. Today, Century Inn presides as the oldest inn in continuous operation along the old thoroughfare.

From stagecoach passengers to wagoners, the guest list at the inn has been long and varied. In May 1825, the Marquis de Lafayette took breakfast here. Andrew Jackson was twice a guest at Century Inn. The second time was on February 1, 1829, as he was on his way to Washington, D.C., for his inauguration as the seventh president of the United States.

It was in 1945 that Dr. Gordon Harrington and his wife, Mary, purchased the inn and began acquiring antiques suitable to its history. Their son, Gordon, and his wife, Megin, are the innkeepers today. As part of their continuing efforts to maintain a decor in keeping with the inn's past, Mary and Megin once hand-stenciled the walls in the bar, using the patterns of Moses Eaton, a recognized stenciling artisan of the early 1800s.

Likewise, executive chef Jim Shaw has researched the foods available to and served by our Pennsylvania ancestors. The menu at Century Inn reflects, but is not limited to, those traditional American dishes. Choices such as Thomas Jefferson's Peanut Soup and Syllabub are offered. We found the Shepherd's Pie and the Cottage Pie deliciously traditional in flavor and plentiful in quantity as luncheon entrées. The traditional Turkey with Savory Stuffing is always on the dinner menu. Or you might try Apricot Quail, filled with chestnuts and wild rice, or Duck Brackenridge, served with Port, Cranberry, and Currant Glaze. Also appealing are the Penn Forest Fillet Medallions, grilled to your specifications and coated with Dark Cherry and Black Walnut Sauce.

Whether you dine in the elegant Music Room, the sunny Garden Room, or the cozy Keeping Room at a table near its large fireplace, the atmosphere and the food will take you back to days of yore. And should you want to extend your enjoyment beyond a delicious meal in one of the five historic dining rooms, this twenty-room stone house can accommodate up to nineteen overnight guests. Although Century Inn is closed for general dining from Christmas through late March, it does host special events such as a Valentine's weekend, business meetings, and weddings during those months.

WILD MUSHROOM STRUDEL

1 shallot, chopped fine
½ cup white wine
4 ounces shiitake mushrooms, chopped coarse
4 ounces oyster mushrooms, chopped coarse
4 ounces crimini mushrooms, chopped coarse
4 ounces button mushrooms, chopped coarse
1 cup heavy cream
1 package Pepperidge Farm puff pastry sheets, thawed according to package directions

Preheat oven to 400 degrees. Place shallots and white wine in a small skillet. Heat on medium until wine is almost completely reduced. Add mushrooms and cream to skillet. Continue heating on medium until reduced by ¾. Open pastry sheets flat. Place ½ of mushroom mixture on each pastry sheet so the sheets can be folded over the mixture lengthwise. Seal edges with a fork. Cut small slits in the top to allow steam to escape. Bake on an oiled cookie sheet for 15 minutes until dough is puffed and lightly browned. Remove from oven and cool slightly before slicing into portions. Serves 8.

SYLLABUB

juice of 1 lemon
½ cup white wine
zest of 1 lemon, chopped fine
2 cups heavy cream
¼ cup powdered sugar

Combine lemon juice, wine, and zest. Place cream and sugar in a chilled bowl and begin whipping. When cream starts to stiffen, very slowly add lemon juice mixture. Continue whipping until mixture is stiff. Use a pastry bag with a star tip to pipe mixture into wine glasses. Serve chilled. Serves 6 to 8.

Whispering Springs

15305 KUTZTOWN ROAD
KUTZTOWN, PA 19530
610-683-7310

Whispering Springs Restaurant & Pub caught my eye as I drove along Kutztown Road while out exploring without Debbie. The imposing stone walls and colonial blue balustrades and shutters were enhanced by large carriage lamps on either side of the front door. The main dining room, known as the Kemp Room, has paneled walls, original fireplaces, and tabard draperies at each window, all of which contribute to the colonial feel. There are two other period dining rooms here as well.

Seated in the Kemp Room, I chatted with owner Greg Poletti about the restoration of this 1740 landmark. He told me that his children had refinished the beautiful poplar tabletops and that his sister-in-law was the interior decorator. It was clear that the whole family had done a terrific job of re-creating the colonial heritage in every room.

The tradition of great food and attentive service began over 250 years ago. Daniel Levan built his home in 1740. Soon afterward, it became the first tavern in the area, known as a safe haven for travelers seeking refuge from Indian raids. Levan's Tavern was expanded in 1765 to accommodate the growing number of patrons who passed through its doors.

Many notable figures of the American Revolution, such as the Marquis de Lafayette and George Washington, passed along this road and stopped to dine or sleep as they went to and from sessions of the Continental Congress, which met in York. Records show that John Adams lodged here on September 25, 1777.

After forty-five years of keeping the inn, Daniel Levan sold the business to his son-in-law, George Kemp, who promptly renamed the inn after himself. The Kemp Hotel was kept in the family for five generations. In fact, Luther Kemp, the great-great-great-grandson of Daniel Levan, represented the proud family in 1978 when the structure was placed on the National Register of Historic Places.

After the Kemps' tenure, the inn was renamed Whispering Springs. In 1997, the Polettis added their touch when they began to offer contemporary American cuisine in this relaxing colonial atmosphere. The varied menu offers choices such as a Lemon Pepper Chicken Sandwich, a variety of Gourmet Pizzas, and tasty entrée selections such as Shanghai Shrimp and Scallops and Grand Marnier Poached Salmon. I opted for the Maryland Crab Cakes with Garlic Parmesan Red Potatoes. The selection of warm, home-baked Bread that accompanied this dish was incredible, and the Hawaiian Pineapple Butter was as delicious as it was unusual. For dessert, I opted for the Chocolate Caramel Pecan Fudge Cake, which was everything a chocolate dessert should be.

❦ FISH CHOWDER ❦

3 tablespoons plus ¾ teaspoon olive oil
½ cup onion, diced coarse
½ cup red bell pepper, cut into ½-inch squares
14 ounces red potatoes, cubed
1 cup water
1⅞ cups seafood stock
7 tablespoons dry white wine
dash of Tabasco sauce
½ teaspoon dried basil
3 tablespoons plus ¾ teaspoon tomato purée
½ teaspoon salt
½ teaspoon pepper
⅔ cup canned tomatoes, diced
2½ ounces clams
3 ounces shrimp, peeled and deveined
2½ ounces scallops
3 ounces catfish
1 pound mussels
2½ scallions, diced

Heat olive oil in a large soup pot and sauté onions and peppers for 10 minutes until soft and translucent. Add potatoes, water, stock, wine, Tabasco, basil, tomato purée, salt, and pepper. Cover and simmer for 15 minutes until potatoes are cooked. Add tomatoes. Cover and simmer for 15 minutes. Wash shellfish and remove muscle from scallops. Add shellfish, catfish, and mussels to other ingredients. Cover and cook for 15 minutes. To serve, pour into bowls and garnish with scallions. Serves 8.

THAI CRAB CAKES WITH CILANTRO PEANUT SAUCE

Crab cakes

1¼ pints fresh breadcrumbs
1 pint bean sprouts, chopped
½ cup green onion, chopped fine
½ cup cilantro, chopped coarse
¼ cup fresh lime juice
¼ teaspoon ground red pepper
2 large eggs
2 egg whites, beaten lightly
2 pounds lump crabmeat
cooking spray
Cilantro Peanut Sauce (see next column)

Combine first 9 ingredients in a medium bowl; cover and chill for 1 hour. Divide mixture into 8 equal portions and shape into ½-inch-thick patties. Spray a cookie sheet with cooking spray. Place crab cakes on sheet and bake at 350 degrees for 10 to 15 minutes until golden brown. Serve with Cilantro Peanut Sauce. Serves 8.

Cilantro Peanut Sauce

¼ cup red wine
⅓ cup granulated sugar
¼ cup soy sauce
1 teaspoon red pepper, crushed
¼ teaspoon salt
2 cloves garlic, minced
¼ cup cider vinegar
¼ cup creamy peanut butter
½ cup fresh cilantro, chopped
¼ cup fresh mint, chopped

Combine first 8 ingredients in a small saucepan and bring to a boil, stirring frequently. Remove from heat and stir with a whisk until smooth. Cool mixture, then stir in cilantro and mint. Yields 1 cup.

CHADDS FORD INN
EST. 1736

US 1 AND PA 100
CHADDS FORD, PA 19317
610-388-7361

The menu at Chadds Ford Inn is a creative combination of traditional dishes and the eclectic cuisine expected by modern diners. Shepherd's Pie appears alongside Saffron Scampi Linguine, while Wild Mushroom Soup is served as frequently as Clam, Spinach, and Roasted Red Pepper Dip. Nibbling on Poppy Seed Rolls flavored with a hint of garlic, we had difficulty deciding from which century to dine. Ultimately, the past won out. The Shepherd's Pie, topped with Garlic Mashed Potatoes, was delicious. Very filling, it would have sated the appetite of long-ago travelers.

It was the year 1703 when Francis Chadsey, a Quaker from Wiltshire, England, purchased five hundred acres from William Penn's commissioner. That acreage encompassed most of what is now Chadds Ford. When Chadsey's eldest son, who signed his name as John Chad, came of age in 1717, he took over the responsibility of operating his father's estate. That responsibility included running the ferry that crossed Brandywine Creek.

When Chad turned the family home into a tavern in 1736, the area was known as Birmingham. However, those seeking directions were usually told to go to "the tavern at Chad's fording place." The name gradually caught on, and Birmingham became Chadds Ford.

Upon Chad's death in 1760, his nephew Joseph Davis took over the tavern. During the Revolutionary War, it was Davis who entertained colonial officers in the days prior to the Battle of Brandywine, which took place near Chadds Ford on September 11, 1777. During that entanglement, colonial soldiers were forced to retreat to the Chester area. British forces swarmed the village and plundered everything in their path. The destruction to the tavern was so severe that Davis was considered to owe no property tax on it. The tavern was not issued a license to operate again until 1810. The inn has been in continuous operation since that time.

Chadds Ford Inn has seen a great deal of American history through the years. Countless Indians, settlers, and soldiers have passed these doors. Martha Washington was a guest as she made her way from Mount Vernon to spend the winter at Valley Forge. General Lafayette visited the inn on his return to the battlefield in 1825. The artists who have found comfort here include Howard Pyle, Peter Hurd, and three generations of the Wyeth family—N. C., Andrew, Henriette, and Carolyn. Their work graces the walls of Chadds Ford Inn today.

Much of the inn remains as it was when Joseph Davis rebuilt it after the Revolutionary War. Throughout most of the structure, lighting is provided by candlelight only. The fireplaces and the plank flooring are original. The draperies hanging in the deep-set windows have patterns reminiscent of crewel needlework done by ladies of a bygone era. Truly, lovers of history will not be disappointed here.

TOMATO ONION SOUP

4 large onions, sliced
¼ cup garlic, chopped
1 teaspoon brown sugar
¼ cup basil, chopped
2 teaspoons thyme
1 bay leaf
¼ cup port wine
2 16-ounce cans peeled tomatoes, chopped
2 12-ounce cans chicken stock
salt and pepper to taste
garlic croutons

In a large skillet, sauté onions, garlic, sugar, basil, thyme, and bay leaf in wine until onions start to brown. Add tomatoes, stock, and salt and pepper. Bring to a boil. Continue simmering until ready to serve. Garnish with garlic croutons. Serves 6 to 8.

POPOVERS

5 eggs
2 tablespoons butter, melted
2½ cups half-and-half
¾ teaspoon salt
2 cups flour
¾ teaspoon baking powder

Combine eggs, butter, and half-and-half in a large mixing bowl. Gradually add salt, flour, and baking powder; continue mixing for at least 10 minutes. Pour into greased muffin tins, filling them ¾ full. Bake in a preheated 375-degree oven for 12 to 15 minutes until golden brown. Yields 12 Popovers.

BEEF AND PORTABELLO CHILI

2½ pounds prime rib, cubed
2 large red peppers, diced
2 large green peppers, diced
1 bunch scallions, chopped
2 large onions, diced
2½ pounds portabello mushrooms, diced
½ bunch cilantro, chopped
1½ cups garlic, chopped
2 cups chili powder
½ cup cumin
¼ cup coriander
1 tablespoon Tabasco sauce or favorite hot sauce
1 tablespoon green Tabasco sauce
1 tablespoon cayenne pepper
28-ounce can whole peeled tomatoes
46-ounce can V-8 juice
¼ cup chocolate sauce
1 cup espresso
salt and pepper to taste

Combine first 14 ingredients in a large skillet or a Dutch oven and sauté until meat is browned. Add remaining ingredients and cook for 2 hours. Serves 12.

The HISTORIC FARNSWORTH HOUSE RESTAURANT & INN

415 BALTIMORE STREET
GETTYSBURG, PA 17325
717-334-8838

Jennie Wade was Gettysburg's only civilian fatality during the fierce battle fought here during the Civil War. She was shot in her home, located at the bottom of Baltimore Hill. It is believed that a Confederate sharpshooter holed up in the garret of Farnsworth House accidentally shot her. He and his comrades lay prone at a small, low window in the house, trying to shoot Union troops as they crossed Baltimore Hill. The hundred-plus bullet holes from return fire scattered across the south wall and the front of the building support the veracity of this.

The original structure dates to 1810. A brick addition constructed by John McFarland was placed at the front of the house in 1833. During the Battle of Gettysburg, the home was occupied by the Sweeney family. After the battle, the structure was renamed in honor of Elon John Farnsworth. Captain Farnsworth was promoted to brigadier general on the eve of the battle. After the failure of the Confederate army during Pickett's Charge on July 3, 1863, Farnsworth's regiment was sent against the right flank of Longstreet's Confederate position. This ill-fated

maneuver resulted in the death of Farnsworth and sixty-five of his men.

The house passed into the hands of the George E. Black family by the early 1900s and subsequently opened as a lodging house. From that time until the present, the home has served in that capacity. In 1972, it was purchased by the Loring H. Schultz family. Restoration to the home's Civil War–era appearance began at that time.

Large portraits of the commanding officers at the Battle of Gettysburg, General Robert E. Lee and General George G. Meade, hang above the fireplaces in the authentically restored downstairs dining rooms. The low-ceilinged Lee Room was the original 1810 structure. We dined by candlelight in the Meade Room, crafted from the 1833 addition. Photos by famed Civil War photographer Mathew Brady were on the walls, alongside many relics from the battle. The tables were set with pewter goblets and plates engraved with a Farnsworth House likeness. Waitresses in period dress further enhanced the ambiance.

Mamie Eisenhower, the widow of President Dwight Eisenhower, was often a dinner guest at Farnsworth House when she was in the area relaxing at her nearby farm. She frequently ordered the Flounder and was very partial to Hot Fudge Sundaes for dessert.

We chose to sample food more closely tied to the home's early years. Upon ordering, we were served Corn Relish and Pickled Watermelon Rind, along with Spoon Bread and Jenny Wade Bread. Whipped Butter and Adams County Apple Butter were brought as accompaniments. Served in its own crock, the white cornmeal Spoon Bread was tasty and different from any other we'd tried. It's one of the many items on the menu derived from recipes left by great-great-grandmothers. Karen tried another such example of early cookery, ordering the house specialty, Game Pie. It was made from turkey, pheasant, and duck, blended with mushrooms, bacon lardoons, Red Currant Jelly, and long-grain and wild rice, all covered with a golden egg crust. Very tasty, it was served in its own oval pewter casserole. Likewise, Debbie's Chicken Pot Pie came in an individual pewter porringer. We agreed that the Pumpkin Fritters that came with our meals were the highlight of our experience—quite a statement about a totally delicious evening.

HAM AND BEAN SOUP

6 cups water
½ pound Great Northern beans, soaked overnight in
  cold water
2 teaspoons salt
1 small onion, chopped
pinch of white pepper
1 teaspoon parsley flakes
¼ cup ham, chopped

Place all ingredients in a large saucepan. Bring to a boil, then lower heat. Cover and simmer for 2 to 4 hours until beans are soft. Serves 8.

RUM CREAM PIE

1¼-ounce packet unflavored gelatin
¾ cup cold tap water
4 egg yolks
½ cup sugar
3 tablespoons rum
2 cups heavy whipping cream
9-inch graham cracker piecrust
1 square unsweetened chocolate, grated or shredded

Soften gelatin in water. Heat over low heat until dissolved, then set aside to cool to lukewarm. In a mixing bowl, beat egg yolks and sugar until light and fluffy. Stir gelatin, then rum into egg mixture; mix well. Place in refrigerator. Whip cream until it stands in soft peaks. Fold cream and egg mixture together. Spoon into piecrust and refrigerate. Garnish with chocolate. Yields 1 pie.

101 SKYLINE DRIVE
FARMINGTON, PA 15437
724-438-8594

It was 1806 when Secretary of the Treasury Albert Gallatin suggested a National Road, prompted by his own difficulties in traveling to Washington from his home about twenty miles from where Summit Inn is now located. The year 1813 saw construction begin on the National Road, which opened for public use in 1818 and remained the primary way west until the advent of railroads. The road was renowned for the number and excellence of its taverns. When the state of Pennsylvania began making improvements to its section of the National Road, wealthy Uniontown residents formed the Summit Hotel Company with the goal of building a mountain resort of "exceptional quality and durability." Summit Inn, which sits atop Chestnut Ridge, is the realization of that goal.

Since 1907, guests have enjoyed the atmosphere and the quality craftsmanship of Summit Inn. Although computers have replaced the handwritten register, you can still announce your arrival to the staff at the same spot where many notable personalities signed in before you. If you consult the register page from August 19, 1918, you'll find that Henry Ford, Thomas Edison, John Burroughs, and Harvey Firestone were at Summit Inn for a meeting of "America's Science Wizards." Photographs and news clippings displayed along the hallway commemorate the event.

Carefully preserved Mission-style furniture has provided generations of guests a comfortable place to sit and chat or enjoy the enormous fieldstone fireplace. Antiques abound, from a Steinway piano to an elaborately carved coatrack to Tiffany lamps, all reminders of the inn's illustrious past. The lobby's grand staircase, leading to the guest rooms, is a sight to behold. Just be careful. It's said that President Warren G. Harding once took an unceremonious tumble here.

The dining room, decorated in soothing teal and peach, is just off the lobby to the left of the staircase. We had a delicious and filling breakfast of French Toast and Popeye's Favorite, a three-egg omelet made with spinach and mushrooms.

Sated, we toured the inn. Although we were most impressed with the spacious rooms, we were continually drawn back to the wide flagstone veranda, as a warm breeze invited us to sit and enjoy the breathtaking vista across the outdoor pool and on toward the Laurel Highlands in the distance. There are many nooks and crannies from which to savor the panorama, including the popular deck area, where guests may select from a luncheon menu that includes such items as Chicken Provençal, Santa Fe Chicken, a Turkey Reuben, the Club Summit Sandwich, and Balsamic Marinated Portabello Mushroom served over Capellini. As tempting as it was to linger, other work beckoned us. We'd like to go back for lunch or dinner on a clear day to learn whether it really is possible to see all the way to Pittsburgh from atop Chestnut Ridge.

PASTA PRIMAVERA WITH ROASTED GARLIC AIOLI

16-ounce package capellini noodles
2 cups fresh garlic, minced
½ cup vegetable oil
2 cups sherry
4 sticks butter
4 cups vegetables (carrots, zucchini, yellow squash, red or green peppers, mushrooms, or other vegetables of your choice), julienned

Cook capellini according to package directions. While pasta is cooking, sauté garlic in vegetable oil until golden. Add sherry and reduce until almost dry. Whip in butter to make the aioli. Sauté vegetables in aioli until cooked al dente. Drain pasta and toss with vegetables. Heat to desired temperature and serve. Serves 4.

PEANUT BUTTER CHEESECAKE WITH OREO CRUMB CRUST

Oreo Crumb Crust

1¾ cups Oreo crumbs
¼ cup sugar
½ cup butter, melted

Combine Oreo crumbs and sugar. Add melted butter and mix. Press firmly into a 10-inch cake pan.

Cheesecake

7 eggs
3 egg yolks
2⅓ cups sugar
5 8-ounce packages cream cheese, softened
1 cup heavy whipping cream
1½ cups creamy peanut butter

Cream eggs, additional yolks, and sugar until sugar is dissolved, adding eggs and yolks slowly 1 at a time. Cream the cream cheese in a separate bowl; add to egg mixture and combine. Add whipping cream and peanut butter and whip until blended. Pour into crust and bake at 325 degrees in a hot-water bath for about 1 hour and 20 minutes. Let cool completely before cutting. Serves 12 to 16.

505 BRIDGE ROAD (PA 113)
COLLEGEVILLE, PA 19426
610-489-1600

Valentine Hunsicker, a farmer, a weaver, and a deacon of the second Mennonite church in the United States, emigrated from Switzerland and established his homestead in Skippack and Perkioming townships in the year 1725. Many years later, after defeats at Brandywine and Germantown, Washington's tattered troops camped near this location before retreating to their winter quarters at Valley Forge. Some accounts say that the Hunsicker farmhouse was used as a hospital for wounded soldiers.

For 170 years, this 225-acre farm nestled along Perkiomen Creek was maintained and improved by members of the Hunsicker family. At the turn of the twentieth century, the farmhouse was expanded to provide room for boarders and travelers. The year 1902 saw the addition of a kitchen, which allowed the farmhouse to begin functioning as one of the best hotels and restaurants in the area. It was known at that time as The Lily of the Valley. Through the twentieth century, the name changed several times— Millside Inn, Hill Creek Inn, and The Eagle's Nest, in honor of Philadelphia Eagles football players who came over from their nearby training camp.

Since 1980, with the unveiling of Gypsy Rose

Restaurant, Mr. Gail Mitchell has tried to recapture the eighteenth-century feeling established by Valentine Hunsicker so many years ago. Old-fashioned wainscoting shines throughout. The dining tables are each draped with a different country-print cloth. The main dining room looks out over Perkiomen Creek and the lovely grounds of the restaurant. Floral-fringed hanging lamps and floral cloth draped at the ceiling bring the greenery inside as well. The bar area, more rustic, has a large wraparound pine bar. Rough-hewn beams overhead and interesting light fixtures that appear to have been made from copper make this central area of the restaurant an appealing stop-off point.

The menu is American and includes everything from Burgers to Roast Prime Rib. Shark is a regular feature, prepared with Cajun Breadcrumbs and Lump Crab Sauce. Lump crab also appears in the Veal Ursinus, which consists of medallions of veal, crab, asparagus, and artichoke hearts in a sauce of white wine and roasted bell pepper. The plentiful Sunday brunch includes a wide range of breakfast offerings, entrée choices, and vegetable accompaniments.

We experienced Gypsy Rose for a quiet Saturday lunch. House-cured Salmon Gravlax and the Nelson New Yorker, a chicken breast served on Herbed Foccacia with fontina cheese and a roasted red pepper, were our choices. Our server was very pleasant and very interested in our research for the book, wishing us luck as we made our way to the creek-side garden area. As we followed the meandering creek, we mused about just whose footsteps we might be following.

CHICKEN PHILADELPHIA

2 3-ounce packages cream cheese
2 tablespoons green onion, chopped
pinch of garlic powder
salt and pepper to taste
6 6-ounce chicken breasts
6 5-by-5-inch puff pastry squares
1½ cups brown sauce
1 tablespoon freshly ground black peppercorns
1 tablespoon brandy

Preheat oven to 350 degrees. In a small mixing bowl, combine cream cheese, green onion, garlic powder, and salt and pepper. Set aside. Make a slit in each chicken breast, forming a pocket. Fill each pocket with 2 tablespoons of the cream cheese mixture, then wrap each breast in a puff pastry square. Place chicken on a greased pan and bake for about 40 minutes until golden brown. Meanwhile, combine brown sauce with ground peppercorns and brandy and heat through. Serve over chicken breasts. Serves 6.

CRAB CAKES

2 cups Imperial Sauce (commercial)
6 tablespoons milk
½ cup fresh breadcrumbs
½ teaspoon baking powder
½ teaspoon Old Bay seasoning
16 ounces lump crabmeat
3 tablespoons clarified butter

Mix all ingredients except butter gently in a bowl. Form into 12 equal cakes. Melt butter in a large sauté pan. Sauté crab cakes until brown on both sides. Serve on a bed of lettuce with cocktail or tartar sauce. Serves 6.

HISTORIC PANTALL HOTEL

135 EAST MAHONING STREET
PUNXSUTAWNEY, PA 15767
814-938-6600

Punxsutawney Phil, the weather-predicting groundhog, has been going about his business on February 2 since 1887. Just one year younger, The Pantall Hotel is equally enjoyable—and it's accessible year-round! Built by Theo Pantall in 1888, at the height of the logging industry, this Victorian structure was one of thirteen hotels in Punxsutawney at the turn of the century. After many years of neglect, restoration began in 1970 under the ownership of the Barletta family. On board for much of that time was Pantall's manager, Jane Cunningham. Her love of history in general and this place in particular is evident as she recounts the many changes over the years. Today, Pantall has seventy-five rooms available for overnight guests. Notably, it hosted Bill Murray and Harold Ramis during filming of the popular movie *Groundhog Day*.

The Pantall Hotel's Victorian heritage is readily apparent in the Coach Light Bar. Bartenders serve potables from behind the curly maple, cherry-stained bar, complete with ornate columns, arches, and dental molding. In its earlier years, this part of the hotel was a pretty rough place. Originally, there was a trough around the bar, complete with running water, for expectorating. That is long gone, but the original tile floor remains, along with some of the stories. Tales about Hans Olson, a partner in the Olson & Fisher Drilling Company during the early 1900s, abound. According to legend, his practice was to meet diamond merchants here, roll their diamonds dice-style onto the bar, then choose the ones he wished to purchase.

The Coach Room is open for breakfast, lunch, and dinner. Antique hutches, collectors' plates, and framed prints line the walls. The lengthy menu includes favorites such as Swiss Steak and Chicken and Biscuits. The cost is modest. Diners can order an entrée such as Chicken and Gravy—served with Mashed Potatoes, a choice of Coleslaw or Applesauce, and a Roll—for less than you'd believe.

After lunch, we wandered through the hotel. The original marble baseboards are evident throughout the main floor. The old carved staircase sits just behind the lobby. Many of the windows throughout the lobby and the dining area still have their original glass. Partially boarded up for many years, they have recently been restored to their original condition. This allows diners to look out over the park next door, where a community bandstand is frequently in use during the warm months. The park is lined with northern maple trees; due to their age, they are frequently damaged during storms. But standing front and center in the park is a groundhog carved from a stump, salvaging what was left of one such tree in celebration of Punxsutawney's claim to fame.

❦ SPINACH BALLS ❦

2 10-ounce packages frozen, chopped spinach
½ cup butter, melted
1 cup Parmesan cheese
2 cups Pepperidge Farm herb stuffing
1 onion, grated
2 large eggs
¼ teaspoon thyme
dash of pepper

Cook spinach and drain well. Place all ingredients in a large mixing bowl; mix with hands until well combined. Roll into 1-inch balls and place on an ungreased cookie sheet. Bake at 350 degrees for 15 to 20 minutes until firm but not dry. Yields 2 dozen appetizers.

❦ ❦ ❦ ❦ ❦ ❦

❦ GLAZED LEMON NUT BREAD ❦

4 tablespoons butter or margarine, softened
¾ cup sugar
2 eggs

2 teaspoons lemon peel, grated
2 cups all-purpose flour, sifted
2½ teaspoons baking powder
1 teaspoon salt
¾ cup milk
½ cup walnuts, chopped
2 teaspoons lemon juice
2 tablespoons sugar

Cream together butter and ¾ cup sugar until light and fluffy. Add eggs and lemon peel; beat well. Sift together flour, baking powder, and salt; add to butter mixture alternately with milk, beating until smooth after each addition. Stir in walnuts. Pour into a greased 8½-by-4½-by-2½-inch loaf pan. Bake at 350 degrees for 50 to 55 minutes until firm. Let cool in pan for 10 minutes. Combine lemon juice and 2 tablespoons sugar; spoon over top of loaf. Remove from pan and let cool. Wrap and store overnight. Slice to serve. Yields 1 loaf.

Note: Orange peel and orange juice may be substituted for the lemon peel and lemon juice.

❦ ❦ ❦ ❦ ❦ ❦

OLD US 22
LENHARTSVILLE, PA 19534
610-562-8520

For those of you who enjoy diner-type fare, Deitsch Eck is the place for you. The menu, which includes items such as a Grilled Ham Sandwich and a Patty Melt, has something for everyone among its thirty-four sandwiches and thirty platters. The platters are served with two vegetables, homemade Bread, and butter. Vegetables and side dishes such as Pepper Cabbage and Cottage Cheese with Apple Butter show the Amish influence on the area. Shoo-Fly Pie tops the list of desserts, which are predominantly homemade. We each had a mug of Apple Cider and a serving of Apple Blueberry Crumb Pie as we sampled the Pennsylvania Dutch tradition.

The Deitsch Eck Restaurant is located on the site of the Washington Hotel, which served travelers during the late 1800s and early 1900s. Soon after the turn of the twentieth century, a fire destroyed the hotel, which was replaced by the present brick building in 1914. It became known as the Lenhartsville Hotel, where rooms went for as little as a dollar per night. According to the hotel's old menus, Iced Shrimp were priced at thirty-five cents, Clam Chowder at twenty cents, and Snapper Soup at twenty-five cents. Coffee, Tea, and Milk were offered at the unbelievable price of a nickel! Although the prices have certainly changed, one thing about the restaurant has not. The business philosophy that appeared on the hotel's original menu is printed on today's menu as well. "But, as we are subject to human imperfections, we stand ready to listen to any reasonable complaint and to rectify any shortcoming brought to our attention," it reads.

Johnnie Ott, a well-known Pennsylvania Dutch artist, was one of the owners and the chef of the Lenhartsville Hotel. During his tenure in the kitchen, the restaurant was listed in a Duncan Hines publication entitled *Adventures in Good Eating.* Later, in 1985, the restaurant was featured in *On the Road with Charles Kurault.*

One of the biggest drawing cards here is the artwork of Johnnie Ott. His paintings, including those of Pennsylvania Dutch hex signs, line the walls of the restaurant. One signifies "*Willkommen,*" or welcome. Another says, "What's wrong?" challenging guests to figure out what is incorrect about the two pictures located in the front corner of the dining room. We got all but one of the tricky pictures, though we won't reveal what we discovered, so as not to spoil the surprise if you stop by for a bite someday. Across the hall in a second dining room are more of Ott's paintings, along with photographs of him at work. This room houses the building's mahogany backbar, around which is an old tile trough. An intricate tin-tile ceiling and red-and-white picnic-style tablecloths round out the room's decor.

In 1971, the Pennsylvania Dutch Folk Culture Society changed the name from the Lenhartsville

Hotel to the Deitsch Eck Hotel. Deitsch Eck translates as "Dutch Corner," which is apropos, since the building stands just off Interstate 78 at the corner of Old US 22 and PA 143.

Owner Steven Stetzler began working at Deitsch Eck in 1988, at the age of sixteen. At that time, he was a cook's assistant and a dishwasher. Before graduating from high school in 1991, Steve dabbled in most of the jobs involved in the restaurant business, including managing the facility. Steve then left for college, where he pursued an associate's degree in hotel, restaurant, and institutional management. In January 1993, the society approached Steve about returning to Lenhartsville to manage the property, since he was familiar with it. Four years later, it offered him the opportunity to buy Deitsch Eck, which he did, thus completing the journey from cook's assistant to owner of this restaurant he knows so well.

BUTTERMILK CUSTARD PIE

2 cups sugar
4 tablespoons flour
4 eggs
4 tablespoons margarine, melted
2 teaspoons vanilla extract
1 cup buttermilk
9-inch deep-dish piecrust, unbaked

Preheat oven to 350 degrees. Combine first 6 ingredients in a bowl and mix with a wire whisk. Pour into pie shell and bake for about 45 minutes until middle doesn't jiggle. When middle

seems firm, remove pie from oven and cool. Serves 6 to 8.

CANDIED SWEET POTATOES

½ cup plus 2 tablespoons light brown sugar
¼ cup dark brown sugar
⅞ cup hot water
5 tablespoons pancake syrup
¼ cup flour
3 tablespoons margarine, melted
4 to 6 sweet potatoes

Preheat oven to 300 degrees. In a double boiler, combine light brown sugar, dark brown sugar, water, syrup, flour, and margarine. Stir occasionally. Remove from heat when mixture starts to thicken. While mixture is thickening, peel sweet potatoes and place them in cold water. Remove from water and cut into 1-inch pieces, then place pieces back in water. (Keeping peeled sweet potatoes in cold water keeps them from becoming wrinkled.) Drain sweet potatoes, place them in a large roasting pan, and pour thickened mixture over top. Place in oven and turn heat to 375 degrees. After 45 minutes, stir sweet potatoes carefully and check for softness by poking with a sharp object. Continue baking until a knife goes into and out of sweet potatoes smoothly. Sweet potatoes will be very hot when taken out of oven and will continue to cook slightly after being removed. Serves 6.

The Sun Inn
1758
Restaurant

THE SUN INN RESTAURANT
564 MAIN STREET
BETHLEHEM, PA 18018
610-974-9451

The Sun Inn's guest list over the years reads like a veritable who's who. It's not surprising, considering that the inn dates back to 1758. The attractive stone building, constructed by the Moravians in their traditional style, originally marked the northern edge of town. Its red-tile mansard roof was a beacon that told weary travelers miles away that food and shelter were finally within reach.

Many Revolutionary War–era statesmen were guests at the inn, including John Hancock, the Marquis de Lafayette, Ethan Allen, and John Adams. In 1787, The Sun Inn provided a respite for the Marquis de Chastellux and forty other French Academy members. The marquis exuded praise for the "venison, moor-game, the most delicious red and yellow bellied trout, the highest flavored wild strawberries, the most luxuriant vegetables." Jimmy Carter reestablished the tradition of presidential visitors, which started with George Washington and continued with every president through James Buchanan.

The Sun Inn was so popular that it grew from its original two-story facade to a full four stories. Balconies and shops were added during the late 1800s to create an attractive Victorian hotel. However, when The Sun Inn Preservation Society was formed in 1971 to save the building from demolition, its members were not interested in the Victorian phase of the inn's existence. Instead, they focused on returning the inn to its original appearance. Additions were removed, and the first floor was furnished as it looked when John Adams, in a letter to his wife, Abigail, described the place as "the best Inn I ever saw." Costumed guides are available to lead entering guests on a living-history tour of these rooms.

The second floor houses the restaurant. Wide-plank floors and hooked rugs contribute to an appealing setting. A bill of fare from long ago hangs in the restaurant's receiving area. The menu is inspired by dishes from that time, updated slightly to appeal to the modern palate. The soup choices include Governor Morris Crab Soup and Sausage, Potato, and Leek Soup, which Karen selected. Debbie sampled Benjamin Franklin's Almond Trout, which was served with Wild Rice and Sautéed Squash of various types.

Lunch was a serene experience. We ate in a dining room with plaster walls of the very faintest sage green. Pewter candlesticks with large hurricanes were part of the table decor. Windsor chairs provided the seating, and tin lanterns alight in the deep-set windows added to the ambiance of this historic inn, which is now situated right in the middle of town.

GOVERNOR MORRIS CRAB SOUP

12 cups water
½ cup crab base
½ red pepper, diced
½ green pepper, diced
½ yellow pepper, diced
16-ounce can jumbo lump crabmeat
2 tablespoons butter
4 tablespoons flour
2 cups heavy cream

Bring water to a boil. Add crab base and peppers and bring back to the boil. Cook until peppers are tender, then add crabmeat. Melt butter in a small saucepan and add flour to make a roux. Stir roux into soup to thicken. Add heavy cream, heat briefly, and serve. Serves 10.

BENJAMIN FRANKLIN'S ALMOND TROUT

2 tablespoons butter, divided
2 tablespoons almonds, sliced
2 8-ounce rainbow trout fillets, deboned
3 tablespoons almond de menthe
1 cup heavy cream

Heat 1 tablespoon of the butter in a skillet. Add almonds and trout and cook for 2 minutes. Place ½ tablespoon butter on top of each fillet. Put trout on a small broiler pan and broil for 7 to 10 minutes. To make sauce, light almond de menthe in a medium saucepan. After flame goes out, add cream. Reduce until thickened, stirring constantly. To serve, place a fillet on each of 2 plates and top with sauce. Serves 2.

Restaurant Index

Recipe Index

Spinach Pesto, 43
Tabasco Tartar Sauce, 234

Corn

Baked Corn, 49
Corn Fritters, 38
Maryland Crab and Sweet Corn Chowder, 60

Cornish Game Hens

Apple-Stuffed Game Hen, 128
Roast Game Hens Stuffed with Wild
   Mushrooms, 63

Crab

Crab Cakes (Gypsy Rose Restaurant), 282
Crab Cakes (The Logan Inn), 168
Crab Cakes with Gourmet Sprout and Seaweed
   Salad, 88
Deviled Crab Cakes, 234
Governor Morris Crab Soup, 288
Lobster and Crab Crepes, 130
Lobster, Shrimp and Crab Casserole, 45
Maryland Crab and Sweet Corn Chowder, 60
Sherried Crab Spread, 68
Soft-Shell Crabs with Cherry Tomato Salsa, 170
Thai Crab Cakes with Cilantro Peanut Sauce,
   274

Desserts

Apple Dumplings, 76
Banana Flambé, 206
Bananas Foster, 155
Cherries Jubilee, 206
Ganache Torte with Pecan Crust and Caramel
   Sauce, 80

Ginger-Almond Crème Brûlée, 34
Homemade Biscotti, 252
Lemon Bars, 248
Lemon Tart with Blueberry Sauce, 64
Peach Shortcake, 191
Phyllo Tartlets with Lime Curd and Berries, 153
Syllabub, 271
Zabaglione Con Lo Spumante, 252
See also Bread Pudding, Cakes, Cheesecakes,
   Chocolate, Ice Cream, Pies, Pudding

Dips

Artichoke and Spinach Dip, 244
Artichoke Dip Cynthia, 214
Savory Mediterranean Dip, 140

Duck

Chambord Roasted Duckling, 70
Duck Huli Huli, 27
Seared Muscovy Duck Breast Salad, 138

Eggs

Egg and Cheese Dressing, 198
Meringue, 82

Elk

Colorado Elk Loin in Swedish Lingonberry and
   Cassis Sauce, 225
Elk and Veal Stock, 225

Fish

Fish Chowder, 273
Fish in Lemon Pepper Brandy Sauce, 216
Grilled Whole Striped Bass, 120
Mahi-Mahi with Spicy Cucumber Salsa, 23

Pan-Roasted Grouper with Spicy Lobster Broth, 109
Potato-Crusted Halibut, 143
Red Snapper in Parchment, 107
Salmon and Rockfish Napoleon with Lemon Grass and Candied Ginger Beurre Blanc, 148
Seafood Pappillotte, 110
Smoked Bluefish Pâté, 258
Stuffed Fillet of Flounder, 238
See also Salmon, Trout, Tuna

Fruits

Baked Brie with Fruit, 214
Bosc Pear Armagnac Granita, 157
Fruit Vinaigrette Dressing, 47
Orange Chutney Glaze, 204
Orange Ginger Ice Cream, 116
See also Apples, Blueberries, Cherries, Lemon, Mangoes, Peaches

Ham

Ham and Bean Soup, 278
Ham Loaf, 198

Ice Cream

Bosc Pear Armagnac Granita, 157
Orange Ginger Ice Cream, 116
Turtle Sundae, 189

Lamb

Herb-Encrusted Rack of Lamb, 130

Lemon

Glazed Lemon Nut Bread, 284
Lemon Bars, 248

Lemon Grass and Candied Ginger Beurre Blanc, 148
Lemon Tart with Blueberry Sauce, 64

Lobster

Lobster and Crab Crepes, 130
Lobster Martiniquaise, 66
Lobster, Shrimp, and Crab Casserole, 45

Mangoes

Chilled Creamy Mango Soup, 132

Mushrooms

Asian Mushroom and Leek Soup, 14
Beef and Portabello Chili, 276
Blue Cheese Mushroom Ragout, 149
Chanterelles Crostini, 269
Drunken Mushrooms, 223
Italian Portabello Appetizer, 232
Mushroom Spread for Tea Sandwiches, 58
Pork Tenderloin Dijonnaise Shiitake, 155
Portabello Mushrooms Stuffed with Artichoke Mousse, 112
Saffron Risotto with Shiitake Mushrooms, 172
Stuffed Portabello Mushroom, 176
Tortellini and Shiitake, 72
Wild Mushroom Bisque, 138
Wild Mushroom Strudel, 271
Wild Rice and Mushroom Soup, 20

Nuts

Sweet and Tangy Nuts, 128
Walnut and Pecan Caramelized Brie, 70
Walnut Poulet, 104

Venison

Grilled Medallions of Venison, 22
Pumpkin Seed-Crusted Loin of Venison with
    Peppercorn-Pear Glaze, 11

Zucchini

Zucchini Blossom Tempura with Red Bell
    Pepper Sauce, 6